CAMBRIDGE STUDIES IN AMERICAN LITERATURE AND CULTURE

The Puritan conversion narrative

CAMBRIDGE STUDIES IN AMERICAN LITERATURE AND CULTURE
EDITOR: ALBERT GELPI, *Stanford University*

Other books in the series
ROBERT ZALLER: *The Cliffs of Solitude*
PETER CONN: *The Divided Mind*
STEPHEN FREDMAN: *Poet's Prose*

The Puritan conversion narrative

The beginnings of American expression

PATRICIA CALDWELL
Department of English, Brown University

CAMBRIDGE UNIVERSITY PRESS
Cambridge
London New York New Rochelle
Melbourne Sydney

Published by the Press Syndicate of the University of Cambridge
The Pitt Building, Trumpington Street, Cambridge CB2 1RP
32 East 57th Street, New York, NY 10022, USA
296 Beaconsfield Parade, Middle Park, Melbourne 3206, Australia

First published 1983

Printed in the United States of America

Library of Congress Cataloging in Publication Data

Caldwell, Patricia.

The Puritan conversion narrative.

(Cambridge studies in American literature and culture)

Bibliography: p.

Includes index.

1. Puritans–New England–History–17th century. 2. Puritans–England–History–17th century. 3. Conversion–History of doctrines–17th century. 4. Spiritual life–History of doctrines–17th century. 5. New England–Church history. 6. England–Church history–17th century. 7. American prose literature–Colonial period, ca. 1600–1775–History and criticism. I. Title. II. Series.

BX9354.2.C34 1983 248.2'4'0974 82–22772
ISBN 0 521 25460 4

To Sarah

CONTENTS

PREFACE

This study attempts to explore a body of materials that has not usually figured in considerations of our literary heritage: the testimonies of spiritual experience that Puritans delivered in the gathered churches of Old England and New England between the 1630s and the Restoration in order to qualify for church membership. Few of these "relations" of religious conversion have survived, and on the American side there is only one large and significant body of so-called conversion narratives. This is a collection of fifty-one "Confessions" given at the First Church of Cambridge, Massachusetts, between 1637 and 1645, and recorded in a small private notebook by the minister of the church, Thomas Shepard. With the kind permission of the Trustees of the New England Historic Genealogical Society, which owns Thomas Shepard's notebook, it has been possible for me to study these rare confessions at first hand. I wish to thank the society and its former director and librarian, Dr. James B. Bell, for permitting me the use of this invaluable document and for allowing me to quote directly from my own transcription of its contents in a few instances. In those cases where my own reading of a particular word or words is given, or where I have interpolated my own interpretation of the Shepard material, I have so indicated. All other citations of the Shepard document are from George Selement and Bruce C. Woolley's modern edition, *Thomas Shepard's "Confessions,"* published in 1981 by the Colonial Society of Massachusetts (*Collections,* vol. 58). To the Colonial Society's editor of publications, Frederick S. Allis, Jr., I am much indebted for generous advice and assistance.

I am grateful to the American Antiquarian Society, Worcester, Massachusetts, for permission to quote the manuscript of Richard Mather's "An Apologie of the churches of New-England" from the society's Mather Family Papers.

The Massachusetts Historical Society has kindly allowed me to cite two manuscripts from its collection: Richard Bernard's "Of the visible Church of Christ under the Gospell" and Richard Mather's "A Plea for the Churches of Christ in New England."

I am indebted to the Mrs. Giles Whiting Foundation, the National Endowment for the Humanities, and the Brown University Faculty Development Fund for generous support during the writing of this book.

PATRICIA CALDWELL

Brown University
January 1, 1983

INTRODUCTION: MRS. ELIZABETH WHITE AND THE PROBLEM OF EARLY AMERICAN LITERATURE

WHO WAS MRS. ELIZABETH WHITE?

On the fifth day of December in the year 1669, Elizabeth White, a well-to-do young woman who had been married for twelve years and who had already borne at least one child, lost her life in giving birth to another. Among the belongings that were found in her chamber after her death were some personal writings that were later to be printed – at different times in Boston, Glasgow, and London – in a format both familiar to, and popular with, the saintly readers of the day. The work appeared under the title *The Experiences of God's Gracious Dealing with Mrs. Elizabeth White. As they were written under her own Hand, and found in her Closet after her Decease,* December 5. *1669;* directly beneath the title the publisher provided – again, in familiar seventeenth-century style – an illuminating portion of Scripture: "Psal. 66. 16 *Come and hear all ye that fear God, and I will declare what he hath done for my Soul.*"[1]

The Experiences of Mrs. Elizabeth White is only one of many such accounts that circulated on both sides of the Atlantic during the first few decades of the Puritan gathered churches (those that restricted their membership to professed believers). Although it is not known whether Mrs. White wrote her narrative to gain membership in a church, her story bears many earmarks of the formal conversion "relation," that is, a testimony of personal religious experience that had to be spoken or read to the entire congregation of a gathered church before admission as evidence of the applicant's visible sainthood. Like many such testimonies, hers progresses from ignorance and self-deception to "notional knowledge," to "bitter grief" for sins, to terror of the devil and of

1 This was one of the proof-texts most frequently cited to support the dissemination of religious experiences, appearing, for example, on the title page of all four surviving editions of Bunyan's *Grace Abounding* (1666–88).

"being consumed in some strange Manner"; her soul hangs on "the Word preached and read," catches a glimmer of "some secret Supports from the LORD," oscillates between those "sweet supports" and fear of "Delusions"; takes temporary refuge in "Duties"; sees its overwhelming "Vileness" and yearns to cast itself entirely upon "Christ Jesus that sure Foundation"; here patrols the borders of despair, there struggles toward "some Pin-hole of Hope." Out of this excruciating vacillation, suffusing the drama almost to the end, springs at last a cautious comfort in the "Unchangeable" God and a final listing of five "Evidences," given "as a further Testimony of my Interest in Christ, by the Effects of my Faith." In short, a preliminary dissection reveals within this narrative a skeletal structure that looks indistinguishable from that of any other conversion story. Here is the expectable sequence of sin, preparation, and assurance; conviction, compunction, and submission; fear, sorrow, and faith.[2]

It is not, after all, surprising that in the 1660s a young woman might seriously anticipate dying in childbed; that she might want to leave behind a memoir of her religious experiences, either as a testimony to her own sainthood or as a teaching witness for her children; that the adventure of her twice-born soul might follow, at least on the surface, the general contours of the "morphology of conversion" laid down by the early Puritan divines; and that such experiences would almost surely find a publisher to help feed "the inordinate appetite of that age for 'good books' " and "guides to godliness."[3] And yet, the story of Mrs. Elizabeth White is a remarkable one – not so much for the bare theological content of the narrative, nor even so much for its vivid personal details, as for its placement in the history of American literature. *The Experiences* appears not only in the standard listings of books printed in early America but also in the most complete bibliog-

2 The "morphology of conversion," a phrase apparently coined by Edmund S. Morgan, is amply explained in his *Visible Saints: The History of a Puritan Idea* (Ithaca: Cornell University Press, 1963), pp. 66–73, 90–2. See also Norman Pettit, *The Heart Prepared: Grace and Conversion in Puritan Spiritual Life* (New Haven: Yale University Press, 1966), under the names of individual ministers, and Darrett B. Rutman, *American Puritanism: Faith and Practice* (Philadelphia: Lippincott, 1970), pp. 99–106. For earlier, broader-based discussions of the process of regeneration against the Renaissance background and in terms of the Puritan temperament, see Herschel Baker, *The Wars of Truth: Studies in the Decay of Christian Humanism in the Earlier Seventeenth Century* (Cambridge, Mass.: Harvard University Press, 1952), pp. 204–11, and Perry Miller, *The New England Mind: The Seventeenth Century* (Boston: Beacon Press, 1954), pp. 25–34, 50–3.

3 Louis B. Wright, *Middle-Class Culture in Elizabethan England* (Chapel Hill: University of North Carolina Press, 1935), p. 228.

raphy of American autobiographies. Moreover, the work is treated (as a revised conversion narrative) in Daniel B. Shea, Jr.'s *Spiritual Autobiography in Early America,* a major study of the genre in the colonial period, and it is cited (as a "diary") in at least one other recent study of colonial New England.[4] In effect, a small but definite niche is now established for Mrs. White in the museum of minor American authors.

It is, therefore, all the more startling to discover that Elizabeth White was not an American Puritan. On the contrary: with her husband, Thomas White, she lived and died far away from Boston, in the hamlet of Caldecot, in the parish of Newport Pagnell, in the county of Buckingham, England, and there is no indication anywhere that she ever set foot on the American strand.[5] Some of these facts may be gleaned from

4 Charles Evans, *American Bibliography,* 14 vols. (Chicago and Worcester, 1903–59; rpt. ed., New York: Peter Smith, 1941), 2:195; Clifford K. Shipton and James E. Mooney, eds., *National Index of American Imprints through 1800: The Short-Title Evans,* 2 vols. (n.p.: American Antiquarian Society and Barre Publishers, 1969), 2:993; Louis Kaplan, comp., *A Bibliography of American Autobiographies* (Madison: University of Wisconsin Press, 1961), p. 310; Daniel B. Shea, Jr., *Spiritual Autobiography in Early America* (Princeton: Princeton University Press, 1968), pp. 183–7; Emory Elliott, *Power and the Pulpit in Puritan New England* (Princeton: Princeton University Press, 1975), p. 185.

5 Edward Arber, *The Term Catalogues, 1668–1709 A.D.; with a Number for Easter Term, 1711 A.D.: A Contemporary Bibliography of English Literature in the reigns of Charles II, James II, William and Mary, and Anne . . . ,* 3 vols. (London: By the Author, 1903), 1:70, provides, under the heading "A Catalogue of Books Printed and Published at *London* in *Easter* Term, 1671," the following title: "The experiences of God's gracious dealing with Mrs. Elizabeth White, late wife of Mr. *Tho. White,* of *Coldecot* in the county of *Bucks;* as they were written under her own hand, and found in her Closet after her decease: she dying in Child-bed, *December* 5th 1669. In Octavo. Price, sticht, 4d." No extant copy of this first edition being reported, Donald Wing does not list it in his *Short-Title Catalogue . . . 1641–1700,* 3 vols. (New York: Columbia University Press, 1951). He does record editions in 1696 and 1698 published in Glasgow and lists the 1671 edition in *A Gallery of Ghosts: Books Published Between 1641–1700 Not Found in the "Short-Title Catalogue"* ([New York]: Modern Language Association, 1967). The work has slipped into the American canon by virtue of its publication in Boston during the Great Awakening in 1741, perhaps at the instigation of Thomas Prince, as Shea suggests (*Spiritual Autobiography,* p. 184). Prince's personal copy of this edition is the one now held by the Boston Public Library and the only reported copy in the United States. Kaplan's bibliography purports to include works of "authors born in the United States, who lived abroad," and "authors born outside the United States who lived in this country for an appreciable period" (p. v), but there is no evidence that Mrs. White fits either category. Her name does not appear in the Boston Registry Department's *Boston births, baptisms, marriages and deaths, 1630–1699* (Boston, 1883), nor in Clarence Almon Torrey, "New England Marriages

Edward Arber's record of the title page of the first (and now lost) London edition of Mrs. White's memoir, and from the same source it may be surmised that the Whites – "Mr." and "Mrs." – were gentlefolk and that Mr. White outlived his wife. These clues are corroborated by chronicles of Buckinghamshire, which trace the history of the White family's Caldecote [*sic*] Manor from William the Conqueror's day (and incidentally suggest that it was an impressive place: According to an 1862 report, "there seems to have been a mansion here in former times: a portion of the moat still remains").[6] The record shows that the manor, which was about a mile from Newport,[7] was sold in 1541 by a family named Hanchett to a John White and that by 1600 it was in the possession of a succession of Thomas Whites, beginning with John's great-grandson. The latter's son, also Thomas, died lord of the manor of Caldecote in 1670, and his son Thomas is known to have made a will in 1678.[8] This younger Thomas – presumably the "Mr. *Tho. White,* of *Coldecot*" who was still alive in 1671 when the memoir was published – was almost certainly Elizabeth's husband.[9]

But apart from these sparse facts, or supposing that we did not have even this much information, what can actually be known about Mrs. Elizabeth White? And why, beyond the satisfaction of setting the record

Prior to 1700," Xerox copy (Boston: New England Historic Genealogical Society, 1971). Inaccuracies about the death date have slightly compounded the problem: Evans, Shipton, and Kaplan report it as 1660; the Boston Public Library catalogue gives 1699; the correct year is 1669.

6 James J. Sheahan, *History and Topography of Buckinghamshire* (London, 1862), p. 457.

7 Newport Pagnell was an important post for Parliamentary forces (and therefore for radical Puritans) during the Civil War. "An old muster roll shows that John Bunyan was one of the Newport garrison for two or three years, and it has been inferred that he gained his conceptions of a fortress in his 'Holy War' from his experiences at Newport" (John Parker, ed., *Records of Buckinghamshire, . . .* [Aylesbury: Architectural and Archaeological Society for the County of Buckingham, 1903], p. 406). Bunyan probably served under Sir Samuel Luke, the original of Butler's Hudibras, who was Commonwealth commander there for three years. Another Newport friend of Bunyan was John Gibbs, the town's first nonconformist minister. Vicar of Newport from 1652 to 1660, he was removed at the Restoration, whereupon he gathered his flock in a barn and preached to them there (Clement Shorter, *Highways and Byways in Buckinghamshire* [London: Macmillan, 1910], p. 302). Gibbs may well be "the Minister of the Parish" Mrs. White refers to in her memoir.

8 William Page, ed., *The Victoria History of the County of Buckingham,* vol. 4 (London: St. Catherine Press, 1927), p. 417.

9 Unfortunately, the White family pedigree (in W. Harry Rylands, ed., *The Visitation of the County of Buckingham Made in 1634 by John Philipot, Esq.* [*et. al.*] [London: (Mitchell, Hughes & Clarke, printers), 1909], p. 127) stops before this generation.

straight, is it important that we understand her and her one small contribution to our literature?

Both questions are best answered by the work itself, for the elusive Mrs. White or, more properly, her meaning in literary history is capturable not in the external data but in the text that she wrote and in a comparison of that text with other narratives of conversion from the period. The intriguing point that such a comparison demonstrates is that English saints like Mrs. White are not indistinguishable from the New England Puritans when it comes to expressing their religious experiences. In important ways, their testimonies sound different both in factual (or historical) reference and in literary character and technique. Even if we knew nothing about Elizabeth White, her narrative should tell us that she never crossed the ocean.

The differences are meaningful even if Mrs. White's *Experiences* cannot be established definitely as a strict church "relation."[10] When the White document is seen against the vast panorama of English spiritual autobiography,[11] it quickly becomes apparent that the work has much in common with the kind of conversion narratives being given in English churches at the time.[12] Like them, it is fairly concise (eighteen and a half printed pages, of which only twelve are strictly narrative), con-

10 Shea claims that the document "diverge[s] from the usual seventeenth-century pattern in order to revise testimony originally given for church membership" (*Spiritual Autobiography*, pp. 183–4), but Mrs. White herself is silent on the subject. She does append to her experiences three "Reasons why I write them": for "sweet Supports to me in a Time of Darkness"; for "Remembrance" of "that which is good"; and to "testify my Obedience to God and his Word." Apropos of the last reason, she writes, "I have been often called upon to see that my Principles be right, and to make sure my Evidences for Heaven," but she does not say when or how she was thus "called upon." (*The Experiences of God's gracious Dealing with Mrs. Elizabeth White* [Boston, 1741], p. 20. All subsequent references are to this edition, and appear in the text by page number.)

11 A most comprehensive treatment of the genre in England is Owen C. Watkins, *The Puritan Experience: Studies in Spiritual Autobiography* (London: Routledge & Kegan Paul, 1972). See especially the extensive bibliography, pp. 241–60. Mrs. White's *Experiences*, however, is not listed. I have not yet found mention of her in any study of English spiritual life or literature.

12 Among these, the largest and most representative group comprises sixty-one relations from Henry Walker's Independent congregation at Martins Vintry in London; it was published there as *Spirituall Experiences, Of sundry Beleevers* in 1653. Two smaller collections from the same period are thirty-eight "Examples of experience" from John Rogers's Independent congregation in Dublin, included in his book on church discipline, *Ohel or Beth-shemesh: A Tabernacle for the Sun* (London, 1653); and "Choice Experiences," in Samuel Petto, *Roses from Sharon* (London, 1654). Subsequent references are to these editions and, where clarity permits, appear in the text by page number.

fines itself exclusively to the parts of the subject's life that exhibit the work of grace in the soul, and depends heavily on scriptural reinforcement. It ends with a formal statement of numbered "evidences" of faith (a common practice in Henry Walker's London congregation) and a recital of "my Principles," containing the kind of doctrinal material often "professed" by candidates following the testimony of religious experience in the church. And though it is more detailed and to some degree more introspective than most publicly delivered relations,[13] it is not, like a confessional diary, a free-form, running chart of the writer's spiritual temperature. Nor is it, like some more elaborate and didactic spiritual autobiographies, a demonstration of God's Providence at work in history or experimental evidence of the truth of the writer's teachings. It is, or purports to be, a straightforward attempt to testify to the personal experience of conversion as precisely and persuasively as possible.

All these generic characteristics are found in the conversion narratives of New England as well.[14] What immediately strikes the reader as different, however, is the factual content – actual items of historical reference. Mrs. White's narrative is silent on all the points we might expect to find (and do find) in the New English materials. There is no word of a move to America nor (for she might have been born and reared there) any talk of people and places in New England; whereas every American conversion narrative is thickly laced with the names, personalities, and activities of ministers in the New England pantheon from Bulkly to Weld. A tiny detail almost clinches the matter: In the midst of her doubts, Mrs. White says, she was advised by a friend "to read *Sheperd's sincere Convert*." No American conversion narrative ever refers to any minister, living or dead, without the title of "Mr." or "Dr."; but even

13 Hereafter, the word *relation*, meaning story, narrative, testimony, or confession, appears without quotation marks. These words are used interchangeably, although the word *confession* has one other technical meaning, to be discussed in Chapter 1.

14 The major collection, and the chief object of this study, is *Thomas Shepard's "Confessions,"* ed. George Selement and Bruce C. Woolley, *Collections of the Colonial Society of Massachusetts*, vol. 58 (Boston: The Society, 1981), containing fifty-one testimonies given between 1637 and 1645 at the First Church of Cambridge, Massachusetts. Six more relations from Cambridge and from Malden, Massachusetts, were recorded by Michael Wigglesworth in his *Diary . . . 1653–1657*, ed. Edmund S. Morgan (New York: Harper, Torchbook, 1965; rpt. ed., Gloucester, Mass.: Peter Smith, 1970), pp. 107–25; and twenty-three relations given at Wenham and Chelmsford, Massachusetts, between 1644 and 1666 are in *The Notebook of the Reverend John Fiske, 1644–1675*, ed. Robert G. Pope, *Collections of the Colonial Society of Massachusetts*, vol. 47 (Boston: The Society, 1974). A few other New English narratives will be cited as they appear in the discussion.

if this were not so, her impersonal use of his last name reveals that Mrs. White assumes a distance from "Sheperd" that would not be possible for any New England Puritan, even after Shepard's death.[15] A final and decisive item of evidence is that, early in her story and just before her marriage in 1657, Mrs. White went "to the Minister of the Parish, to be Examined before I was admitted, and finding my self able to Answer him, I thought all was well with me then, and so unworthy I went to the Lord's Table" (p. 4). Such an event – acceptance at the Lord's Supper before effectual conversion and a public relation of it – is unlikely to have happened in New England in the 1650s. But even if it had, Mrs. White's use of the term *Parish* means that at the time she was in England, not in New England, where the parochial system was unpalatable to Congregationalism.[16] Twelve years after the time of this incident, she was dead; yet nothing in the narrative suggests a subsequent trip to America – an event so central, even traumatic, for American Puritans that only a handful of them fail to discuss it. Mrs. White was not in New England before her marriage, and she was not in New England after her marriage.

Factual content aside, the inward, literary qualities of these narratives by English and American saints also strike the reader as strangely different from each other. Although all Puritan conversion narratives share some basic literary techniques – a heavy reliance on Scripture, a certain amount of objective self-examination and orderly arrangement – real contrasts emerge in structure and theme and in the symbolic modes employed to knit them together. In the end, these elements add up to what can only be described as a marked difference in tone or in "feel."

15 Cf. James Fraser (a Scottish Presbyterian minister writing around 1670): "I read Shepherds Sincere Convert in one of my calm fits, . . . but I had not read four Leaves of him when I was thrown on my Back" (*Memoirs* [Edinburgh, 1738], p. 41, cited in Watkins, *Puritan Experience,* p. 59).

16 This is the passage on which Shea bases his assertion that Mrs. White is revising testimony originally given for membership, presumably in a New England congregation (see n. 10, above). There are two questions: (1) Is it a revised church relation? (2) Was the original delivered in a New England church? The second question is easier to answer. Apart from the decisive word *Parish,* Mrs. White's private examination by the minister alone is more suggestive of the Old than of the New England way. In the latter system, private examination had to be followed by public testimony; in England, church practices varied considerably during the Commonwealth period. As for the first question, Mrs. White's visit to the minister appears on the second page of her narrative and is followed by all her subsequent experiences, chronologically arranged. The bulk of her story, therefore, cannot be a revision of anything she said to the minister. Nevertheless, I agree with Shea's general view that this is some kind of conversion relation. A strong possibility does remain that the work grew out of testimony offered for admission to an English gathered church later in her life, although she does not say so.

Perhaps we can pin down this elusive quality if we now look at Mrs. White's story in more detail.

MRS. WHITE'S "EXPERIENCES"

The theme of Elizabeth White's memoir, not surprisingly, is deliverance; and much of the action is framed in images of constraint and release. At the outset, she presents herself as a creature in bondage to sin, enthralled by ignorance and folly ("I was a great lover of Histories, and other foolish Books, . . . so bewitched by them, that I could not forbear") and, even worse, by her own fallen nature ("I was but like a Wolf chained up, which keeps its Nature still" [p. 3]). Even when she thinks she has made some progress she finds that she is still enslaved by her own self, having merely substituted "righteous Self" for "sinful Self." Forced to wander in the endless maze of futile "Duties," she is in "a worse Condition than at the beginning" and one that "I plainly saw . . . but how to get out of it I knew not" (p. 8). When at last the trap begins to spring, it is because she is able to give over her self; then, in a series of accelerating climaxes (but continually interspersed with relapses), she feels herself released and elevated by "this free Grace of GOD in chusing me before the Foundation of the World was laid" (p. 16); and this is the "plot" of her confession.

All this is very familiar, for every story of Christian redemption is a story of deliverance, and many of them use imagery like this. What makes Mrs. White's version immediately interesting is her selection of particular situations or events to carry her toward the realization of her spiritual rebirth. These events are exclusively those of her life as a woman, in particular, some details surrounding the birth of her first baby. The saga of Mrs. White's soul proceeds through the "stations" of her feminine progress in life: her marriage, her pregnancy and "delivery," nursing her infant and then weaning it, her apprehensions about bearing children, and a final, eerily accurate dream prediction of her own death. It is a female story, not just in a social but in a biological sense, and in some ways a female parable, an extended metaphor derived from the universal experiences of women's lives that draws its power, to a great extent, from those experiences[17] – even though the "audience" for the parable may be only Mrs. White herself.

If the "deliverance" theme of Mrs. White's *Experiences* is universally Christian, its structure is just as typical in the way it represents the basic motion or "shape" of that deliverance. One scholar has described all religious experience as "a succession of disclosures" within which there

17 See Sallie TeSelle, *Speaking in Parables: A Study in Metaphor and Theology* (Philadelphia: Fortress, 1975).

is "a downward and an upward movement or an outward and a return journey," roughly corresponding to a question and an answer.

> In the first phase there is the emergence and formulation of a need . . . The subject becomes aware of his own lack of symbolic meaning, [and] enters into a disclosure experience in which this lack is experienced in its depth and power. . . In the second phase the question is converted into an answer. The downward or outward movement merely raises and states the existential question while the upward or inward movement provides a response creative of integration within the subject as a result of the establishment of a harmonious relationship with the sacred beyond.[18]

Similarly, Owen C. Watkins defines "the normal pattern of a Puritan conversion" as

> peace, disturbance, and then peace again. Bunyan said of *Grace Abounding,* "It is a Relation of the work of God upon my own Soul, even from the very first, till now; wherein you may perceive my castings down, and raisings up; for he woundeth and his hands make whole" . . . The casting down and raising up, the wounding and making whole, referred to the two landmarks . . . conviction of sin and coming to Christ.[19]

Mrs. White's story plays some variations on these basic patterns, but, here again, all of them are allied in some way with a movement "down into" and "up out of" her own body and self. This is one reason that childbirth is an effective linchpin for the story – a physical and spiritual experience both intensely inward-turning and outward-moving at the same time. At a deeper level, beneath the entire surface of the story, the basic motive force is one that pulls Mrs. White – or, to use her own good Puritan word, *draws* her – through all the roles life gives her to play and toward something beyond. Thus in the first part of the narrative there is a slow outward motion away from the men in her life – from her father, then from her husband, even from her minister – and inward into her "Closet" and "into my own Heart" (p. 9), where the gestation of a need, the disclosure of her own "lack," reaches its most intense expression – and must ultimately be answered.

In this first section she begins as something of a feral child, a "Wolf" clothed in an outwardly "Mild" girlish sheepishness, with no real life and little to say for herself despite her father's efforts "to bring me up in the Nu[r]ture and Admonition of the Lord" (p. 3). It is only near her marriage time that she begins to awaken to any genuine religious

18 Thomas Fawcett, *The Symbolic Language of Religion* (Minneapolis: Augsburg, 1971), pp. 171–2.

19 Watkins, *Puritan Experience,* p. 37.

awareness, however limited: "I remember about a Month before I was married, my Father would have me receive the Sacrament of the LORD's Supper, and I was very willing to it; until I considered what was requisite to be in those which did partake thereof" (p. 4). Faintly apprehending what is at stake, she begins to suffer virginal doubts about her own worthiness to approach this awesome contact with God, but she is caught in a kind of archetypal bind, "loath to disobey my Father, and more loath to eat and drink my own Damnation." She soon deludes herself, however, with "some notional knowledge of things" and pins her hopes on marriage, "thinking that when I was married, I should have more leisure to serve God." Mrs. White's premarital state, her life with father, is occasionally illuminated by some primal glimmerings of truth, but at best she learns a kind of childlike Old Testament obedience to "legal" appearances while somewhat ingenuously looking forward to a New Testament state of things in which everything will be better.

She then goes to the minister of the parish and actually gains admittance to the Lord's Supper. Only briefly thereafter is she able to indulge her complacency, for suddenly the Lord "broke my false Confidence, and swept away my refuge of Lies"–an abrupt, almost violent breakthrough that happens, appropriately enough, "about a Quarter of a Year after I was married, in the Year 1657" (pp. 4–5). Moreover, "it was at this Time [while she was attending a sermon] that God did begin to manifest his Love to me, as I trust, in my effectual Vocation; here the Lord was pleased to open my Heart, as he did the Heart of *Lydia*" (p. 5).[20] The intimacy of her earthly union thus accompanies, if it does not trigger, her first yielding to a genuine intimacy with God.

This habit of conflating different forms of love, long understood as characteristic of mystical religious expression, is not uncommon in Puritan writers. Anne Bradstreet's poems, written to her husband but often read as addressed to another Bridegroom, are only one case in point; and the great preacher John Cotton is described as exclaiming of his wedding day, " 'God made it a day of double marriage to me!' "–since "it was then, that he first received a comfortable assurance of God's love to his soul . . . and this comfort continued with him, in

20 See Norman Pettit, "Lydia's Conversion: An Issue in Hooker's Departure," *Proceedings of the Cambridge Historical Society for the years 1964–1966*, pp. 59–83, for the significance of Lydia (Acts 16:14–16) in conversion theory. It is hard to pin down Mrs. White's technical position in terms of Pettit's "orthodox" and "preparationist" camps. Though her story is one of gradual conversion rather than of "seizure," her own will plays no part in the process, and by calling her vocation "effectual" at this early point, she stresses God's initiative; all of which puts her closer to "orthodoxy."

some happy measure, through the residue of his days."[21] But for Cotton, his "day of Union" with Elizabeth Horrocks was the consummation of a long conversion that had begun years earlier. Not so for Mrs. White, whose marital union is only the prologue to the real action.[22] In fact, "my Husband," who has been prominent in the first few pages of the story, has only one more scene to play (he invites the minister to pray with his wife, who turns flustered and speechless because she feels herself still a "Stranger to God"), after which both men disappear, nevermore to be seen.

Father, husband, and minister all having played their parts, Mrs. White is now left alone upon the stage for a long siege of inner turmoil, of wrestling with grief for sin, doubts of election, and fear of hypocrisy. In Pamela-like seclusion, she dwells in the chambers of her house, seemingly accompanied only by her own arguments and counterarguments, her alternating comforts and delusions, guilts and fears, scribbling down scriptural passages and "laying" them in her "Closet" for encouragement; clinging to "Duties"; and finally, reluctantly, both attracted and repelled, trying to give over to love, yet doubting all the while. This long anxious period of waiting is so much like the self-absorptive waiting of pregnancy – as if something were gestating inside her, something both joyous and dangerous – that we are not surprised when Mrs. White tells us that that is her condition: "Once when I was in great Fear least my Heart should grow dead, and when I was with Child, I was much dejected, having a Sense of my approaching Danger, and wanting an Assurance of my everlasting Happiness." But these very fears, of death and danger both physical and spiritual, mark the turning point of the story. For Mrs. White, the "existential question" (must I die?) is answered, quite literally, in the affirmative, because of course she must "die," must go down, before she herself can be reborn. In this second and climactic section, Mrs. White is "dejected," that is, literally thrown down (the repetition of the words "I lay in my Bed," "now I was in Bed," "as I lay," has an almost ritual quality), and in the labor of childbirth, aided by the "begetting" Word of God, she feels for the first time the joys of deliverance.

21 A[lexander] W[ilson] M'Clure, *The Life of John Cotton* (Boston, 1846), p. 29.

22 John Winthrop's experience was similar: "I married into a family . . . in Essex; and living there sometimes I first found the ministry of the word to come to my heart with power (for in all before I found only light)" ("Christian Experience," *Winthrop Papers*, vol. 1, 1498–1628 [(Boston): Massachusetts Historical Society, 1929], p. 155). But it took Winthrop twelve more years fully to experience conversion.

> But whilst I was considering of these Things, I had this Scripture set home with abundance of Sweetness, Psal. 53. 15. *Call upon me in the Day of Trouble, and I will deliver thee, and thou shalt glorify me:* And in the Time of Extremity this Word was set home upon my Heart again, and my good GOD made me to Experience the Truth of it in a wonderful Manner, for I had speedy Deliverance beyond my Expectation, which filled my Heart and Mouth with Praises to the LORD. (p. 10)

It is important to note that even (or especially) here Mrs. White's mode of expression is right in the Puritan tradition of scripturalism. Describing an extremely personal and potentially dramatic event, she transmutes it into the reenactment of a biblical truth with, in effect, the Word as her midwife: the Word that in Christian theology embodies, in the Second Person, the creative and regenerative powers of God.

> Of his own will begat he us with the word of truth, that we should be a kind of firstfruits of his creatures. (James 1:18)

Moreover, the scriptural imagery of redemption sometimes takes the form of literal childbirth:

> Because the creature itself also shall be delivered from the bondage of corruption into the glorious liberty of the children of God.
>
> For we know that the whole creation groaneth and travaileth in pain together until now.[23] (Rom. 8:21–2)

This last passage of Scripture serves to remind us that Mrs. White's experience of childbirth is also a deliverance from everything that has happened "until now" in the narrative itself. It is the culmination of her movement away from (Old Testament) father, husband, and all the other elements of her ordinary life before "birth." Finally, it is worth stating explicitly what we have been assuming all along: That this is, like Cotton's "double marriage," a double birth, of Mrs. White's child and of herself. This needs to be stated because the imagery is so intertwined, and so inherently meaningful, that it is easy to lose the separate allegorical strands.[24] It can be seen in this passage, as well as in those following in which the child is suckled and weaned, that the baby is

23 The Greek word συνωδίνω, translated in the New Testament as "travaileth in pain together," means literally, "to have (parturition) pangs in company [i.e., sympathy] with."

24 Cf. Bunyan's very different allegorical birth-dream, in which he squeezes through a narrow passage "with great striving"–head first, then by the shoulders, then by the whole body–to get through a wall to a sunny mountainside where the true Christians are gathered. Unlike Mrs. White, Bunyan has to interpret each item: the mountain is the church, the sun is the face of God, the wall is the Word, the narrow passage, Jesus Christ. (*Grace Abounding to the Chief of Sinners,* ed. Roger Sharrock [Oxford: Clarendon Press, 1962], sec. 53–5, pp. 19–20.)

really another version of Mrs. White – that it is made to stand for her and to mirror her experiences.

This is why, having relapsed into a kind of postpartum struggle with Satan that first takes form in a frightening vision, Mrs. White gets only temporary relief from nursing the infant. It is like turning to herself for support (especially since a newborn baby, in a very real sense, still *is* part of its mother), so that she soon is visited by Satan himself. In a way, she is still struggling with the flesh. It is no wonder, then, that she can get, quite literally, no "Promise" of rest, even with the help of Scripture.

> But as I lay in my Bed, I thought I saw three Men before me, and it was presently suggested to me that these were the three Persons in the Trinity; O then I was very much troubled, but I knew I was under a Temptation, and therefore cryed to the LORD for Help, but was not presently delivered from it; . . . but now I was in Bed, and knew not what to set about for the present, at last I resolved to try to Suckle my Child, which I did, and then lay down again, and found that I was pretty well freed from that Temptation, . . . but as I lay, I thought Satan stood before me, asking where I could find a Promise for Sleep, at present I could not think of any, but after some study this was brought into my Mind, *The Lord will give his Beloved Sleep:* This Word comforted me, but yet I could not all that Night get any Sleep, but still thought I saw Satan laughing at me. (pp. 11–12)

Mrs. White had found, immediately after her delivery, that she was still "tempted to think my Faith was false" and, no doubt still under the spell of childbirth, that "I laboured what I could to encourage my self in the LORD my God" (p. 11). It is now clear that all kinds of "labor" on behalf of the self have become futile. Any illusions about operating under one's own power or turning to one's own self for help have been dispelled. Only now, helpless and supine – when "I expected nothing but Death" and yet, like a good Puritan, was "beginning to think more seriously of my Change [i.e., death]" and was resting not in "Assurance" but in "good Hope" – is she given the strength to answer Satan. Whereupon, she gets her long-sought rest, falls asleep, and is finally lifted from the body altogether (in the one way possible short of death): by a dream that synthesizes the Old and the New Testament, beginning and end, the promise to Jacob and its fulfillment in Revelation, wherein she is drawn up to heaven and momentarily touched by "the sacred beyond."

> My Heart made Answer [to Satan], it is true, I have no Assurance, but I have cast my self wholly upon the Lord Christ, and in him only is my Hope, and here will I Rest, and if I perish, I perish, but sure I am such shall not perish, for Christ hath promised them eternal Life. Thus being assisted by the Lord, I vanquished Satan for that Time: And being thus at Peace, I quickly fell asleep, and dreamed there was a

> Ladder set upon the Earth, whose rop reached to Heaven, and I thought I was to go up that Ladder into Heaven, and that as fast as I got up, I was pulled down again, which caused me to shed abundance of Tears, fearing that I should never get up, and I tho't something from above drew me by the Arms, but I could not see what, but at last I thought I was in Heaven, where all Tears were wiped from mine Eyes, and I was filled with Rejoycing, but when I had been there a little while, I thought I was to go back again to the Earth, and this very much troubled me: But then I thought I heard a Voice saying, it would be but for a little while, and that I should die in Child-bed,* and that the Night before I died, I should have full Assurance; this very much rejoyced me, (and I was very desirous to know of what Child I should die) but that was denied me upon this Account, because I should be always prepared, but when I did awake I was filled with inexpressible Joy, earnestly longing to be Dissolved, and to be with Christ, which was best of all. (pp. 12–13)
>
> * *Which accordingly came to pass about twelve Years after her Marriage.*

We shall return to this dream; but for the moment, without even attempting to analyze it very closely, we can perceive its fervency and a kind of nervous vibrancy that echoes but surpasses everything else in the foregoing narrative. Despite a certain vagueness of imagery and guardedness of language (both of which subdue any undue "enthusiasm"), the dream achieves a poetic reality – partly because of the deeply reverberating myths embedded in it, partly because of the excited, almost staccato rhythm of the prose – that heightens its impact over that of any of the earlier events or scenes. If we now look back at the childbirth passage, which is about a real, concrete event, we can see how abstract and placid it appears by contrast. But here, in a dream, the words spill out in a long chain of emotion-charged, energetic phrases, incessantly pushing forward to the final joyous promise: "to be Dissolved, and to be with Christ," which is "best of all" – perhaps also, to the speaker, most real of all.

As if to drive home this final point, there is another crisis, precipitated by the very last, and in some ways the most painful, stage of the birthing process, the weaning of the baby.

> And since my Child was weaned, I was in such a State of Deadness and Darkness, that I thought if I was ever raised out of it, I should never question my Condition again; I was tempted to think that the Scripture was not the Word of GOD? I had let out my Affection in a wonderful Measure to my Child, and yet my Lord forsook me not, but dispelled my Darkness, and filled me with Rejoycing; O what shall I render to Him? (p. 14)

Those who know the Puritans well are familiar with their concept of "weaned affections," but seldom do we see such a literal rendition of it.

And this passage, which virtually draws the story to a close, is something of a gloss on the entire narrative, because it makes clear that Mrs. White herself is the weaned child,[25] just as she herself has been the newborn child, the sleepless child, the tearful child. In the end, the entire story has been about the process of weaning – from her girlish dependence on worldly books and on her well-meaning but ineffectual father; from her have-your-cake-and-eat-it illusion "that when I was married, I should have more leisure to serve God"; and even from the affection, the very mother's milk that she has "let out" to her child – so that she can be dependent on God alone, lifted up and carried aloft to him.

> But this is my Comfort, God is Unchangeable, who I trust will carry me through all the Difficulties I shall meet with here below, and I trust will ere long bring me to the Enjoyment of himself, where I shall be past Sinning and Sorrowing. (p. 14)

To this promise, Mrs. White adds only a brief list of internal "Evidences": love to God, love to the brethren, desire to serve God, love to the Word of God, and admiration for the grace of God, at which she exclaims:

> I can never sufficiently admire it, while I am here in the Body, which makes me long to be dissolved, that so I might know it more clearly, and be swallowed up in the eternal Admiration of it. (p. 16)

This is the end of Mrs. White's story proper; and whatever else may be said about it, it is a proper ending. Mrs. White has completed the circuit of motion. She has experienced a lack and has felt it fulfilled in "a harmonious relationship with the sacred beyond." The structure is complete.

At first glance this does not seem very impressive. We might reasonably expect any story of deliverance to be complete in the Aristotelian sense, to have a beginning, a middle, and an end. Completeness is also demanded by the regenerative patterns of movement that Fawcett and Watkins describe – the kind of "casting down and raising up" made explicit in Donne's metaphysical "geography" or Bunyan's allegory, and the "peace, disturbance, peace again" that might be said to represent the primal dramatic plot. But we also know that it is hard to write *Finis* to any Puritan version of life on earth – that it is hard to reconcile a literary standard of completeness, wholeness, and roundness with Puritanism's conviction that the better the man, the more continually he

25 Cf. John Winthrop, "[The Lord] showed mee the emptines of all my guifts, and parts; left mee neither power nor will, so as I became as a weaned child" ("Christian Experience," p. 159). Winthrop may be thinking of Ps. 131:2, "my soul *is* even as a weaned child."

lives on a knife edge in an endless process of wayfaring and warfaring, a ceaseless testing by the vicissitudes of life, a perpetual self-examination, and a vigilant, restless, wide-awake watch against the "security," self-deception, and sleepy complacency that – so Thomas Hooker warned – invariably make men "goe to hell with a dreame."[26]

Mrs. White, of course, does have a dream – not only has it, but goes to heaven with it; and it is this very dream that helps her to make her story a coherent whole. Indeed, it is hard to imagine just how a narrative like hers might have made a satisfactory end without the dream. Theoretically, the knottiest problem in trying to conform the structure of any conversion narrative to the actual experience would be how to convey, with convincing power, the essence of a spiritual event that manifests itself in the material world but starts and ends elsewhere; one that is felt in the temporal bodily existence but can be "assured" only beyond its bounds. The dream, traditionally a bridge (or a ladder) between two worlds, with all its complex capacities for translating the inner life into concrete, communicable symbols, is obviously one key to this dilemma.

Yet students of Puritan sermons and treatises know that dreams are not traditionally part of the *ordo salutis* and that a deep suspicion of "revelations and dreames" is firmly established in Puritan psychological theory. Orthodox Puritan preachers like Thomas Hooker insisted that an omnipotent God had decided for his own good purposes not to communicate with men in extraordinary ways that might depart from the objective revelation of Scripture – especially Scripture as "opened" by the ministers within the safe confines of the church.

> It is true, the Lord can worke above meanes: we know also God can appoint other meanes for to call the soule, but . . . we must not looke for revelations and dreames, . . . in common course Gods Spirit goes with the Gospell, and that is the ordinary meanes whereby the soule comes to be called. God can make ayre nourish a man, but he doth not.[27]

Moreover, in England by the 1650s many of the worst fears of the moderates were coming true: Ranters, Antinomians, Quakers, and sectaries of all sorts seemed to be putting man in the room of God and doing so by appealing to dreams, visions, voices, and personal revelations. "Extraordinary" experience began to be seen as an insidious means to uphold the authority of the self over both civil and ecclesiasti-

26 Thomas Hooker, *The Saints Dignitie, and Dutie* (London, 1651), p. 67.
27 Thomas Hooker, *The Soules Vocation or Effectual calling to Christ* (London, 1638), pp. 62–3, cited in Miller, *New England Mind: Seventeenth Century*, p. 290.

cal restraints and even over the objective revelation of the Bible–a particularly dangerous and subversive delusion.[28]

What, then, is Mrs. White–who uses her Bible with faithfulness and prudence and who is not a wild enthusiast–doing with a vision and a dream in her conversion narrative? And why is she having the particular kind of dream that we have seen–scriptural, orderly, reasonable enough as dreams go, yet so otherworldly, so resigned, so melancholy as to seem not very "Puritan" at all? Even John Bunyan, the most fervently pious and emotionally sensitive of souls, very much given to dreams, visions, and voices–even Bunyan marches resolutely forth after his conversion to a vigorous life of preaching, political action, and worldly suffering. But we have seen that Mrs. White's entire story, not just her dream, moves relentlessly away from this world and from the energetic, urgent involvement with it that supposedly made the Puritan character so distinctive. What are we to make of this?

It may be helpful to take the testimony of other witnesses, since many other English conversion narratives were taking the same general tack as Mrs. White's, and were doing so a decade and more before she wrote her narrative, with the ministers' apparent approval. For example, a number of dreams appear in relations of religious experience from Henry Walker's Independent congregation in London. Many of these are brief and rather tame: Æ.L., a typical speaker, receives in her dream no grand revelation but simply an inspiration to use the more ordinary "means" of prayer:

> I fell into a slumber, . . . in which I heard as it were a voyce from heaven speaking to my heart, and saying thus, *Aske of God a perfect upright heart to walke in his presence;* which when I was more fully awake, I tooke to be the motions of Gods Spirit upon my Conscience, which did fill me with much joy, provoking me to pray to the Lord to grant mee that grace. (p. 46)

But in Walker's group there is also a handful of longer, more poetical dreams on the order of Mrs. White's. One of the most elaborate and affecting is by T.M. (presumably a man, since he was put out to be an apprentice), who related his experiences on July 25, 1652. Before he described his dream, T.M. reported that he had been hearing "great Disputes amongst some persons about Episcopacy, Presbytery, Independency, and the like, which made me question with my owne thoughts, which was the true way to worship God." Unable to resolve his "perplexity of spirit" and wondering "what would be the end of my

28 See Watkins, *Puritan Experience,* pp. 96, 144–59; and Christopher Hill, *The World Turned Upside Down: Radical Ideas during the English Revolution* (New York: Viking, 1972), pp. 72–4, 235, 286–7.

troubles," he was tempted to despair of salvation. Then he lay down on a bench and had this dream.

> I was in a green Meddow, where I saw various formes of Creatures, some furious and fell, others very pleasing, yet all of them seemed monstrous, and changed their shapes often.
>
> And beholding my selfe alone in the middest of them, I was grievously troubled, and then there appeared a great red Dragon; before it came at me, there appeared a little Childe, and it was put into my armes, which was so beautifull and comly that I admired it, and for the present was so taken with beholding it, that it put the feare of the Dragon for the present out of my minde.
>
> But the Dragon afterwards drew neere, and sorely affrighted me, but both my selfe and the childe were taken away, and carried up an high hill, and the Dragon pursued us; and being often ready to fall in running up the hill, I feared that the Dragon would catch me, but my strength being come to me, I got up to the top of the hill, and the Dragon made up the hill after me.
>
> When I was got to the top of the hill there appeared a brightnesse from Heaven, which gushed forth like a flash of Lightning, and split the Dragon in peeces, at which I rejoyced exceedingly.
>
> Then the Childe was put into my armes againe, and I asked it what was its name; it said, *Emanuel;* I asked it, who was its father; it said, *I am;* I asked, who was its Mother; it said, *Eternity;* I asked, from whence he came, he said, *from my Father out of Heaven;* I asked to whom he came, and what was his errant here; he said, *to save that which was lost, and returne againe;* I asked him, if he would dwell with me while he stayed, hee said, *he could not be detained according to that frame and figure he was in, but after death he would dwell with me in another frame;* the thought of death grieved me, but the childe bid me *not to weepe at it, for in this world, that which is beauty must be destroyed, & that which is contemptible must be exalted.*
>
> I saw my selfe very contemptible, and poore, and troubled, and in these thoughts the childe was taken away from me. (pp. 370–3)

The reader will recognize the derivation of these images from the twelfth chapter of Revelation and recall that in that chapter "a woman clothed with the sun" (taken to represent both Israel and the Christian Church), "travailing in birth, and pained to be delivered," is confronted by "a great red dragon" that threatens to devour the child as soon as it is born. But the child, born "to rule all nations with a rod of iron," is caught up into heaven; the woman flees into the wilderness; Michael and his angels fight the dragon and cast him, "that old serpent, called the Devil [later called 'The Accuser'] . . . out into the earth."

This chapter of Revelation was traditionally interpreted as a portent or sign for the encouragement of Christians under persecution, and, along with the rest of the Book of Revelation, it was a favorite of the millenarians. But T.M. seems to have incorporated its symbols into his dream as much for personal comfort amid the broils and confusions of the times as for political reasons. Surrounded by the conflicting claims of various church polities and, undoubtedly, much millennial talk,[29] he seems to have internalized the country's anxieties as well as the scriptural resolutions of them. It is worth noting that he considerably subdues the fierceness of the Revelation chapter: Rather than lingering over the warfare imagery, he swiftly dispatches the dragon and expands the role of the "beautifull and comly" child, dreaming that he takes it in his arms and imagining a dialogue with the child that enhances the promise of the dream both musically (building to a climax in ever-increasing line lengths) and scripturally (incorporating some of the most consolatory verses of Matthew and Isaiah). The strongest emotion in the dream is not fear of the dragon but sadness at the removal of the child and all that it represents out of "this world" and into the next. If the dreamer is a millennialist, he seems not to be a rabid Fifth Monarchist, for he dreams not of Christ's triumphant return to earth (or to England), not of wide-scale upheaval, but of his own inner longing to dwell with "beauty."[30]

29 On the widespread belief that the millennium was at hand, see Hill, *World Turned Upside Down,* pp. 77–8, 153–4, and *Puritanism and Revolution: Studies in Interpretation of the English Revolution of the 17th Century* (New York: Schocken Books, 1958), pp. 323–8. For an excellent discussion of the intellectual milieu in which millenarianism was "only one aspect of an almost universal belief in the constant intervention of supernatural forces" in human affairs, see B[ernard] S. Capp, *The Fifth Monarchy Men: A Study in Seventeenth-century English Millenarianism* (London: Faber & Faber, 1972), pp. 16–22. Capp points out that recent scholarship stresses "the normalcy and the wide extent of millenarianism in England in the seventeenth century" (p. 19).

30 Capp's study demonstrates that one could well be a millenarian without holding to Fifth Monarchism, which was a smaller movement using millenarian ideas to justify "violent political action and sweeping social changes" (p. 20). Yet Capp summarizes the conversion narratives from the Walker and Rogers congregations (pp. 94–8) on the grounds that, although both groups were "independent not Fifth Monarchist, . . . the membership was probably fairly similar" (p. 98). Be that as it may, neither his reading nor mine turns up anything "violent" or explicitly political in the narratives. Moreover, Henry Walker, T.M.'s minister, was no extremist: He was an Independent, a Cambridge man, admitted to orders by Laud, and a fierce opponent of the Quakers. His pastoral writings are notable for their emphasis on spiritual comfort, an emphasis I find reflected in the testimonies of his flock. On the other hand, Walker's friend Vavasor Powell, who wrote the commendatory "Epistle" introducing *Spirituall Experiences,* was a radical Welsh Baptist who later did become a staunch Fifth Monarchy man. John Rogers, minister of the Dublin Independents, also later turned to Fifth Monarchism. One can only rest on Christopher Hill's assertion that we cannot "impose too clear outlines on the

After he awakens, T.M. is somewhat "Distracted" and "perplexed" by all this, "seeking to understand what I had seen"; and he finds the comforting answers in Scripture, especially in those passages that promise to the weak and the helpless future surcease from trouble and pain. Among these, again, are Matthew (11:28, "Come unto me all yee that are weary and heavie laden, and I will give you rest") and Isaiah (40:11, "I will gather my Lambs with my armes, and gently lead those that are with young").[31]

T.M. related his experiences in the later years of the Commonwealth, and Mrs. White wrote near the end or after the Restoration; yet both reflect the bittersweet melancholy, a yearning for refuge, solace, and a happy ending, that tinges all of these English materials. Some members of Walker's congregation and of John Rogers's Dublin church speak of suffering in the wars of the 1640s, of battle wounds, husbands shot, children taken, lack of bread and water; and they seem to have had enough of struggle and strife.[32] There is much talk about affliction, distress, trouble "too much to bear"; a great deal about children; gratitude to God for the relief of pain, removal of burdens, "peace," "deliverance," and – a constant refrain – "comfort," especially the comfort of church fellowship. Although each speaker dutifully lists his "evidences" – love to the saints, joy in the ordinances, and other alleged transformations in the person's emotions and attitudes – there is neither substantive nor stylistic evidence that people are experiencing (or want to experience) new perceptions, new levels of apprehending reality, in short, becoming the "new creatures" that Paul said all men in Christ would be. The church is more frequently and fervently spoken of as a shelter, a place of rest and security after crosses and afflictions, than as a place of triumphant activism in the praise and service of God on earth. (John Megson, in Dublin, bluntly orders his priorities when he tells the congregation, "I *desire* to be of this Church, for God shall *adde such as shall be saved*" [p. 416].)[33]

It is worth noting that the most frequent scriptural citation among

early history of English sects, . . . in this period things were much more blurred. From, say, 1645 to 1653, there was a great overturning, questioning, revaluing, of everything in England. . . . Men moved easily from one critical group to another" (*World Turned Upside Down,* p. 12). It is this "overturning" that T.M. and his fellows seem to have responded to.

31 The exact wording is T.M.'s. He appears to be citing the King James Version (hereafter cited as KJV) but not verbatim.

32 "*Experience of* Frances Curtis," Rogers, *Ohel,* p. 412[11], "*Experience of* Andr. *Manwaring,* Major," ibid., p. 412[2], and "Experience of M.W.," Walker, *Spirituall Experiences,* pp. 8–18, are typical.

33 He is paraphrasing Acts 2:47: "And the Lord added to the church daily such as should be saved."

Henry Walker's membership is the soothing twenty-eighth verse of Matthew, chapter 11: "Come unto me, all *ye* that labour and are heavy laden, and I will give you rest."[34] The Geneva Bible defines the "all ye" of this verse as those who "fele the waight, & grief of your sinnes and miseries" – exactly the refrain that we have noticed in the general run of the narratives. Only a few verses earlier, Jesus has thanked the Father "because thou hast hid these things from the wise and men of vnderstanding, and hast opened them vnto babes."[35] The Geneva Bible hereupon directs the reader to Luke 10:21, where a marginal note explains, "He attributeth it to the free election of God, that the wise & worldlings knowe not the Gospel, & yet the poore base people vnderstand it." Apparently there is a particular appeal in such Gospel passages for people who feel themselves poor and base and weighted with miseries – who feel themselves, in short, to be "babes."

We know that the Commonwealth period and the early years of the Protectorate were marked by the rising power of sectarian views and the spread of millennial activism. We know that politics and religion went hand in hand during "the explosive political atmosphere of the sixteen-fifties,"[36] especially in Quaker and Fifth Monarchist circles. But when we look to the religious expression of the Puritan folk (not Quakers, whose mode of discourse is different and falls outside this discussion),[37] the chief literary manifestation of all this turmoil seems to be an equal and opposite reaction: the emergence of a counterdemand and a heartfelt longing for peace and safety, for comfort, and, in a word, for assurance. And many people unreservedly claim – or, more probably, need to claim – that they have received it. Thus, in Dublin:

> But now I live in *Christ,* and I can *positively* say, I have *faith,* and am *sure* in *Christ* to be saved, and looke upon none else. (Edward Hoar, p. 412[4])
>
> I have had ever since a *full assurance* of Gods love to me in *Christ.* (Dorothy Emett, p. 413)
>
> The Lord at last came and . . . assured me of *love in Christ.* (John Chamberlain, p. 412[9])
>
> And I am *sure of my pardon* in *Jesus Christ.* (Francis Bishop, p. 399)

34 Some use the Geneva Bible, which gives, "all ye that are wearie & laden, and I wil ease you."
35 The KJV gives, "wise and prudent, and hast revealed them unto babes."
36 Christopher Hill, *The Century of Revolution: 1603–1714* (New York: Norton, 1961), p. 168.
37 See Jackson I. Cope, "Seventeenth-Century Quaker Style," in *Seventeenth-Century Prose: Modern Essays in Criticism,* ed. Stanley E. Fish (New York: Oxford University Press, 1971), pp. 200–35.

abundant amends for all the uneasiness and hardship thou canst suffer in the way.[39]

Christopher Hill has said that "the quietist, pacifist tendency increased as Puritanism turned into non-conformity" after 1660.[40] But the gradual subsidence of the revolutionary impulse, the longing for peace and stability that culminated in the Restoration of the King, the shift of religious hope from England to heaven, all these seem to have an expressive counterpart (or prolepsis) in English narratives of conversion throughout the Interregnum years not only in what people say but in the way that they say it: in the kind of dream imagery, the kind of finished narrative structure, even the consolatory scriptural references they employ. The overall feeling in the religious expression of ordinary English Puritans is therefore not as rigorous and muscular as we are sometimes told to expect from the tough-minded saints.[41] Frances Curtis, one of the Dublin group, conveys another strain of English Puritanism at this time when in her conversion narrative she implores (echoing Prov. 18:14), "*a troubled spirit, who can bear?*" (p. 412[10]).

In such an atmosphere, Mrs. White's spontaneous use of "feminine" materials – the only ones she has – can be seen as an expression of more than just her own personal experience. It is almost as if an earlier phase of the seventeenth-century English temper has reappeared in another form: that phenomenon of Jacobean life that Norman Rabkin describes as "the new loss of faith in the old order." Rabkin points out that Jacobean tragedy increasingly "presents helpless men whose heroism is ironically qualified by the contexts in which they live," until the playwright John Webster "signifies the final helplessness of his tragic protagonists by making them women."[42] Mrs. White's womanly drama (though of course essentially a comedy and not a tragedy) has that helpless quality – one that is not wholly accounted for by the Calvinist outlook but seems also to have to do with the sense of a changing "order." It is not a doctrinal deviation, for the text betrays no serious departure from orthodox Puritan thought. It is a mood, an atmosphere, a complex of feelings, an undercurrent of desire.

We are told that for the Puritans the grand promise of Christian

39 Cited in Hill, *Century*, pp. 250–1.

40 Ibid., p. 170.

41 On the Puritan as "a new man, self-confident and free of worry, capable of vigorous, willful activity," see Michael Walzer, "Puritanism as a Revolutionary Ideology," in *Essays in American Colonial History*, ed. Paul Goodman (New York: Holt, Rinehart & Winston, 1967), pp. 60–2.

42 Norman Rabkin, ed., *Twentieth Century Interpretations of "The Duchess of Malfi": A Collection of Critical Essays* (Englewood Cliffs, N.J.: Prentice-Hall, 1968), p. 4.

redemption is to be born again to a new, adult life, to be able, as Christian says, "to quit myself like a man," to put away childish things and to face whatever is to be faced. It is this understanding and the living of it, not just his piety and emotional sincerity, that make John Bunyan so powerful a writer. But Mrs. White's work seems to represent the power of a different Christian appeal: the command to become as "babes" in order to enter the kingdom of heaven.[43] Bunyan's conversion comes upon him in roadways, doorways, shops, and fields; Mrs. White's, in her house and in her bed. For Bunyan, "walking brought him closer to heaven."[44] Mrs. White must be lifted up, in a dream.

It is not our task here to judge the value or authenticity of these experiences but rather to recognize that it is her experience, not his, that seems to exemplify an outlook and a need that find expression in English conversion narratives. And for the most part, these narratives do seem to serve the need. Their loose but conventionalized framework provides a shape and a reinforcement for the speaker's sense of order and completeness. At the same time, the ministers, whatever their political motivations, encourage a certain freedom and emotionalism: Dreams and visions convey what otherwise might be inexpressible or even inadmissible evidence. And because the end of conversion is perceived more in terms of psychological benefit than epistemological discovery, the speaker, no matter how humble and how little trained in the art of rhetoric, is usually able to put together some kind of coherent prose narrative about what God has done for him, the very process of doing which may help to reassure him that he is indeed saved. Mrs. White writes down the evidences of God's "Work in me and for me," she says, so "that GOD may have the Glory of his own Grace: . . . for of my self I am not able to think a good Thought, speak a good Word or do a good Action" (p. 21). But if this is so, then writing about God's work is also his work; speaking a good word for God, she must know that God is enabling her to speak.

In fact, Mrs. White's dream can be read symbolically as a restatement of this subliminal assumption, as a recapitulation of the narrative strategy (even if unconscious) not only of particular passages but of the larger structure of the story. In the dream, there is a ladder set upon the earth, its rope (presumably divided into steps) reaching to heaven, and as fast as Mrs. White gets up those steps, she is pulled down again. This is not a bad description of the way language, or any narrative structure

43 Many Puritan preachers, of course, described the converted person as "a new-born babe in Christ," from 1 Cor. 3:1. See also 1 Pet. 2:2.

44 Joan Webber, "Donne and Bunyan: The Styles of Two Faiths," in *Seventeenth-Century Prose,* ed. Fish, p. 508.

made of language, works to try to express the ineffable. One needs to climb up it step by step, presuming to reach the unknown by way of the known, but one keeps falling down again or, at least, never quite gets there by this architectural route. In the end, one must *be* drawn up by "something from above . . . but I could not see what." That something, in literary as well as theological terms, can only be – for Mrs. White and presumably for her readers – the assurance that lies at the end of the story and that, once seen, reveals itself as having been there all along. It is "this free Grace of GOD in chusing me before the Foundation of the World was laid, so unworthy a Creature as I am." Without that assurance, all the steps of the narrative would have been worthless, that is, unconvincing; with it, they are infused with meaning and conviction even though in themselves they cannot carry the mind or the reason across that mysterious gap into the heart of the experience. By exemplifying all this in its own symbolic terms, the dream "justifies" the narrative and is a fit ending for it.[45]

What all this adds up to is a certain willingness, or even a desire, to settle for human limitations, even in the possession of grace. Mrs. White tells the story as clearly and sequentially as she can and that is enough for her. She builds her story out of the ordinary materials of her woman's existence, automatically allegorizing it in an unselfconscious way. She seldom apologizes for inarticulateness, never struggles with the language or strains for a figure; she states unequivocally that through grace, "the LORD hath . . . rightly informed my Judgment" (p. 19). She feels free to say, at the end of her story, that there is an end to striving: "I am sure my greatest Grief is that I can Love [God] no better, and in this Case GOD will accept the Will for the Deed" (p. 15). She might just as well have said the same thing about her narrative of conversion.

But few American Puritans at the time would have been at ease saying either one of these things.

45 No claim is made for completeness, much less exhaustiveness, in this discussion. For example, the dream of Jacob's ladder is also cited in studies of the mystical experience of prayer. It is worth noting that "prayer for spiritual blessings without faith that those blessings will be granted implies a doubt of God's power and is equivalent to unbelief" (Robert Middlekauf, *The Mathers: Three Generations of Puritan Intellectuals, 1596–1728* [London: Oxford University Press, 1971], p. 6). Here again, the assurance of the end is a necessary precondition, even though no conditions can be put upon God. Fawcett also points out that Jesus puts an end to all symbolism by being "in himself Jacob's ladder, the manifestation of God and so the way to the Father" (*Symbolic Language of Religion*, p. 233). In these terms, the dream recapitulates the transition from the old to the new dispensation. An early, personal prefiguration of that transition occurs when Mrs. White leaves father for husband.

ACROSS THE OCEAN

In our preliminary reading of English relations of religious experience, nothing so far has been startlingly inconsistent with what we know about the general expressive contours of Puritan spirituality. It is only when we look across the ocean at the New English counterparts of these narratives that we begin to see complex, and even contradictory, elements that make us realize how inaccurate it is to treat "Puritan spiritual autobiography" (or any subgenre of it) as a monolithic, predictable body of expression.

For example, when people stood up in the churches of Massachusetts Bay to testify to their religious experiences, there were certain potentially symbolic aspects of their lives that they did not seem to find pertinent. When women tried to articulate their experience of conversion, they seldom resorted to talk about children and childbirth;[46] and though some of them mentioned their husbands, most neither dwelt on nor allegorized their experience of marriage. Even fewer of the men spoke of their wives and children, and none dwelt at length on his occupation, except, significantly, one or two seafaring men. Certainly nobody ever spoke of dreams. To judge by the early conversion narratives of New England, no one, during the first thirty years of the colony, ever had a dream at all – excepting, of course, the one publicly permitted dream: the dream of America.

Much has been written and said about "the American dream"; perhaps too much. But it is impossible to discount, when reading the conversion stories of New Englanders, the fact of America as a central, even obsessive concern of the imagination, and one that is inextricably bound up with each person's notion of, hope for, and recapitulation of his or her own experience of salvation. In the first generation of settlers, the obsession emerges concretely in the figures of sea, ship, towns, churches, and ministers and indirectly by intricate scriptural reference; in the second generation, it is transmuted into an excruciating self-consciousness about the first generation; but it is always there, shaping the narrative and irradiating it with the speaker's hope to be pure and new and whole in a new and holy place. If the central symbols of both English and American narratives revolve around the concept of heavenly deliverance, it still must be stressed that the American version of deliverance is imaginatively mediated and substantively affected by a real geographical place.

46 Yet the figure, like that of the "new-born babe," was often used by preachers: "A person must know whether he has grace first of all by his own experience, 'as a woman that is breeding a Child feels such qualmes and distempers, that shee knows thereby shee is with Child' " (John Cotton, *A Practical Commentary . . . upon The First Epistle Generall of John* [London, 1656], p. 196, cited in Miller, *New England Mind: Seventeenth Century*, p. 51).

None of this should be news to students of American Puritanism. Yet it bears repeating, and close examination, in the context of the conversion narrative, if only because of the persistent assumption that a work like *The Experiences* of Mrs. White can somehow be read as a product of the New England mind, despite its obvious indifference to the one experience that is most centrally American.

It may be worthwhile, then, to sample here at least one literary formulation of the American migration experience, from the chief source of first-generation narratives: the Thomas Shepard collection from the First Church in Cambridge, Massachusetts. Between 1637 and 1645, Shepard recorded the relations of twenty-two women, twenty-eight men, and one unidentified person, and forty-two of them talked in one way or another about the shift from England to America. They provide several subtle and even contradictory variations on the theme; but for our present purposes, it will be useful to examine a narrative that uses the migration in just the way we might expect: as a keystone in the structure of deliverance.

About Katherine, "Mrs. Russel's maid," nothing is known, and her "Confession," like most of the relations in New England churches, tells us very little about her.[47] All we know, and perhaps all we need to know, is in her narrative. We can probably assume that, as a maid, Katherine is a young woman of fairly humble background, and this may have something to do with the fact that her story is closest to the English type that we have been looking at. It is similar in two ways: The story is complete; and its "happy ending" is in the transition from self to self-surrender – with the one crucial difference that the transforming event in the story is the trip to the new world.

Katherine's narrative has the conversion "shape" that we saw earlier: Its motion is a sort of hybrid of the down–up and outward–inward. In fact, the story falls into three segments, the first and third of which are like mirror opposites. In the first half, as we would expect, the emphasis is on sin, legal "terror," and her own external actions; at the center is the passage to America; at the end, new perceptions, self-surrender, and "a great lifting up of my heart to the Lord."

It is interesting to see how important the verbs are in distinguishing one section from another. At the outset, the sense of self-willed movement is strong: "I went on in ignorance," "I went to an aunt," "I sought the Lord," "I followed the word," "But to go back, I would not," "I sought that ministry," "continued two years," and so on.

47 *Shepard's "Confessions,"* pp. 99–101. Except where clarity may be impaired, subsequent references to the Shepard document appear in the text by page number.

But in the last section, almost all the verbs have to do with perceptions rather than actions: "heard," "hearing," "saw," "seeing," "thought," "found Christ to me." In the first section, even negative verbs are active: "I questioned," "I doubted," "I fell"; in the second, passive ("I was troubled") or privative ("could not get victory"), and in the final moment, the verb is altogether transformed into a substantive: "a great lifting up." By means of these verbs, the protagonist moves through the plot from a condition of doing to a condition of being or abiding. And between these two conditions, the critical ritual event is the passage over the ocean, a passage taken because, after all the searching, going, looking, following, and seeking in Old England, the speaker hopes that "here the Lord might be found."

In the central passage, the important alliance of migration with conversion is revealed not only by the word *call,* with its weighty religious significance, but also by the selection of scriptural references.

> And thought here the Lord might be found, and doubtful whether I had a call to come because I was to leave my friends. Hence I remembered that Scripture – I'll be with thee in the first waters* – and I knew I should be armed like Jacob in all straits to have a promise. And in our way when ready to be cast away, stand still and see salvation of God,† then heard Lord is my portion.‡ So I came hither. (pp. 100–1)
>
> * Isa. 43:2. † Exod. 14:13; 2 Chron. 20:17. ‡ Ps. 73:26; 119:57; 142:5; Lam. 3:24; Ps. 16:5.

At the center of this passage is Jacob; it is as if the speaker can perceive a "call to come" only when she likens herself to the public and collective figure of Israel. Katherine undoubtedly has in mind the beginning of the forty-third chapter of Isaiah, which is the "calling" of Jacob.

> But now thus saith the LORD that created thee, O Jacob, and he that formed thee, O Israel, Fear not: for I have redeemed thee, I have called *thee* by thy name; thou *art* mine.
>
> When thou passest through the waters, I *will be* with thee.

Having established the "waters" imagery, Katherine continues it by next citing the fourteenth chapter of Exodus. A modern reader is likely to skim over this connection; but Katherine is speaking directly out of the most dramatic moment in Exodus, knowing – as her audience surely does – that just after Moses tells the people, "Fear ye not, stand still, and see the Salvation of the Lord" (which she quotes), God parts the waters of the sea for the Israelites. Katherine's final citation is from Lamentations, an odd-seeming choice for someone who is describing a deliverance; until we realize that she has chosen the one chapter therein that represents the turning point from lament to thanksgiving, to trust that "hopeful waiting is justified."[48]

> *It is of* the LORD's mercies that we are not consumed, because his compassions fail not.
> *They are* new every morning: great *is* thy faithfulness.
> The LORD *is* my portion, saith my soul; therefore will I hope in him.
> The LORD *is* good unto them that wait for him, to the soul *that* seeketh him.

Because all these Scriptures are cited only in fragments, it is easy for the reader to overlook them. But clearly, for the speaker and for her audience, it was possible to evoke a great range of scriptural meaning with only a few key words. All these echoes of the Word seem to exercise a transforming power on the outcome of the story, just as they presumably operated on Katherine herself during the voyage, taking her from doubt of her "call" to embark through confidence that the trip was justified. Having gone so far "down" and "out" through her ordeal that she was even "ready to be cast away" on the ocean, the speaker is now ready to move upward toward the fulfillment of John 6:37: that "him that cometh to me, I cast not away."[49] The words "So I came hither" signal the start of this upturn in Katherine's story: henceforth, the coming to Christ *is* coming to the new world, where, hearing Shepard preach, Katherine first perceives sin as "sicknesses" to grieve over and understands the "will" to Christ as futile. The weak one now sees that she cannot "get victory" over "very strong" sin but can only submit (like Mrs. White) to "a great lifting up."

> And hearing of coming to Christ and Christ will not cast away,* which was a great lifting up of my heart to the Lord. And I heard though Judas forsook all, yet he had not Christ for his last end and that there I took my rest . . . so I found Christ to me. (p. 101)
>
> * John 6:37.

Only in the new world are such perceptions discovered. And this may be why the promise of the first Gospel, Matt. 11:28, cited in the first part of the story while Katherine is still in Old England (we recall that this is the favored passage in Henry Walker's London congregation), does not prove satisfying until it is transformed, in New England, into the last Gospel's promise, John 6:37. Again, it is worth

48 Harvey H. Guthrie, Jr., "Lamentations," in Charles M. Laymon, ed., *The Interpreter's One-Volume Commentary on the Bible* (Nashville: Abingdon, 1971), p. 405. I assume that Katherine's primary reference is to Lamentations (not to the Psalms), since it alone matches her words exactly.

49 Katherine echoes the Geneva Bible version of St. John, although her Exodus citation appears to be from the KJV. All subsequent scriptural references in the discussion of Katherine's narrative are from the Geneva Bible.

recalling the contexts of these passages. We have seen that Matt. 11:28 is a promise of ease and rest to "the poore base people" – those that "fele the waight, & grief of your sinnes and miseries." Now, Katherine has earlier said that in Old England she found such "particular promises" unsatisfactory: They left her still "under terror." But John 6:37 is absolutely clear, direct, and starkly unequivocal about who comes to God, and how.

> All that the Father giueth me, shal come to me: and him that cometh to me, I cast not away.

To drive the point home, the Geneva Bible provides a crisp marginal note: "God doeth regenerate his elect." It is no longer a question of feeling the weight and terror of sin (though she must) or of doing anything (though she has) but of being done to and of finding that her "coming" is a foregone conclusion. What has happened between the imperative "Come vnto me" of Matt. 11:28 and the declarative "All that the Father giueth me, shal come" of John 6:37 is the stripping away of all self-dependency by passing through the waters, quite literally, of affliction. The old world was effort and doing; the new world, forsaking all and thereby finding "rest." And as the narrative progresses, the syntax mirrors this exchange, from the opening phrase to the concluding one, from

> First I went

to

> Christ to me.

We have gone into some detail about this conversion story to clarify several points of difference from the English narratives. First, we saw that in England the "movement" through conversion is often described in personal terms: Mrs. White's story moves down into and up out of her own body and self; many of the church relations move outward through personal experiences of family life, economic vicissitudes, warfare, and so on, and inward through dreams, visions, or just a sudden inexplicable realization of being personally saved. But the movement here is not personal; any passage through the stages or roles of the speaker's own life is overshadowed by her movement through a vast geography, both physical and spiritual, as well as through an expansion (at least momentary) of the private person into the public figure of Israel.[50] Second, that movement is much more closely knit with Scrip-

50 These conflations of two kinds of geography and personality involve the pervasive literary problem that Sacvan Bercovitch describes as peculiar to American Puritanism: the transformation of a spiritual journey into an actual

ture than is the movement of an English narrative. Of course, all Puritan use of Scripture grows out of the idea that men are saved by the gospel. In both English and American narratives, a piece of Scripture "comes" to explain or illuminate the meaning of an experience, and sometimes, as in Mrs. White's childbirth passage, the scriptural reference quite explicitly mediates the experience – as we saw, it acts as a midwife to the deliverance. But there is seldom a discernible architectural pattern of scriptural use in an English narrative. Throughout the story, Mrs. White's numerous biblical citations are not ordered in any particular way. In Walker's congregation, biblical citations are often grouped at the end of the narrative as an example of the "comfort" Scripture has brought to the believer. But many of the New England saints follow and elaborate on the practice we have glimpsed in Katherine's story: Scriptural passages become structural elements of the narrative, and there is, so to speak, an actual movement of the narrator through the Bible, almost as through a physical space. When this movement works well, it provides, as for Katherine, a kind of ideal old world–new world transition, translated into satisfying literary form by a strong reliance on the creative internalization of Scripture. This movement toward a satisfying end, both spiritual and literary, gives her common ground with the English saints, despite the genuine differences in technique.

But hers is not the only pattern in New England conversion narratives. There is another, a pattern of asymmetry or discontent, usually launched by the ritual statement that "after I came hither I saw my condition more miserable than ever," or "since I came hither that hath been my grief that I walked no more closely with God in the place where I came," or "at last came to New England and found heart and all ordinances dead," or "and when she came hither she found her heart . . . full of perturbation and distress."[51] Such complaints echo so insistently that they constitute almost a ceremonial incantation; in fact, they seem to become established as a new literary convention. A certain emotion begins to be connected with the migration: a kind of grim, gray disappointment that emerges in conversion stories as an almost obligatory structural element. Overlaid with this emotion, New En-

historical one, resulting in "aesthetic tensions . . . between symbolism and allegory" (*The American Puritan Imagination: Essays in revaluation* [Cambridge University Press, 1974], p. 13). We have still to deal with that problem. For the moment, we are only illustrating those things that New England conversion narratives try to do that English ones do not.

51 *Shepard's "Confessions,"* pp. 90, 43, 143; Fiske, *Notebook*, p. 44. Henceforth in this Introduction, all citations of conversion narratives are from the Shepard group.

gland becomes a kind of allegorized character. Sometimes it is a Slough of Despond:

> I thought to go back but I considered – is this my spirit[52] and straitened and so I fell upon myself and justified God in what He had done or should. And I saw a vexing in all I did and my life was a death and when I knew not to do my eyes were to Him and I considered though hope fail yet Lord undertook for me . . . And I thought I was lost and unsupported and I thought Lord had left me to be so. (p. 191)

Sometimes it is an Enchanted Ground:

> And so came to New England. I forgot the Lord as the Israelites did . . . And so saw sloth and sluggishness so I prayed . . . And the more I prayed the more temptation I had. So I gave up. (p. 140)

> And so I came to this place and coming by sea and having a hard voyage my heart was dead and senseless . . . And though I had some affection yet stuck nothing by me. (p. 179)

> But after this I was in a benumbed condition. (p. 177)

But it is not the Immanuel's Land it was expected to be:

> And in old England, seeing ordinances polluted, my soul desired to be there where Christ is feeding of His flock in this place. But saw many stumbling blocks yet prized, yet since I came hither my heart hath been straightened for God. (p. 87)

There are, in fact, so many "stumbling blocks" in these Cambridge conversion stories that the reader is forced to ask just what the trouble might be. Perhaps we can never know whether people were "really" having so much difficulty being converted or whether their expectations for the new world were inevitably doomed to defeat by dreary reality. But we can ask why people are talking about their experiences in this particular way, and why there is an urgency in the language that seems to reflect some larger, more pervasive dynamic in the narratives as a whole.

> And so when I desired to come hither and found a discontented heart and mother dead and my heart overwhelmed . . . And in this town I could not understand anything was said, I was so blind, and heart estranged from people of people [*sic:* God]. (p. 183; interpolation mine)

> Hence I desired hither to come thinking one sermon might do me more good than a hundred there. And hearing children would curse

52 The phrase *is this my spirit* is my reading. Selement and Woolley omit the word *this*.

> parents for not getting them to means but I found not what I came for hither and found no rest my heart was so dead. (p. 185)

"I found not what I came for hither": This is the cryptic cry, sometimes only implicit, in most of the narratives and may be a clue to that underlying dynamic. One applicant bluntly spelled out her understanding of what the elusive problem really was when she testified that in Old England,

> hearing a sermon that feeling follows faith of saints and I labored to feel it and Lord making way for New England I thought I should find feelings. (p. 78)

This unfulfilled desire to "find feelings," which cannot be "labored" for but which simply do not come upon one (as they did for Mrs. White and Katherine), is what pulsates through most American conversion stories and seems to give them their distinctive flavor. For instance, Mr. Sparhawk (Nathaniel Sparrowhawk),[53] who was a deacon of Shepard's church from 1639 to 1647, describes what seems to have been a genuine religious experience while he was still in Old England.

> Sometimes the Lord, especially in a fast day morning, refreshed my heart at Dedham and so God inclined my heart to close with the Lord most. But on the fast day morning, desiring to be alone and to bewail my condition and there entreating reconciliation, the Lord revealed Himself so as never before with abundance of the sweetness of Himself, which rejoicing made me to break out to weeping and hardly could I refrain from speaking to others to let them see what Lord had done. (p. 63)

Yet he undercuts it at once ("But that day he found least of God") and nothing in the subsequent narrative returns to this pitch of spiritual joy. Instead, the rest of Mr. Sparhawk's relation unravels in a string of rather sad, confused emotions connected with the move to New England; he has trouble putting it into words ("I cannot remember many things which I cannot now express myself"), a difficulty shared by many of his fellows; and finally the story stops without, somehow, really concluding: "And I have entreated the Lord to help my unbelief and other things whereby I found my heart enlarged" (p. 64).

The shape of many such stories becomes increasingly amorphous after the arrival in New England. Like Mr. Sparhawk, many others seize on the "since-I-came-hither" convention, offering the same limp and irresolute endings, leaving the shape undefined.

53 Selement and Woolley give some names both as Shepard originally recorded them and in modernized form. This study uses the original names, with the modern alternates indicated on the first reference.

> So I heard of Christ's little ones begot by promise* and so I feared I was [not] one. And last lecture day Lord let me see something. (p. 186)
>
> * Matt. 10:42; 18:6, 10, 14; Mark 9:42; Luke 17:2.

> But Lord was pleased in this poor condition to let me hear – Gospel was preached to the poor† and though sin were as crimson yet He would make them as white as snow.‡ But I could not tell what to do and so I remained. (p. 174)
>
> † Matt. 11:5; Luke 4:18; 7:22. ‡ Isa. 1:18.

> Still I am doubting but I know I shall know if I follow on and if He damn me He shall do it in His own way. (p. 143)

These are a far cry from the reassuring conclusions of the English conversion stories. Much of this hesitancy can be attributed, of course, to a fear of enthusiasm, especially after the Anne Hutchinson trials of 1637–8. Yet enough people, like Katherine, do claim a measure of assurance and satisfaction, of "closing with Christ," that we cannot explain everything in terms of fear of clerical strictures. The problem seems to be at least partly one of temperament – as if a certain strain of the collective personality is trying to work itself out in the conversion narrative: a personality that, unlike the English, with its drive toward completion and resolution, is more comfortable with ambivalence and open-endedness. The Englishman ends his conversion narrative with one foot in heaven; his brother starts out for heaven but gets sidetracked in New England, where he continues his seeking but somehow needs to postpone his final salvation. Hence, the "peace, disturbance, peace again" movement never comes to a satisfying close. Like Thoreau walking toward a never-setting western sun, a great number of American Puritans, at least when they express themselves on the subject of their own conversions, either will not or cannot end the story.

The most striking difference between English and American relations of religious experience is this matter of the completeness of the structure; and along with it go questions about the adequacy of the available symbols and even of language itself. On the surface of it, the American tendency to open-endedness would seem to perpetuate a state of literary anxiety: the exact opposite of what the English narrative, in its limited way, achieves. For if the "dream" of New England fails to provide a proper conclusion, where does the speaker – where does the *story* – go from there? It is a question – but it is also a challenge – that the English narrative does not raise.

In any case, a preliminary survey like this suggests that it is neither useful nor accurate to lump together English and American conversion narratives, despite the undisputed fact that a shared Calvinist theology undergirds them all.

There are, of course, many historical explanations for the differences we are seeing. First, there is time. American conversion stories begin earlier (indeed, they are thought to be the prototype of the form), and even the latest of Shepard's group predates the Walker and Rogers congregations by six or seven years and Mrs. White by fifteen to twenty years. (On the other hand, the relations recorded by Wigglesworth and many by Fiske are contemporary with the English narratives included in this study. In this second New English group, the migration experience naturally subsides in importance, but closely related factors, as we shall see, take their place, and the pattern of open-endedness, along with a somewhat different use of Scripture, still persists.)

Second, there are obvious differences in the political, ecclesiastical, and basic physical circumstances out of which these narratives emerge. The conversion story in America is thus inevitably tied up with the migration and with expectations about New England. It is also affected by the very fact that it is a requirement in virtually all the churches, and by its central role in the broader New English effort to work out, often with blood, sweat, and tears, the exact nature of the church and the best way to define and gather its membership. In England, the conversion narrative can only blossom after the Civil War, when the gathered churches are free to depart from the parochial system of general membership; but even then, under Cromwell's loose religious settlement, such churches have neither unity nor power, and the relation of religious experience is less a testing instrument in the working out of a polity than it is a vehicle for evangelical comfort and encouragement.

Finally, out of these different situations emerge differences between the preaching being heard in England and America. On both sides, we must take into account the interaction of the people with the kind of preaching they were exposed to and the complex ways in which they processed that preaching through their actual experience.

All these crucial factors will be considered in the next chapters in more detail. But before proceeding on that path, we should define more precisely the literary problem with which we began.

THE LITERARY PROBLEM

How shall we explain the past misunderstandings about the provenance of Mrs. Elizabeth White's memoir? Surely they are partly attributable to the scattered nature of the bibliographical records. Yet a text is usually the most reliable key to itself, and this text clearly speaks with an English accent: an accent, however, that may not be audible if there is not a settled habit of listening for it. The Mrs. White mix-up suggests that our twentieth-century ears are not yet habitually attuned to the differences between English and American expression in the seventeenth century; and this is so despite the massive scholarly efforts of recent years to delineate the special characteristics of early New English culture.

This is not to say that our earliest literature is not taken seriously and studied sensitively. That there is a genuine literary realm here, and one that embraces more than the accumulated "thought" or "ideas" of the time, is a truth that surely has been rescued by now from the supposed neglect of Perry Miller, whose disinterest in the nonrational side of the mind has so often been lamented. Alan Simpson's complaint in 1955 that Miller "told us too much about the Puritan mind and not enough about the Puritan's feelings"[54] has been amply answered by literary (and psychological) studies of increasing sophistication, notably by the work of Sacvan Bercovitch. But still a kind of veil hangs over early American expression, so that, as we have seen, even now an English writer like Elizabeth White is easily mistaken for an American one. The question persists: Why are we in fact without a finer sense of what might constitute a genuinely American tone of voice in the earliest years of our literature?

Some of the answers have been intimated by Norman S. Grabo in his assessment of the largely unrecognized role of aesthetics in early American studies.[55] One of Grabo's most telling points is that historians too often fail to grasp the distinction between discursive and symbolic writing and that even poetry and fiction are used by them as documentary evidence

> to support what we know from other sources. They are read just as any other documents – proclamations, diaries, church records, or formal histories – are read, . . . as if the relationship of words to ideas were identical in both kinds of document.

On the contrary, Grabo explains, the "facts" offered by the symbolic forms of art are different in kind from documentary facts and often more revealing, since art, better than any other human endeavor, embodies not "thought" and even less doctrine but rather "the shape of human feeling" in a given moment of time.[56]

54 *Puritanism in Old and New England* (Chicago: University of Chicago Press, 1955), p. 21.

55 "The veiled vision: the role of aesthetics in early American intellectual history," in Bercovitch, ed., *Imagination*, pp. 19–33. I have borrowed Grabo's "veil" figure, which he uses to represent the putative "artistic debility of colonial literature"; like Hawthorne, Grabo questions whether "the obscurity lies, . . . in the eye of the beholder" (p. 33).

56 Ibid., pp. 26, 33. These distinctions were earlier elucidated by William York Tindall and Northrop Frye among others, but Grabo's essay is notable for its unapologetic application of such ideas to Puritan expression.

Since literary scholars (unlike Grabo's historians) are presumably familiar and comfortable with these propositions, why is it that "even literary historians ignore the artistic side of colonial literature for its more attractive intellectual sister"? It is almost as if the literary people are taking a cue from the Puritans themselves, who, Grabo reminds us, are perceived as distrustful of art and therefore resistant to any conscious recognition of their own capacities for the use of aesthetic form. The odd fact is that Puritan theory is all for plain, logical, explanatory expression, whereas Puritan practice – for example, Edward Johnson's history – betrays "another, quite sophisticated symbolic sense." In the face of this contradiction, it is virtually useless to look to the rhetorical speculations of the Puritans in trying to account for their art.[57]

A decade earlier, in his influential work on symbolism, Charles Feidelson, Jr., encountered the same contradiction and vehemently stressed what he saw as its destructive consequences.[58] In Feidelson's view, the Puritans had a gift for symbolic writing that they themselves did not understand. Obsessed with logical method and mistaking the fundamental nature of both knowledge and language, they feared the possibilities of a conscious "functional symbolism" and choked off much of their own imaginative power – as, for example, Cotton Mather did (according to Feidelson) – under a blanket of "wearisome," "trivial," "grotesque," and "mechanical compilations"; whereas only on rare occasions did images, "all unawares," manage to "quicken into symbols as idea and illustration coalesce[d]." Thus Puritanism nurtured its two unhealthy children: "the furtive and unacknowledged role of artistic method in the American mind" and "the crudity or conventionality of a great part of American literature from 1620 through [1875]."[59]

Grabo, on the other hand, suggests that we bypass the Puritans' theories about the nature of art and postpone any final critical evaluation of their work or their legacy to the culture. Instead, he begins with the simple existential *fact* of Puritan poetical, dramatic, or fictional techniques, and asks us to pose as many questions as possible about why Puritan writers made their particular formal aesthetic choices, and how they imparted the peculiar satisfactions of art (which they undoubtedly did)[60] to their seventeenth-century audiences. He reminds us that

57 Ibid., pp. 24, 25.

58 *Symbolism and American Literature* (Chicago: University of Chicago Press, 1953), pp. 77–101.

59 Ibid., pp. 86, 81, 83, 89.

60 Michael Wigglesworth's *The Day of Doom* offers vivid evidence. See Harrison T. Meserole, ed., *Seventeenth-Century American Poetry* (Garden City, N.Y.: Doubleday, Anchor Press, 1968), p. 37, for an account of the poem's overwhelming popularity. See also Grabo, "Veiled Vision," pp. 25–6, on Wigglesworth.

> if some kinds of "ideas" representing a major aspect of human experience can only be observed in the symbolic forms of art and not at all in discursive statements, then such questions must be answered. But the common explanations of Puritan art discourage intellectual historians from even asking them.[61]

Grabo's approach is not new to literary study,[62] and yet he himself seems to recommend it more for the solution of historical than of literary problems. As the title of his article suggests, he is trying to shake up the attitudes of intellectual historians by showing them how an insight into the nature of art can transform colonial literature into a usable tool for getting at "the Puritan mind" – even when the materials seem to be of little interest to literary history itself! In fact, Grabo carefully draws a line between the two disciplines, intellectual and literary history. Discussing later colonial writers who took Dryden's poetry as a model in spite of their American subject matter, Grabo observes:

> To discount eighteenth-century American verse as weakly imitative of British models may suffice for literary history or even for literary criticism. But intellectual history cannot afford to ignore the fact that the ideas expressed in these poems are as they are because the writers have been conditioned by the forms of others' imaginations, others' feelings. To borrow or inherit a form of verse or a figure of speech may not be significant; to fall heir to a form or figure of thought, however, may have infinite and infinitely subtle consequences.[63]

This seems an unnecessary putting asunder of what should be joined together; but Grabo nevertheless touches the heart of the matter. What he is willing to dismiss (at least for the sake of argument) on behalf of literary scholars is just what they can*not,* any more than intellectual historians, "afford to ignore." The "shape of feeling," the "form or figure of thought," these are inherent (as well as inherited), ineradicably present and alive, in the form of a verse, the figure of speech, the syntax of a sentence, the selection of an image – in the very stuff of literary expression, even if involuntarily introduced.[64] And the trans-

61 Grabo, "Veiled Vision," p. 26.

62 It has much in common with Northrop Frye's thinking in its deemphasis of evaluation and in its wariness of the "intentional fallacy." It is also like archetypal criticism insofar as "it requires close textual readings, like the formalistic, and yet it is concerned humanistically with more than the intrinsic value of aesthetic satisfaction; it seems psychological insofar as it analyzes the work of art's appeal to the audience . . . and yet sociological in its attendance upon basic cultural patterns as central to that appeal" (Wilbur Scott, *Five Approaches of Literary Criticism* [New York: Collier, 1962], p. 247).

63 Grabo, "Veiled Vision," p. 29.

64 "Colonial *belles-lettres,* like other arts, are symbolic expressions, often involuntary, of the artist's emotional framework of ideas" (ibid.).

mission and transmutation of these linked forms always have significant "consequences" for the life of literature.

Should we doubt the validity of that position, we need look no further than *The Experiences* of Mrs. White and the confessions of her American cousins, unimpressive as they may initially appear to be from an "aesthetic" standpoint; for until we can begin to perceive them as cousins and not as twins, we can make no certain claim to our own expressive beginnings. That we have not thus perceived them is as much a literary problem as it is a problem in intellectual history. And it is a problem compounded by the fact that even among the supposedly "plain" and utilitarian forms of colonial literature, the conversion narrative seems the plainest and most utilitarian of all. It would scarcely be considered, and indeed has not been considered, a legitimate part of Grabo's (or anyone's) universe of early American symbolic forms. It is not, in short, thought to be art – even of the awkward Puritan variety.

This is the real reason why Mrs. White has not been better understood. Her work has been misread because it has not been taken to heart as imaginative expression. She has been approached as a documentary writer, a reciter and reporter of certain events for the edification of our intellects – or of her own.[65] That these "events" (and the personality that experiences them) are spiritual and invisible and even mysterious may be overlooked because – so we have been told – virtually all conversion narratives are stiff and formulaic, dutifully conforming to established theological conventions and plowing along in the same old ruts. No one has questioned Edmund S. Morgan's wry observation that New England conversion narratives "demonstrate clearly the familiarity of the narrators with the morphology of conversion, a familiarity produced, no doubt, by a great many sermons on the subject"; nor his conclusion that "the pattern is so plain as to give the experiences the appearance of a stereotype."[66] And no one has reevaluated Daniel B. Shea, Jr.'s diagnosis that

> their subject matter is restricted, . . . their vocabulary is uniform and impersonal, . . . The issue, whether or not conversion had taken place, is never in doubt . . . they indicate how limited the

65 Whether Mrs. White's "Reasons why I write" (see n. 10, above) are head or heart reasons is not easy to decide. In any case, as I have been arguing, there is no need to assume that the narrative does only what it purports to do.

66 Morgan, *Visible Saints,* pp. 90–1. I regret that I, too, have propounded these views of the "more or less formulaic conversion relations" of New England (Patricia Caldwell, "The Antinomian Language Controversy," *Harvard Theological Review* 69:3–4 [July-Oct. 1976]:366). On closer study, I have learned (and try to demonstrate herein) that there were significant and varied uses of the "formula."

Puritan's freedom of movement could be as he prosecuted his inward exploration.[67]

Statements like these stir up some intriguing literary questions; for example, the question of what it means to say that a form of expression works within a convention and whether adherence to a "pattern" or even restriction of subject matter are in themselves detrimental to effective expression. Is it really a stumbling block that "the issue, . . . is never in doubt"? There are many literary forms in which this is so, and besides, we have reason to believe that all conversion narratives do not march inexorably to a heavenly close. Even if they did, are we not obliged, as Bunyan has taught us, to concern ourselves with the way in which the journey is taken? But, we are warned, we know the way, and it is dreary; the "vocabulary is uniform and impersonal," the whole abstract "pattern" determined by "a great many sermons on the subject" (perhaps, we begin to suspect, too many). Here our only response can be a willingness to look very closely at the narratives to see whether they really are stereotypes and whether they are in fact controlled to the point of paralysis by the prescribed signs and stages of conversion.

Such an inquiry is especially important in light of our information about Mrs. White: that she is English, after all, and that she and her countrymen often speak in more conventional ways than do their American counterparts (whom Shea credits with a special bent for "formalistic recitation and mechanical pattern").[68] Hence we are called upon to reexamine the Anglo-American relationship and to try to account for the divergence of expression in new, more precise literary terms; for the present vocabulary – "abstract," "mechanical," "restricted," "uniform," and so on – leaves us unable to explain the variegated feel and color of these narratives in the face of the relatively "impersonal" quality they all do seem to possess. Furthermore, we must take care not to prejudge that impersonal quality without some attention to the nature of the broader confession form of which the conversion narrative is a subgenre, and which Northrop Frye has characterized for us as "introverted, but intellectualized in content."[69] In fact, if we are seriously to consider the charges of abstractness and impersonality, we must do so in light of Frye's definition of the form:

67 Shea, *Spiritual Autobiography*, p. 91. Cf. Robert G. Pope, "Introduction" to Fiske, *Notebook*, p. xvi: "Their substance is remarkably similar, almost a stylized formula of sin and election"; and Roger Sharrock, Introduction to *Grace Abounding*, p. xxxii, on Bunyan's "uniqueness" in departing from the usual "rationalization into stock Calvinist formulae."

68 Shea, *Spiritual Autobiography*, p. 90.

69 *Anatomy of Criticism: Four Essays* (Princeton: Princeton University Press, 1971), p. 308.

that the confession, "intellectualized" though its content may be, is "inspired by a creative, and therefore fictional, impulse"; that the goal is to build up an integrated inward pattern, often a pattern associated with something larger than oneself; and that the realization of that pattern ultimately meets a personal, felt need. Hence we find that

> nearly always some theoretical and intellectual interest in religion, politics, or art plays a leading role in the confession. It is his success in integrating his mind on such subjects that makes the author of a confession feel that his life is worth writing about.[70]

The process, then, involves some kind of creative organization of materials at least partly theoretical and intellectual but aimed toward the satisfaction of a need to feel something or to feel it in a certain way. This loose and possibly oversimplified description at least helps us to remember that the conversion narrative may be approached as a literary form, an imaginative construct that comes about in order to fulfill – in its peculiar way and in no other possible way – an aim, an end, a need. If the form looks impenetrable and inartistic because "the language of discourse and the symbolic constructs of art seem indistinguishable"[71] in it, we probably should ask what needs are served by this particular confluence of modes and, above all, how those needs are different, or become different, on the facing shores of the Atlantic.

That there are differences, we have already discovered. The raw experiences of a Mrs. White could well have happened outside England, but the imaginative reconstruction that she fashioned from them could not have issued from America. It is the burden of this study to ask why this should be so and to locate some of the first faint murmurings of a truly American voice, emerging from little-known, ordinary people in community who, during a few decades in our history, tried to act on the idea that their lives were worth writing – or talking – about. Their minds saturated with the Bible, struggling to express in an unfamiliar public arena their most vital and private religious concerns, they somehow started to speak "New Englandly" – not on the eve of the Revolution and not at the turn of the century but from the first moment the Puritans alighted on the hopeful, holy land of America.

70 Ibid., pp. 307–8.
71 Grabo, "Veiled Vision," p. 33.

PART I

THE CONVERSION NARRATIVE AS A FORM OF EXPRESSION IN THE PURITAN GATHERED CHURCHES

By the breath of the Lord,
a Congregation is gathered together.

John Cotton, *The Way of Life*

1

ORIGINS

Nobody knows who gave the first full-fledged conversion narrative – or when, or even where it was heard. Like all forms of art and nature, the Puritan conversion story evolved; it did not spring full-blown from the brain of a creator, either divine or human. And, as with many points of Congregationalist discipline, the barn doors were a long time shutting: Although the practice was skimpily referred to during the developmental years of the 1630s, and more widely acknowledged and discussed in published documents throughout the 1640s, the fullest articulation of a rationale for relations only appeared long after they were well on the way out – notably in Cotton Mather's *Magnalia Christi Americana*.[1] In consequence, despite years of scholarly research and speculation, no one has yet found a sure way to pinpoint the exact place on the scale where the three major standards for these testimonies first coalesced: namely, (1) relation before the entire congregation of (2) a genuine experience of conversion (not doctrinal "knowledge" or "belief"), which (3) was required of all who would join the church.[2]

1 2 vols. (Hartford, 1855), 1:327–8; 2:67–76, 243–7.

2 Edmund S. Morgan's *Visible Saints* is the classic historical work on the subject and the indispensable source for understanding the subtle development of the idea that an elect church could and should "test" the inward spiritual estates of all its members. Morgan's virtually indisputable thesis is, in part, that the early reformed churches required nothing more of prospective members than an outward "profession of faith," an understanding of basic doctrine, and a visibly "godly conversation" (i.e., conduct), in the hope that a church made up of such would contain the greatest possible number of truly elect members; that the troublesome test of "experience" for evidence of genuine conversion and true "saving faith" only emerged during the New England settlement, probably about 1634 and probably at the instigation of the most venerated New England minister, John Cotton; and that the administration of such tests was then exported back to England. Though even Morgan has been unable to trace the practice to its precise origins, he records some provocative speculations on the matter, to which this chapter is indebted.

Conversion narratives were aptly described in the Cambridge Platform of 1648 as both "personall & publick,"[3] and between the two words lay a vast territory of contradiction and unease that for fifteen years had rendered this one of the most controversial points of church polity between the Congregationalists and the Presbyterians. It was "personall" because it represented the speaker's own inner experience, his own feeling "of God's manner of working upon the soul in conversion."[4] It was "publick" because it was required of all who would become church members in full communion (entitled to all privileges, especially that of partaking of the Lord's Supper) and because it had to be delivered before and voted upon by the entire membership.[5] In fact, the full-fledged relation made up a three-sided figure: for the speaker, it was meant to be not a set of doctrines intellectually assented to but a living experience of the heart, voluntarily told in his or her own words; for the audience, it was meant to be not just a passive absorption of information but a spiritual act – of hearing, of rendering the "judgment of charity,"[6] and of receiving (sometimes rejecting)[7] a "living stone" for the temple; and for the "Militant-visible-

3 Williston Walker, *The Creeds and Platforms of Congregationalism* (Philadelphia: Pilgrim Press, 1960), p. 223.

4 Ibid.

5 The elders were permitted to deliver the relations of those, especially women, who felt "excessive fear"; but the Cambridge Platform clearly preferred "*relations, & confessions* personally [made] with their own mouth" (ibid.).

6 *Iudicium charitatis* is a theological term that is interpreted, broadly speaking, in two ways: as a readiness to judge people favorably unless there is clear evidence to the contrary (St. Thomas Aquinas's view); and, more specifically, as a readiness to assume the sainthood or elect state of a person who is baptized (Luther's view) or of one who confesses the faith, takes the sacraments, and leads an outwardly upright life (Calvin's view). For a thorough discussion of the concept, see Baird Tipson, "Invisible Saints: The 'Judgment of Charity' in the Early New England Churches," *Church History* 44 (December 1975): 460–71. New England's critics claimed the judgment of charity was incompatible with a "test" of inner sainthood; her apologists claimed charity protected the system from exclusivism and harshness. See John Norton, *The Answer To The Whole Set of Questions of the Celebrated Mr. William Apollonius* . . . ed. & trans. Douglas Horton (Cambridge, Mass.: Harvard University Press, Belknap Press, 1958), pp. 39–41.

7 Thomas Lechford's contemporary (and critical) account of New England church practices claimed that members "often" took exception to the "expressions" of candidates and prevented their admission (*Plain Dealing; or, News from New England,* ed. J. Hammond Trumbull [Boston, 1867; rpt. ed., New York: Garrett Press, 1970], p. 28). John Cotton, Thomas Weld, and others counterclaimed that members were admitted with leniency: "If they can give any evidence . . . its sufficient" (Weld, *An Answer to* W[illiam] R[athband] . . . [London, 1644], p. 24). But Thomas Hooker abandoned the practice partly

church," it was the closest thing in this world to a guarantee of the purest possible membership.

Over this last point, battles raged throughout the 1640s, when Presbyterians were struggling to reorganize the English church according to their own practice and meeting resistance on various fronts from a small pro-Congregationalist or "Independent" force within the Westminster Assembly. Both sides cited the New England way to substantiate their views, and fierce vituperation ensued, particularly over the knotty question of how far mere men could hope to go in merging the visible with the invisible church. Yet despite the vast amounts of paper and ink expended on the subject, relatively little was said in these tracts about the genesis of the practice of requiring conversion narratives. By the time the presses were going, relations were a fact of church life, and, as Samuel Eliot Morison remarked in another connection, no one at the time thought to circulate a questionnaire among the churches to help historians three hundred years later.

Of course, to the Puritan divines who advocated a relation of religious experience for church membership, the original point on the scale was clearly at the very beginning, with John the Baptist and the apostles. In support of their contention that in the admission of members "there is . . . reason for trying of them that profess themselves to be beleivers," the framers of the Cambridge Platform cited (as had two of them, Richard Mather and John Cotton, in earlier arguments) such cases as that of John the Baptist baptizing the people on confession of their sins (Matt. 3:6), the eunuch of Ethiopia baptized by Philip after his profession of faith in Christ (Acts 8:37), the three thousand baptized at Jerusalem (Acts 2:37–41), and Paul rejected by the disciples at Jerusalem until they were persuaded of his conversion

because of what he felt were "curious inquisitions and niceties" by the membership concerning candidates (Morgan, *Visible Saints,* p. 107). In an unpublished letter some time after 1636, Richard Mather indicated that many *were* trying and failing: "All [who are found unworthy] are kept out though they offer themselves to bee taken in. And hence it is that many are in the Country and not members of any church" (R[ichard] Mather Papers [Massachusetts Historical Society], "A Plea for the Churches of Christ in New England," December 1645, p. 365). Yet there is no hard evidence of wholesale rejections – only some scattered cases, for example in the Dedham and Wenham church records. The outstanding case is that of the attempted gathering of a second church at Dorchester in 1636, at which a delegation of ministers, elders, and magistrates (there were no ordinary members involved) led by Thomas Shepard found the confessions inadequate. The full story is in John Winthrop, *The History of New England from 1630 to 1649,* 2 vols., ed. James Savage (Boston, 1825; rpt. ed., New York: Arno, 1972), 1:183–4 ("Mo.2.1.1636"). See also John A. Albro, *The Life of Thomas Shepard* (Boston, 1847), pp. 210–22.

(Acts 9:26).[8] These were some of the standard, but arguable, proof-texts, and they were relentlessly countered by the Presbyterians' assertions that in none of these cases had the baptized persons been "tried" or "examined" to demonstrate that they had been truly converted and possessed inward saving faith, something only God could know. The English "conformable puritan," Richard Bernard, insisted that, on the contrary, these very texts showed that Christ required only two things of those who would "become a Church": "professing that they did believe [Act. 8. 37.]" and "to be baptised [Act. 2. 41 & 8. 38]."[9] The Scottish Presbyterian Robert Baillie, the fiercest and most voluble opponent of the New England way, called the argument from Acts 8 a "very grosse" fault, in that (as he interpreted John Cotton's writings),

> profession of faith is made a certain argument of true grace and sanctification. Will any of our Brethren bee content to admit their members upon so slender termes as *Philip* or any of the Apostles did require of their new converts? Will the profession that Iesus is the Christ, or such a confession of faith as *Simon Magus* and all the people of *Samaria* men and women, after a little labour of *Philip* among them, could make, be an evident and convincing sign of regeneration?[10]

The opponents of conversion narratives thought that the example of Simon the Magician was a strong counterblow to the Congregationalist position, because after his baptism, Simon proved to have an ungracious heart (Acts 8:9–13, 18–22). The same was true of Ananias and Saphira (Acts 5:1–10), who were also repeatedly brought into the argument. If tests for effectual, inward calling were indeed required in the scriptural cases cited (and the Presbyterians doubted that anyway), what use were they, if even in apostolic times such members as these were allowed to slip through? The repeated response was that God did not require the apostles or the churches to know truly the hearts of men as long as "in judgement of charity they conceived them all to be saints, and faithfull, . . . when they did admit them" and when members proved to be false proceeded against them.[11]

But no matter: Even with the most compelling example, that of Paul (although his conversion experience was related to the disciples by Bar-

8 Walker, *Creeds and Platforms,* pp. 222–3; Richard Mather, *Church-Government and Church-Covenant Discussed* (London, 1643), p. 23; John Cotton, *The Way of the Churches of Christ in New-England* (London, 1645), p. 58.

9 "Of the visible Church of Christ under the Gospell," April 1, 1637, fol. 11r, Bernard Papers, Massachusetts Historical Society, Boston.

10 *A Dissvasive from the Errours Of the Time* (London, 1646), p. 173.

11 John Cotton, *Of the Holinesse of Church-Members* (London, 1650), p. 32.

nabas and not by himself),[12] none of the scriptural arguments served to persuade the Presbyterians that the apostles actually required of converts a demonstration of saving faith by personally and publicly talking about their spiritual experiences. Moreover, no Congregationalist seems to have produced for purposes of argument any clear evidence of such an actual practice in the more recent or contemporary reformed churches, and we can only assume from this omission either that there were no such cases to be cited (as Morgan does) or that the supporters of the practice had reason not to call attention to them (it would hardly have enhanced their cause to cite separatist church practices). The one pale reference to the contemporary churches is in an unpublished treatise by Richard Mather, written around October 1638 in reply to Bernard's criticisms of the public examination of candidates for admission to New England churches. Bernard had questioned public tests both of doctrinal knowledge and of religious experience, but in his answer Mather implied that the public part of the examination concerned only matters of "faith, and good knowledge, in the principles of religion." And this was the practice, he said,

> not onely . . . here but in Sundry parish churches in England: where the Godly ministers will not admit any to the Lords Table till they bee able to give an intelligent answer to the Questions of the Catechisme: . . . Who would thinke that you should find matter of exception, against such a practise in us, which soe the substance, findeth soe full and publike approbation, amongst yourselves, at home?[13]

But Mather did not try to claim that "an intelligent answer" to the minister's questions was a testimony of religious experience. He did, however, imply (in a different section of the treatise) that in New England a confession of "Gods manner of dealing with them, in their conversion" was to be made by candidates "at least to some of the brethren."[14] Here he sounded vague as to whether this, like the doctrinal test, was a matter for full public examination. But in any case, he

12 Hence this text was often cited to support recommendations or testimonies by church members on behalf of the "godly conversation" of candidates for admission.

13 "An Apologie of the churches of New-England, against the Exceptions of Mr Richard Bernard, minister of Batcombe, in Summersetshire," Mather Family Papers, American Antiquarian Society, Worcester, Massachusetts, pp. 7–8. It will be recalled that Elizabeth White went "to the Minister of the Parish, to be Examined before I was admitted" (*Experiences,* p. 4). Mrs. Stedman, in the Shepard group, also speaks of having to "declare my condition" to the minister in Old England (*Shepard's "Confessions,"* p. 102).

14 "Apologie of the churches of New-England," pp. 5, 4.

did not attempt to justify the practice on the basis of anything that English or Continental churches were doing at the time.[15]

This does not mean, however, that between first-century Jerusalem and seventeenth-century Boston there is nothing but a blank when it comes to the emergence of conversion narratives. For if we look carefully at the scanty but tantalizing evidence, we can discern in different places the elaboration of certain trends that at least laid a foundation – that opened up the possibility – for a situation in which ordinary men (and women) would be asked to stand up in the churches and talk "in their own words and way" to their fellows about the most important and personal inner experience of their lives.[16] As unprecedented and even presumptuous as such a "test of saving faith" might have seemed (and might still seem) from a theological standpoint, it is not so shocking when viewed as a literary phenomenon. As an idea about expression, communication, and "performance," it has visible roots within a powerful reformed church tradition that did give new importance to verbal activity on the part of the individual believer, demanding that his skills be exercised, as we have said, both personally and publicly. Personally, because conscious understanding was to replace what the reformers viewed as a "Popish" mumbling and babbling of set prayers and recitations. Publicly, because believers voluntarily entered into a verbal covenant (at least in some churches) and, removed from the

15 There is evidence that some early nonconformist ministers began a custom of gathering covenanted groups within their congregations to watch over one another and in some cases to receive the Lord's Supper together; but the method of gathering is unclear. See Morgan, *Visible Saints,* p. 19, n. 34 and pp. 75–8.

16 We are told that in the public assembly, women were often excused, their experiences being read for them by the elders, who had first examined them privately (Lechford, *Plain Dealing,* pp. 22–3; Weld, *Answer to* W.R., p. 21). Lechford reported that Salem was an exception. Edward Johnson flatly stated that "women speak not publikely at all" (*Johnson's Wonder-working Providence: 1628–1651,* ed. J. Franklin Jameson [New York: Barnes & Noble, 1910], p. 217). John Cotton seems to have been averse to women speaking, except to answer an offense ("The Keys of the Kingdom of Heaven, 1644," in *John Cotton on the Churches of New England,* ed. Larzer Ziff [Cambridge, Mass.: Harvard University Press, Belknap Press, 1968], p. 144; Winthrop, *History,* 1:110 [Sept. 4. 1633.]). Considering the Pauline admonition against the practice (1 Cor. 14:34), it is hard to believe it was permitted at all; yet the narratives by women in the Shepard, Fiske, Walker, and Rogers groups all appear to have been made publicly. Many references to women relating their experiences may be found in English church books, most of them unpublished; but see, for example, H. G. Tibbutt, ed., *Some Early Nonconformist Church Books, Publications of the Bedfordshire Historical Record Society,* vol. 51 ([Bedford]): By the Society, 1972). See also n. 5, above. For "their own words and way," see n. 60, below.

auricular confessional, subjected themselves to communal judgment and discipline: As John Cotton pointed out, "wayes of truth seeke no corners."[17] From the early sixteenth century, reform rested on the priesthood of *literate* believers – English Bibles in hand, ears open to the sermon, ready to "teach the lawes of Christ, and talke and reason for the maintenaũce of them," to "exhorte, moue, and stirre vp," to "appoint, counsel, and tell one another their dueties."[18]

Thus, while John Cotton was largely responsible for the establishment of conversion narratives in the Massachusetts Bay churches and perhaps as well for the form they were to take, some stirrings along these lines were going on long before his arrival in Boston in September 1633. The evidence suggests that no one man could be responsible, despite "the authority . . . (especially Mr. Cotton) had in the hearts of the people."[19] Perhaps it is not unfair to say that Cotton brought to a boil a pot that had been set to simmering a long time earlier.

Of the two aspects, the "personall" and the "publick," it was the "publick" nature of relations as a form of communication that first had to define itself. There was already, in the separatist churches, an incontrovertible precedent for the importance of communal consent in the principle of founding a church on a written covenant subscribed to by all. But before there could be such a thing as an open testimony of personal religious experience, an idea had to take shape that the entire congregation was to be involved not only in the taking of a covenant together but in whatever additional steps might come to be required in the admission of church members. This may have happened as far back as the early Puritan church at Frankfurt. Morgan reports that this church, founded in 1554 by English exiles from Queen Mary's rule, at first held that "euery one as well men as wemen which desier to be receiued shall make a declaration/or confession off their faithe before the ministers and elders" – *not* before the entire church.[20] But Morgan

17 "The Way of Congregational Churches Cleared, 1648," in *Cotton on the Churches,* p. 260.

18 "Extracts from [Robert] Browne's 'Booke which Sheweth the life and manners of all true Christians,' etc., Middelburg, 1582," in Walker, *Creeds and Platforms,* p. 23.

19 Morgan, *Visible Saints,* pp. 95–100; William Hubbard, *A General History of New England from the Discovery to 1680,* 2d ed., ed. William T. Harris (Boston, 1848), p. 186, cited ibid., p. 95.

20 Ibid., p. 39. As Morgan explains, "a confession of faith was designed to prevent heresy, and it consisted of a statement of consent and agreement to the doctrines of the church" (p. 40). In other words, it was a confession of "historical faith" in the basic tenets of reformed religion and did not purport to arise from an experience of grace in the heart. These personal confessions were

also relates the story of a quarrel in 1603 at the separatist church in Amsterdam, during which one of the disputants, George Johnson, referred to

> the practice [of this same church] at Frankfurt, where, he said, "none/ man or woman/were to be received members without making confession of their faith/also great care was in admitting youth to the supper of the Lord/none being to be admitted/til they were able to make confession of their faith *before the whole congregation*."[21]

According to Johnson, says Morgan, "these same standards had originally prevailed at Amsterdam" as well but had become corrupted. (The Confession of the London-Amsterdam Church in 1596 stated that members "doo make confession of their faith, *publickly* desiring to bee received as members.")[22] Johnson was appalled at the ignorance of candidates for admission and at the fact that the pastor (his brother, Francis Johnson) and the ruling elder "admitted whom they pleased." But if we are to believe him at all (and the 1596 document does support his statement of the practices in his own church), then somewhere along the line in the late sixteenth century Continental separatist churches[23] moved from admission by a doctrinal confession of faith before the church officers to confession before the entire membership. This is not to exaggerate the role of the congregation in admitting members; they may have constituted only a rubber stamp of approval after the requisite private examination by the ministers and elders. Nevertheless, this point (the necessity for "the satisfaction of a multitude"),[24] which later became a major bone of contention with the Presbyterians, was a logical outgrowth of the idea held by some separatists that the membership of a gathered church had the "keys" not only to select its officers but to eject unworthy members: Why not, then, to admit them?[25] In fact, it

versions, of course, of the official statements of doctrine and polity issued by a church or a group of churches, such as the London-Amsterdam Confession or the Westminster Confession.

21 Ibid., pp. 43–4. Emphasis added.

22 Walker, *Creeds and Platforms*, p. 71. Emphasis added.

23 Morgan explains that the Frankfurt church "was Separatist only by circumstance; but later Separatists revered it as a precedent for their own churches" (*Visible Saints*, p. 39).

24 W[illiam] R[athband], *A Briefe Narration of Some Church Courses Held in Opinion and Practise in the Churches lately erected in* New England . . . (London, 1644), p. 9. See also Baillie, *Dissvasive*, pp. 184–5.

25 See "Robert Browne's Statement of Congregational Principles, 1582," in Walker, *Creeds and Platforms*, pp. 14, 25; "The London Confession of 1589," ibid., p. 39. In *Way of the Churches*, p. 64, Cotton defended the public judgment of relations on just these grounds, citing Scripture (not Browne!). See also his "Keys," in *Cotton on the Churches*, Chapter 4.

was from this very church that Henry Ainsworth and a group of his supporters withdrew in 1610 to form another church in Amsterdam because of "their belief that excommunication was to be approved by the whole congregation rather than just by the elders."[26]

In this early period there were nonseparatist exiles as well who would not have disagreed with at least a minimal popular rubber-stamp approach to the question of membership. Robert Parker described the admission policy of reformed churches "beyond seas" (where he lived from 1607 until his death in 1614) in these terms: "The Presbytery doth examine, the people do consent."[27] And Morgan suggests that Henry Jacob's nonseparatist but independent church in London (established in 1616) probably required new members publicly to confess their faith in doctrine before admission.[28] Certainly by 1630 the issue of popular hearing of candidates was a serious point of dispute among nonseparatists. Morgan reports that

> in the peculiar situation of the [nonseparatist] church in the Netherlands, the congregation had the power to elect the minister. In 1630 they attempted to choose as assistant to [the minister, John] Paget the Reverend Thomas Hooker, who apparently believed, in some measure at least, in the Separatist practice of examining candidates for membership . . . Paget defeated the move by making Hooker answer a set of questions . . . [including] "Whether it be lawfull to receave any as Members into the church without publique examination of them before the whole Congregation?" Hooker answered that "some members may be receaved without publique examination, and yet the case may so fall out that some cannot without publique examination."*
>
> * Stearns, *Congregationalism in the Dutch Netherlands*, pp. 27–30, 108.

"Whether the examination Hooker envisaged was of behavior, understanding, or faith," concludes Morgan, "there is not a hint."[29] But whatever Hooker meant by "examination," he was clearly willing to accept the possibility of its "publique" nature (although later, in New England, he strongly altered his views).

Finally, there is a report by John Canne (the successor to Ainsworth's ministry in Amsterdam) that Continental reformed churches some time before 1632 were enlisting the entire congregation's "consent" to new admissions. In *A Necessity of Separation from the Church of England Proved by the Nonconformists' Principles* (1634), Canne described "the manner and order of this joining unto true visible churches" – a version he apparently derived from James Henric's *The Curtaine of*

26 Ziff, *Cotton on the Churches*, p. 367.
27 Rathband, *Briefe Narration*, p. 35.
28 Morgan, *Visible Saints*, pp. 78–9.
29 Ibid., pp. 79–80.

Church-power and Authoritie (1632). (Morgan discovered this book and reports that it "describes admission procedures in French and other reformed churches.")[30] In any case, here is Canne's understanding of those procedures:

> He which is to be received, first is to go to the elders of the church, to be well informed and instructed by them, and to have his cause by them propounded to the congregation; afterwards he is to come himself into the public assembly, all men looking upon him with love and joy, as upon one that cometh to be married, and there he is to make a profession of faith, and to be asked sundry needful questions, to which he having well answered, and being found worthy, by the consent of the whole church is joyfully to be taken into their communion; and this they say was the practice of the primitive churches.[31]

By 1630, then, there was obviously considerable support for witnessing and approval by the whole public body of some kind of performance for church admission – even if that performance was merely the candidate's recitation of fundamental Christian doctrine and assent to the discipline of the church and not at all a matter of the demonstration of inward grace.

But was it mere recitation and/or assent? Even if "propounded" members were not yet speaking in the churches about their inner religious experiences, were they at least speaking in some kind of "personall" or individual way? The answer seems to be yes – if not in terms of personal *experience,* at least in terms of the candidate's own understanding of doctrine.

In line with the Reformation impulse to eliminate mindless ceremony, separatists had long argued, of course, that more was required in a public declaration of faith than "the verball repeating certayne words taught them by rote," as the martyred John Greenwood had put it.[32] "Yea," wrote John Robinson, "a parrot might be taught to say over so many words, yea, the devil himself, though he were known so to be, would not stick for his advantage to utter them, and so might be true

30 Ibid., p. 73, n. 16.

31 Canne, *Necessity,* ed. Charles Stovel (London, 1849), p. 186. Save for the emotional overtones, this is the same procedure described in both Old and New English churches: preliminary examination by the elders, "propounding" to the congregation, followed by testimony. Detailed accounts are in Weld, *A Brief Narration of the Practices of the Churches in* New-England . . . (London, 1645), p. 8; Cotton, *Way of the Churches,* pp. 54–5; Lechford, *Plain Dealing,* pp. 18–29. For a strikingly similar description of such an admission in the early Roman church, see the story of Victorinus in Augustine's *Confessions,* bk. 8, pt. 2.

32 Morgan, *Visible Saints,* p. 42.

matter for Mr. B.'s church."[33] But for all their protestations about the need for individual believers to demonstrate a genuine understanding of the professed doctrines, the separatists said little about just how they went about getting such a demonstration. Presumably there was a question-and-answer procedure of the kind Mather referred to in answering Bernard, and we have seen that John Canne cited evidence of such a method apparently in use by "nonconformists" on the Continent by 1632. Morgan asserts that "in the later [separatist] churches and *possibly* in the earlier ones the ministers, elders, and members questioned the candidate publicly in order to be sure that he understood what he was saying when he made his confession or profession (the terms were used interchangeably)."[34] But how long the business of "examination" and questioning was left only in the hands of the catechizing elders and, more important, how much latitude of expression was possible for the candidate under either private or public "examination" is not exactly known.

A valuable clue comes, however, not from the separatists but from the (at least borderline) nonseparating church in London. Henry Jacob described the formation of his church in 1616 by ten foundation men, each making

> some confession or Profession of their Faith and Repentance, some ware longer some ware briefer, Then they Covenanted togeather to walk in all Gods Ways.[35]

For all its brevity, this is a revealing statement. First, it establishes, at a very early date, that at least the founding members of a gathered church were able, perhaps even encouraged, to speak about their faith *in their own words,* for "some ware longer some ware briefer." This allowance for a little variety of expression, at least in profession of doctrine, shows up later, either in the first gathering or in subsequent admissions of New England churches – for example, in Salem, Dedham, New Haven, and possibly Roxbury – and must have been based on some kind of tradition brought over by the settlers. This growing acceptance of a personal composition or phrasing (however limited) of one's own profession of faith may represent a critical step toward the

33 *The Works of John Robinson, Pastor of the Pilgrim Fathers,* ed. Robert Ashton, 3 vols. (London, 1851), 2:285. "Mr. B." was Richard Bernard, who later disputed with Mather and Cotton; in 1610, he had written *The Separatist Schisme,* to which Robinson was replying.

34 Morgan, *Visible Saints,* pp. 41–2. Emphasis added.

35 In Champlin Burrage, *The Early English Dissenters in the Light of Recent Research,* 2 vols. (Cambridge, 1912), 2:294, cited in Morgan, *Visible Saints,* p. 78. It is this procedure that Morgan thinks "subsequent members" probably followed (ibid., pp. 78–9).

idea of a personal relation of one's own religious experiences.[36] Such, in fact, is what Richard Mather leads us to believe, for in his reply to Bernard he notes that during admission the candidates "of more spirituall abilityes, do of themselves in a continued Speech, declare the Summe of the confession of their faith, in their owne words."[37] Mather doesn't make it clear whether his people are also making their relations of religious experience before the whole congregation (rather than just before the elders or "some" of the brethren), but clearly both kinds of "free-style" speaking were by then going on simultaneously.

In the second place, Jacob clearly separates the "confession or Profession" of faith from the particular church covenant. Morgan makes the important point that the covenant and profession of faith may once have been lumped together but were definitely distinct by the early seventeenth century.[38] The movement from a simple, combined profession-and-covenant, probably read to members for their consent, to a profession separate from the covenant, possibly spoken, read, or even composed by the member himself, is a small step that has great literary repercussions. Eventually the admission procedures were to be broken down into still a third distinct act; but the conversion narrative, or confession of experience, could not be differentiated from the confession of faith until the latter had first emerged on its own. In this respect, Jacob's statement reflects an evolutionary pattern of fission that produces ever more verbal refinements in the stages of admission.

Still another element in Jacob's description may be said to foretell, in a faint but intriguing way, this trend toward the emergence of a third step in the admission process. Here Jacob slightly elaborates on the content of a profession of faith, for he mentions that it includes "Repentance." Granted that the juxtaposition of faith and repentance is hardly surprising in any Christian statement, it is still worth noting that not all the early reformed churches actually used both words in their declarations about membership requirements. Perhaps they felt it was superfluous to do so; nevertheless, in the early sixteenth century, Anabaptist sects specified only that men were admitted to the church "by

36 For the difference between a confession of doctrine and one of experience, see Henry Dunster in *Shepard's "Confessions,"* pp. 156–64. Dunster professes his doctrinal beliefs, then his experience of grace (sometimes it was done the other way around). He is undoubtedly one of Cotton Mather's "few *learned* men" who "have, at their admissions, entertained them with notable confessions of their own composing . . . Nevertheless," Mather assures us, "all this *variety* has been the exactest *unity*" (*Magnalia,* 2:181).

37 "Apologie of the churches of New-England," p. 7.

38 Morgan, *Visible Saints,* p. 41. See, for example, Browne's "Booke," in Walker, *Creeds and Platforms,* pp. 18–20, where covenant and profession seem to be construed as one.

confession and baptism" (just as Richard Bernard later argued they should be);[39] and in the 1550s, the Frankfurt church said only that it required of members "a declaration/or confession off their faithe . . . shewinge him selff fully to consent and agree with the doctrine off the churche."[40] John Smyth, minister of another separatist congregation in Amsterdam in 1606, also defined the "fayth" requisite in members only as "the knowledg of the doctrine of salvation by Christ";[41] and *The Heads of differences* between the separatists of Amsterdam and the Church of England, submitted to King James in 1603, merely stated that the members of a true visible church were "joyned together by voluntarie profession of the faith of Christ."[42] Of course, the faith of Christ and the doctrine of salvation include the concept of repentance for sin, but it is interesting that some churches felt called upon explicitly to place the word *repentance* next to the word *faith*. Hence in 1596 the Johnson-Ainsworth separatist congregation in Amsterdam specified that it received "into our societie all that with faith and repentance come vnto vs willingly"[43] and repeated in 1598 that "none of yeres may be receved into the Churche without free professed fayth repentance and submission unto the Gospell of Christ."[44] And we have just seen Jacob's own statement that the founders of his church in 1616 professed both faith and repentance before joining in covenant. What was once presented as one step, then as two – profession of faith and taking the covenant – is now beginning to look like three.

Were there in fact three steps? Were candidates for admission to Jacob's church, or to the Amsterdam congregations, asked to make separate confessions, one of "faith" and one of "repentance"? And even if they were, how would that affect the question of the provenance of relations of religious experience?

The reason repentance is so important to this investigation is that, according to Judaeo-Christian doctrine, true repentance *is* the key to conversion: "Repent ye therefore, and be converted, that your sins may be blotted out" (Acts 3:19).[45] In both testaments, repentance for sin and confession of sins is equated in some way with the concept of an imme-

39 Walker, *Creeds and Platforms*, p. 3; cf. Browne, ibid., p. 19.

40 [William Whittingham], *A Brieff discours off the troubles begonne at Franckford in Germany Anno Domini 1554* ([Zurich], 1575), pp. 127–8, cited in Morgan, *Visible Saints*, p. 39.

41 Smyth, *Principles and inferences concerning the Visible Church* (1607), p. 13, cited in Morgan, *Visible Saints*, p. 45.

42 Walker, *Creeds and Platforms*, p. 78.

43 Ibid., p. 56.

44 *Certayne Letters translated into English, being first written in Latine* (1602), p. 8, cited in Morgan, *Visible Saints*, pp. 40–1.

45 Cf. Ezek. 18:30–2, Acts 26:20.

diate turning or change. When John the Baptist came, "saying, Repent ye: for the kingdom of heaven is at hand" (Matt. 3:2), he was carrying forward the Jewish prophetic tradition which

> had emphasized the power of repentance in achieving Israel's reconciliation with God. The Talmud preserved that religious conviction: "If Israel were to repent they would straightway be redeemed" (*Sanhedrin* 97b). "Great is repentance which hastens the redemption" (*Yoma* 86b). John . . . applies the concept to the individual, promising the kingdom to those who repent.[46]

One Bible scholar claims that Luke is particularly firm on this point: In his gospel, the Baptist's arrival, "preaching the baptism of repentance for the remission of sins" (Luke 3:3) means that "repentance has become practically synonymous with conversion."[47] In the Second Helvetic Confession of 1566, "Article XIV, *Of Penitence and Conversion,* states the plain doctrine that Repentance is a change of heart."[48] The Westminster Confession reads:

> Repentance unto life is an evangelical grace, . . . By it a sinner, . . . so grieves for, and hates his sins, as to *turn* from them all unto God . . . none may expect pardon without it.[49]

The operation of grace was crucial in Luther's explanation of the reformed doctrine of repentance, which he called "the true meaning of Christianity," and out of his two-stage theory of repentance came a "morphology of conversion" which was, in effect, a model for all the later ones. First, under the work of the law, the sinner saw his sin and was sorry for it; only then, under grace, was he enabled to resolve to amend his life. That resolution was literally the turning point or conversion. That was the point at which the gift of grace could be said to have been bestowed, and if that point was not experienced, the person was left unsaved, in the horrifying state of what the Puritans were to call legal terror.

> We teach faith and the true meaning of Christianity. First, a man must be taught by the law to know himself, so that he may learn to sing: "All have sinned and fall short of the glory of God" (Rom. 3:23); again: "None is righteous, no, not one; no one understands, no one seeks for God. All have turned aside" (Rom. 3:10–12); again: "Against Thee only have I sinned" (Ps. 51:4) . . . Now once a man has thus

46 Walter M. Abbott et al., *The Bible Reader* (New York: Bruce, 1969), p. 647.

47 William Baird, "The Gospel According to Luke," in Laymon, *One-Volume Commentary*, p. 678.

48 Erik Routley, *Creeds and Confessions: The Reformation and its Modern Ecumenical Implications* (London: Duckworth, 1962), p. 75.

49 Walker, *Creeds and Platforms,* pp. 381–2, n. 3. Emphasis added.

> been humbled by the law and brought to the knowledge of himself, then he becomes truly repentant; for true repentance begins with fear and with the judgment of God. He sees that he is such a great sinner that he cannot find any means to be delivered from his sin by his own strength, effort, or works . . .
>
> Now he begins to sigh: "Then who can come to my aid?" Terrified by the law, he despairs of his own strength; he looks about and sighs for the help of the Mediator and Savior. Then there comes, at the appropriate time, the saving word of the gospel, which says: "Take heart, my son; your sins are forgiven (Matt. 9:2). Believe in Jesus Christ, who was crucified for your sins . . ."
>
> This is the beginning of salvation.[50]

One of Luther's striking characteristics is his emphasis on active expression. The sinner doesn't just learn to know himself; he learns "to sing . . . again . . . again." He doesn't just see; he also "begins to sigh" and "looks about and sighs" again. (Similarly, the "saving word" comes and "says" to him as if in response.) There is a sense that the full realization of inward repentance is partly dependent on its being expressed in some outward way; and if this is so, then true repentance should actually give rise to a profession or a "confession of sin." Certainly it would have to infuse any conversion narrative a person would eventually make; but in this early period, before there was such a thing as a true narrative of conversion, the emphasis on repentance might well have pushed confessions very close to that kind of expression, to the borderline between "historical faith" and "saving faith." If repentance was thought to be a particularly important subject for examination, query, or profession in the church admissions procedure, this in itself might encourage an appeal to personal experience. A candidate trying to express or answer questions about his understanding of repentance, of man's sinfulness and need for Christ's redemptive power, might be forced to lay claim to something beyond his intellectual knowledge of the doctrine – namely, as Luther says, knowledge of his own self.[51]

And there *was* good reason why repentance should become an important subject for examination; for this was precisely the point on which the separatists removed from the "false and counterfeit" Church of England, whose

50 Martin Luther, "The Argument of St. Paul's Epistle to the Galatians," in *The Protestant Reformation,* ed. Hans J. Hillerbrand (New York: Harper, Torchbook, 1968), pp. 103–4. See also Routley, *Creeds,* p. 58.

51 No other part of Christian doctrine is, after all, so concerned with self-knowledge as that which treats of sin: "The first step in Christianity is the preaching of repentance and the knowledge of oneself" (Luther, "Galatians," in Hillerbrand, *Reformation,* p. 99).

> people in Their Parish-assemblies, neyther were nor are meet stones for Gods house, meet members for Christs glorious body, vntill they bee begotten by the seed of his word vnto fayth, and renewed by repentance. Their generall irreligious profannes ignorance, Atheisme and Machevelisme on the one side, & publique Idolitrie, vsuall blasphemie, swearing, lying, kylling, stealing, whoring, and all maner of imptetie [impiety] on the other side, vtterly disableth them from beeing Citizens in the new Hierusalem, sonnes of God & heires with Christ and his Saints, vntill they become new creatures . . . the vyalls of Gods wrathfull iudgments are powred vpon them, . . . and [they are] not yet finding grace to repent of and turne from their sinnes.[52]

An argument around 1610 between John Robinson, pastor of the separatist church at Leyden from which the Plymouth pilgrims emigrated, and Richard Bernard, whom we met earlier, illuminates this question of a penitent membership. Bernard, who had recently retreated from the separatist position, and who would conduct the same argument across the Atlantic twenty-five years later with Richard Mather and John Cotton, held that the one doctrinal requirement for church membership had always been a simple profession of belief in the doctrine of salvation: That is, that Jesus was Christ, the son of God, and that life and salvation came only by him. Though in the apostolic churches men were exhorted to repent, Bernard argued, many were not enabled to do so until *after* they were believers and received into the church. In short, to use the common scriptural metaphor, it was not necessary to be a perfectly hewn stone before being laid in the temple. But against Bernard's disjunctions, Robinson was adamant.

> You separate and disjoin those things, which then were, and always should be joined together: and they are faith, and repentance. These two jointly did Christ himself preach, and John the Baptist before him, and the apostles after him: and these two were preached to, and required of every one both men and women, which was admitted into the church, Matt. iii. 2, 6; Mark i. 15; Acts xix. 4; Luke xiii. 3, 5; xxiv. 47; Acts ii. 38; viii. 37; xix. 18. But now, because faith and repentance are inward graces residing in the heart, and known to God alone, which knoweth the heart, and that the profession and confession of them are the ordinary means by which these hidden and invisible graces are manifested, and made visible unto men, there was no cause, but they, which made this profession to men, in sincerity, so far

52 "The Second Confession of the London-Amsterdam Church, 1596," in Walker, *Creeds and Platforms,* pp. 51–2. See also Mather, *Magnalia,* 2:245, for a "pro-relations" argument based on the church tradition of admitting none but the penitent to the Lord's Supper.

> as men could judge, should by men be deemed and acknowledged for true members of Christ, and fit matter for the Lord's house.[53]

This interesting outburst has led David D. Hall to speculate as to whether the early separatists did after all require some kind of "public and explicit 'relation' of effectual calling," something beyond a mere profession of doctrine by which to judge those "hidden and invisible graces."[54] In this connection, we may note the words "profession and confession" on the heels of the words "faith and repentance." Are these synonyms, or do they represent two separate acts: a "profession of faith" *and* a "confession of repentance"? On the same page Robinson makes reference to the admission of members by other means (such as baptism in the case of the children of the faithful), "though they made *neither* profession of faith, *nor* confession of sins" (emphasis added). It sounds almost as if Robinson is thinking in terms of the three steps we postulated in connection with Jacob's church (and the two are almost contemporary) – as if, in short, a confession of sins has taken on a separate importance in the definition of church members; and if so, we may be seeing evidence not necessarily of a conversion narrative but of the first faint possibility for the development of one.

It would be helpful to our inquiry if we could hear some of the early professions or confessions of faith that individuals actually made upon joining the reformed churches of which we have been speaking to see if they actually were giving rise to some kind of "experimental" expression.[55] Not many have been preserved; perhaps the best-known doctrinal profession by a New England Puritan is the rather long and formal one John Davenport delivered at the gathering of his New

53 Robinson, *Works,* 2:284. Cf. Canne, *Necessity,* p. 195: "Who dares affirm that there was one man or woman admitted a member at the constitution of any of these [apostolic] churches, which had been known to be an ill liver, and did not first manifest sound repentance thereof?"

54 *The Faithful Shepherd: A History of the New England Ministry in the Seventeenth Century* (New York: Norton, 1972), p. 26, n. 11 and p. 38.

55 One problem is that for this early period (both in England and in the first churches of New England) we do not know how often such statements were read to candidates for their consent, and how often they read, spoke, or composed their own professions, as in Henry Jacob's church gathering. Cotton Mather reports a traditional belief that "the first Churches of *New England* began only with a Profession of Assent and Consent unto the *Confession of Faith* and the *Covenant* of Communion" (*Magnalia,* 2:244). This does seem to have been the method at the Salem church gathering in 1629 but not in later admissions there. In the case of other early New England churches, the situation is less clear, although we know that the church covenant (following the profession of faith) *was* read to new members. See, for example, Richard D. Pierce, ed., *The Records of the First Church in Boston 1630–1868, Collections of the Colonial Society of Massachusetts,* vol. 39 (Boston: The Society, 1961), pp. 4–5.

Haven church in 1639.[56] But it comes too late for our purposes; by that time, the conversion narrative was an established form on its own. (Though Davenport was a firm advocate of "tests" of saving faith, and presumably gave his own relation at New Haven, it has not come down to us.) Fortunately, we have a version of the earliest general New England confession, and it is briefer, simpler, and probably closer to what the average member was asked to profess in the days before conversion narratives. It comes from Salem, where the first church in the Massachusetts Bay Colony was gathered in 1629: an event, in fact, that has been the subject of some dispute about the extent to which the Leyden-Plymouth group may have exerted an influence.[57] The document was published in Cambridge in 1665, along with the church covenant, by John Higginson, son of Francis Higginson, the pastor at Salem, as *A Direction for A Publick Profession In the Church Assembly, after private Examination by the Elders . . . Being the same for Substance which was propounded to, and agreed upon by the Church of* Salem *at their beginning.* the sixth of the sixth Moneth, *1629.* Although there is some doubt that this particular profession was ever formally adopted, it is thought "to be fairly representative of the type of theologic belief which the candidates for membership in the Salem church were expected to manifest to 'the elders' from the beginning."[58]

In this brief and simple document, there are seven main points of Christian doctrine, expressed in general and conventional language, "Concerning God," "Concerning the Works of God," "Concerning Jesus Christ," and so on. But one of the seven subsections strikes a slightly more personal note, since it is the only one to use the first-person verb, and it is, not surprisingly, the one "*Concerning the fall of Man.*"

> That *Adam* by transgressing the Command of God, fell from God and brought himself and his posterity into a state of Sin and death, under the Wrath and Curse of God, which I do believe to be my own condition by nature as well as any other.[59]

Was this a part of the confession upon which an individual speaker might be given the opportunity to elaborate? According to Nathaniel Morton's *New-Englands Memoriall,* published in 1669, the original confession of faith and the covenant were written out for the thirty

56 See *Letters of John Davenport, Puritan Divine,* ed. Isabel M. Calder (New Haven: Yale University Press, 1937), pp. 68–75.

57 Ziff, *Cotton on the Churches,* p. 14, n. 15; idem, *The Career of John Cotton: Puritanism and the American Experience* (Princeton: Princeton University Press, 1962), pp. 75–80; Hall, *Faithful Shepherd,* pp. 78–86.

58 Walker, *Creeds and Platforms,* p. 114.

59 Higginson, *A Direction,* in Walker, *Creeds and Platforms,* p. 120.

founders and were simply read to them for their consent. But according to Morton, after the first gathering this profession was handled with much more – with a really surprising – variety that might well have opened the way for personal statements of repentance.

> After which, at several times many others joyned to the Church in the same way. The *Confession of Faith* and *Covenant* forementioned, was acknowledged onely as a Direction pointing unto that Faith and Covenant contained in the holy Scripture, and therefore no man was confined unto that form of words, but onely to the Substance . . . And for the Circumstantial manner of joyning to the Church, it was ordered according to the wisdome and faithfulness of the Elders, together with the liberty and ability of any person. Hence it was, that some were admitted by expressing their Consent to that written *Confession of Faith* and *Covenant;* others did answer to questions about the Principles of Religion that were publickly propounded to them; some did present their Confessions in writing, which was read for them; and some that were able and willing did make their Confession in their own words and way.[60]

These final words – "some that were able and willing did make their Confession in their own words and way" – although not, ostensibly, about conversion narratives, are strikingly similar to those used by Richard Mather in explaining the New England admissions procedures to Richard Bernard. Because his answers are somewhat hazy, we cannot be sure whether Mather was or was not referring to conversion narratives when he said "such as are of more spirituall abilityes, do of themselves in a continued Speech, declare the Summe of the confession of their faith, in their owne words"; but we do know, at least, that "their own words and way" was by now a familiar concept.[61]

60 Morton, *New-Englands Memoriall,* cited in Richard D. Pierce, ed., *The Records of the First Church in Salem Massachusetts 1629–1736* (Salem: Essex Institute, 1974), p. xv. Cotton Mather's almost identical account makes it clear that the final sentence refers to speech: some "*orally* addressed the people of God in such terms, as they thought proper to ask their communion with" (*Magnalia,* 1:72).

61 See n. 37, above. Morgan reports that in New England admissions, "though at first the candidate might state his beliefs in his own words, the profession or confession ultimately became standardized" (*Visible Saints,* p. 89). The atrophy of the profession of doctrine was probably a by-product of the development of the profession of experience. In some churches, the doctrinal confession even disappeared. John Fiske's Wenham church, for instance, actually had to reinstate theirs in 1644 (*Notebook,* p. 10). Yet around 1650, Edward Johnson could still say (about the church covenant), "Every Church hath not the same for words, for they are not for a form of words" (*Wonder-working Providence,* p. 216). Presumably this principle would hold for professions as well.

We are now just over the threshold of the New England settlement. We have established the fact that by this time some of the more able candidates for admission were making doctrinal professions of faith more or less in their own words before the assembled membership. We have suggested that the profession of faith was thought of as a confession of faith *and* of repentance, perhaps even in separate parts, and that talk of repentance would very likely lead, sooner or later, to talk of personal experience. Is it possible, then, that Morton, perhaps all unknowingly, was describing in his historical account of Salem something like a protoconversion narrative, a narrative that was not yet required as such but whose occasional delivery depended rather on "the liberty and ability of any person"?

John Cotton is said to have brought all these matters to a head within the first few years after his arrival. Cotton landed in the colony on September 4, 1633, and four days later became a member of the Boston church. John Winthrop's journal shows that Cotton made "his confession according to order, which he said might be sufficient in declaring his faith about baptism." Although the baptismal question represented an important change of heart for Cotton on a crucial point of doctrine, there is no indication whatever that he was delivered of any personal relation of religious experience in joining the church.[62] (In fact, the story of his own conversion is known only because he apparently told it to his eventual biographer and successor, John Norton, who reported it in detail after Cotton's death.)[63] But only one year later, in January 1634/35, Cotton prepared a manuscript entitled "Questions and answers upon Church-Government," which was long afterward to be printed in London as *The True Constitution Of A particular visible Church, proved by Scripture* (1642).[64] This was the earliest of an avalanche of transatlantic exchanges on church polity within which the question of relations of religious experience was going to take on more and more importance over the years. Here, the question had not yet a separate identity but appeared implicitly in the query "What manner of men hath God appointed, to be received as Brethren and members of his Church." Cotton's complete answer was brief and crisp:

> *Answ.* Such as are called of God out of this world to the fellowship of Christ (1) and do willingly offer and joyne themselves, first to the

62 Winthrop, *History,* 1:110–11 (Sept. 4. 1633). For Cotton's change of heart on baptism, see Ziff, *Cotton on the Churches,* pp. 11–12, 18, 19, and Cotton, "A Sermon Delivered at Salem, 1636," ibid., pp. 41–4.

63 *Abel being Dead yet speaketh* (London, 1658), pp. 12–13.

64 On the date of 1634, see Julius H. Tuttle, "Writings of Rev. John Cotton," in *Bibliographical Essays: A Tribute to Wilberforce Eames* (Cambridge, Mass.: Harvard University Press, 1924), pp. 365–6.

> Lord (2) and then to the Church (3) by confession of their sins (4) by profession of their faith (5) and by taking or laying hold of his Covenant (6).[65]

Here were the three steps, all in a row, unmistakably divided by Cotton's logical number system. The confession of sins and the profession of faith were now definitely two separate items. In fact, during the religious revival in Boston that immediately followed Cotton's arrival, and during which, according to Winthrop, "more were converted and added to that church, than to all the other churches in the bay," the aspect of it that impressed Winthrop was that "divers profane and notorious evil persons came and confessed their sins, and were comfortably received into the bosom of the church."[66] Darrett B. Rutman construes this as evidence that "no more than" outward behavior and historical faith were required for church membership,[67] but he does not consider the cardinal question: Just what was in those confessions of sin?

John Cotton has answered this question for us in a general way (although we do not know if his answer applies to the 1633–4 revival). The confession of sin was, or became, a conversion narrative, the story of the work of grace to the soul.

> [Candidates] are called for before the Church, . . . and each one maketh confession of his sinnes, and profession of his faith. In confession of his sinnes (that it may appear to be a penitent confession) he declareth also the grace of God to his soule, drawing him out of his sinfull estate into fellowship with Christ: In the profession of his faith, he declareth not onely his good knowledge of the principles of Religion, but also his professed subjection to the Gospel of Christ, with his desire of walking therein, with the fellowship of that Church.[68]

Cotton wrote *The Way of the Churches* around 1641, and, it is said, he regretted its publication, preferring *The Keyes* to stand as his definitive statement on church polity.[69] Nevertheless, it here contains the clearest description we have of what may be the "missing link" between the

65 *True Constitution*, p. 4. Cotton's English counterpart, Thomas Goodwin, repeated the question and answer almost verbatim in *The Government and Discipline of the Churches of Christ* (unpublished until 1696), in *The Works of Thomas Goodwin*, vol. 4 (London, 1697), p. 30.

66 Winthrop, *History*, 1:121 (December 5. 1633). Sixty-three persons joined in six months (Darrett B. Rutman, *Winthrop's Boston: Portrait of a Puritan Town 1630–1649* [Chapel Hill: University of North Carolina Press, 1965], p. 109).

67 Rutman, *Winthrop's Boston*, p. 109.

68 Cotton, *Way of the Churches*, p. 55.

69 Tuttle, "Writings of . . . Cotton," p. 372; Ziff, *Cotton on the Churches*, p. 26.

profession of historical faith and the profession of saving faith as manifested in a relation of religious experience. Terse as it is, Cotton's pronouncement is unlike any other we have about the New England admission procedures in that it specifies how the churches managed to get from repentance – that word that had begun to look so important fifty years earlier – to "experience." It pinpoints the emergence and the encouragement of a personal relation of the work of grace in order to fulfill a particular need – namely, to make the candidate's words "appear to be a penitent confession." It was not enough to say a lot of words about how sorry you were; you had to speak with *conviction* – from experience. So Richard Mather wrote to Bernard supporting a regenerate membership:

> You demand . . . why should our people bee kept out of the church . . . if they can make confession of their faith, as it is in their common creed, and being asked will say they bee sory for their sins, and do hope in Gods mercy . . . unlesse you can conceave that all such as can say the common creed, and that they are sory for their sins . . . were Saints by calling faithfull brethren (whom onely the Apostle acknowledgeth for fit materials of the church) wee can but wonder why you should presse us, to receave all such? . . . Is there any papist, so ignorant, but can say the common creed? or so impudently prophane, as to deny himselfe, to bee a sinner, or to bee sory also for his sins, to hope in Gods mercy, for the pardon of them, and that hee hath a mind to serve God? or what drunkards, or whoremongers, or the most notorious wicked persons, but will bee ready to say and professe as much?[70]

Over the years, it was taken more and more for granted that a profession of repentance, above and beyond the profession of faith, was the distinguishing factor that made a conversion narrative personally felt and experiential, rather than merely "objective." In 1645, John Norton, explicating the entire matter for the eyes of Europe, answered the urgent question "*How is the confession of one faithful to the church to be made?*" with a crisp distinction between the two parts of the confession. There would be "a profession of faith, that is, of objective faith," and then "a confession of sins, that is, in substance, of the work of experienced faith."[71] And long afterward, Cotton Mather explained the "pro-relations" position of the Cambridge Platform by reminding his readers that a narrative of regenerative experience was perceived by some "as a thing required by the word of God, when 'a confession with the

70 "Apologie of the churches of New-England," p. 9.

71 *Answer To . . . Apollonius,* p. 41. Norton finished writing the book in 1645, but it was not published until 1648.

mouth' and 'a profession of *repentance as well as* faith' and 'a giving a reason of the hope that is in us' is required."[72]

Given the "free aire of a new world," and given the reform emphasis on individualized, conscious verbal performance, and given the definition (going back to people like Johnson, Ainsworth, and Robinson) of the membership of a true church of Christ in terms of genuine, sincere repentance, it was almost inevitable that in New England such a profession of experience would emerge from the profession of faith, even if no one consciously set out to create one. Repentance was the one point of theology on which the lowliest person had a right, not to say a duty, to become an expert – and an expert gets to be one by being *expertus,* tried or experienced. Nothing in the Christian doctrine – neither the Trinity, nor the Creation, nor the Headship of Christ in the church – could be acceptably and safely and directly spoken of by experience as could the Fall of Man – "which I do believe to be my own condition" – a belief of which one could speak both authoritatively and feelingly.

And, in fact, contemporary descriptions of New England admissions do concentrate on the two basic stages of repentance, rather than on the elaborate five- or ten-step morphology of conversion that present-day scholarship claims was demanded in public testimony.[73] Thomas Weld, for instance, wrote that the things demanded in a public relation of a work of grace were simply "*Repentance from dead works, and faith towards God, both of which they insist upon.*"[74] Thomas Lechford, an unfriendly but extremely judicious witness who left us the best detailed account of day-to-day New England church procedures, described "the usuall termes whereupon" members were received as revolving around Luther's two points, legal fear and free grace, mediated by the Word.

> [They testify] that they are true beleevers, that they have been wounded in their hearts for their originall sinne, and actuall transgressions, and can pitch upon some promise of free grace in the Scripture, for the ground of their faith, and that they finde their hearts drawne to beleeve in Christ Jesus, for their justification and salvation, and these in the ministerie of the Word, reading or conference.[75]

Similarly, virtually all the major attacks on and apologies for the New England system characterized relations of religious experience in

72 *Magnalia,* 2:247. Emphasis added.

73 Morgan, *Visible Saints,* pp. 68–72.

74 *Brief Narration,* p. 2.

75 *Plain Dealing,* p. 19. Lechford also stresses the confessional aspect by comparing "such publique confessions and tryals" to "Popish auricular confession," calling them both undesirable "extremes" (p. 21). See Keith Thomas, *Religion and the Decline of Magic* (Harmondsworth: Penguin, 1973), pp. 187–8, on the problems for Protestantism caused by the loss of the confessional.

terms of confession and repentance. One clear example may suffice. It comes from the Presbyterian minister John Ball, who joined the trans-atlantic debate in its early stages. In 1637, "many ministers" in Old England had sent to New England nine questions about church government; these had been answered by Cotton's friend John Davenport in 1639, and in 1640 Ball replied to Davenport's answer. Curiously, nothing in the original nine questions or answers touched directly on the issue of conversion narratives. But Ball's reply suddenly raised the subject, seemingly out of nowhere, in discussing the question of church covenants. Conceding that every church member "hath entred into Covenant, either expresly or implicitely," Ball exclaimed,

> but we never finde that they were called to give account of the worke of grace wrought in their soules, or that the whole Congregation were appointed to be Judge thereof . . . When *John Baptist* began to preach the Gospel, and gather a new people for Christ, he admitted none to Baptisme but upon confession of their sinnes; but we reade of no question that he put forth unto them to discover the worke of grace in their soules . . . [The apostles] received men upon the profession of faith, and promise of amendment of life, without strict inquirie what sound worke of grace was wrought in the soul.[76]

Clearly, Ball did not think a confession of sin or promise of amendment needed to deal with anything more than outward behavior and historical faith (just as Rutman assumes in discussing Cotton's early conversions). But in their reply to Ball, Thomas Shepard and John Allin, like John Cotton and Richard Mather before them, insisted that a confession necessarily involved *inward* repentance.

> Confession of sins, is ever put for true repentance, when there is a promise of pardon made to it, *Prov*. 28. 13. 1 *John* 1. 9. and therefore when he requires confession of sins, was it without remorse or sorrow for it? was it not with profession of faith in the Messiah?

Citing a great number of proof-texts concerning humbling and penitence, they concluded,

> Lay all these together, and let any . . . say, whether this confession was not such a profession of faith and repentance, which a discerning charity ought to take for a worke of grace.[77]

76 *A Letter of Many Ministers in Old England, Requesting The judgement of their Reverend Brethren in* New England *concerning Nine Positions . . . Together with their Answer . . . And the Reply made unto the said Answer,* . . . (London, 1643), pp. 81–2.

77 John Allin and Thomas Shepard, *A Defence of the Answer made unto the Nine* Questions *or* Positions *sent from* New-England *Against the Reply Thereto By . . . Mr. John Ball* (London, 1648), p. 196.

There is an interesting indication that people might have been talking thus about their "remorse" and "sorrow" as a work of grace quite early in Massachusetts Bay – that is, even before Cotton's arrival. The hint comes from Dorchester, the site of a second church established in July 1630, a year after the Salem church foundation. The official records do not begin until 1636, when a new church was organized under the ministry of Richard Mather after the departure of most of the original congregation to Windsor, Connecticut. Nevertheless, we have an excellent witness to the beginnings of the original Dorchester church in the person of Captain Roger Clap, who emigrated from Plymouth, England, at the age of twenty-one, along with the body that had already been joined into "church-estate" (although Clap himself was not yet a member) – the only New England church to gather before sailing to America. "Stout and valiant . . . Clapes, strong for the truth,"[78] long afterward wrote in his *Memoirs* two facts, intriguingly juxtaposed: first, that "I was admitted into the Church Fellowship at our first beginning in *Dorchester* [Mass.] in the Year 1630"; and second,

> Because many in their *Relations* spake of their great Terrors and deep Sense of their lost Condition, and I could not so find as others did, the Time when God wrought the Work of Conversion in my Soul, nor in many respects the Manner thereof; it caused in me much Sadness of Heart, and Doubtings how it was with me, Whether the Work of Grace were ever savingly wrought in my Heart or no?[79]

Nowhere does Clap make it clear just when these relations of great terrors were being given, but he mentions them hard on the heels of his own admission in 1630, making it seem that "many," if not all, prospective members were delivering relations at that time. Clap himself expresses extreme doubts about his own spiritual estate and describes his actual conversion as having occurred some years later – as a matter of fact, after having heard Cotton preach; so that it seems unlikely that he himself would have given an experience of the work of grace as a condition of his own entrance into church fellowship in 1630. If relations were in fact being heard in Dorchester at that time, were they, perhaps, voluntary? We have seen that in early Salem a kind of proto-relation could have developed on a voluntary basis, and Morgan suggests that this may have been the case in Cotton's religious revival at Boston.[80] It may be that the Dorchester people, too, were part of an early movement toward voluntary confessions of experience. This possibility is enhanced by another recollection Clap records in his memoirs

78 *Johnson's Wonder-working Providence*, p. 229.
79 *Memoirs of Roger Clap. 1630* (Boston, 1844), p. 24.
80 *Visible Saints*, pp. 98–9.

concerning public conversion testimonies. Again he provides no dates, but the *Annals* of Dorchester assigns this description to the very early years, 1631–2.[81]

> O how did Men and Women, young and old, Pray for Grace, beg for *Christ* in those Days; and it was not in vain: Many were Converted, and others established in Believing: many joined unto the several Churches where they lived, confessing their Faith publickly, and shewing before all the Assembly their Experiences of the Workings of God's Spirit in their Hearts to bring them to *Christ:* which many Hearers found very much Good by, to help them to try their own Hearts, and to consider how it was with them; whether any work of God's Spirit were wrought in their own Hearts or no? Oh the many Tears that have been shed in *Dorchester* Meeting-House at such times, both by those that have declared God's Work on their Souls, and also by those that heard them.[82]

It must be remembered that Roger Clap was a very old man when he wrote this memoir, probably in the 1680s, and that his avowed purpose was "to tell God's wondrous Works" to his children at a time when New England's famous piety was felt to be fast fading away. Thus, what time and memory did not distort, desire might well have adorned. But even if his account is taken with a grain of salt, its tone and its syntax do suggest a certain variety and looseness in these early conversions and church admissions. "Many" joined, confessing their faith and "shewing" their experiences – but were "those that . . . declared God's Work on their Souls" required to do so? Clap doesn't say, but he conveys an impression of fluidity and spontaneity; and if he is indeed talking about the very early 1630s, before relations were fully established, it is plausible that these were voluntary testimonies.

Even more striking is Clap's version of the significance of these relations: They helped and encouraged those who heard them "to try

81 James Blake compiled the *Annals of the Town of Dorchester* (Boston, 1846) during the early eighteenth century, and we cannot be sure about the authority of his dating procedures for the early period. He had Clap's manuscript at hand, but apparently it did not date this passage. Thomas Prince obtained the Clap manuscript from Blake and had it printed in 1731 for the first time. (The 1844 edition of Clap's *Memoirs* cited herein is a literal copy of the 1731 version.) But Prince also corrected and annotated his own copy of the work and rearranged it in what he judged to be proper chronological order. Alexander Young based his reprinting of Clap on the Prince corrections, and thus used Prince's date of 1633 for this "revival" passage (Alexander Young [ed.], *Chronicles of the First Planters of The Colony of Massachusetts Bay From 1623 To 1636* [Boston, 1846], p. 354). Prince is right *if* Clap is referring to Cotton's 1633–4 revival, but Clap does not say so and does not mention Cotton at all until several pages later.

82 Clap, *Memoirs,* p. 21.

their own Hearts" and deeply affected their emotions. Assuming this is not sheer propaganda, it seems to corroborate another of Morgan's suggestions, namely, that conversion narratives were an outgrowth of prophesying – that practice of spontaneous exhortation by laymen, following the regular sermon, which was widely used in reformed churches, including Plymouth's (but soon discouraged in Massachusetts Bay after the Antinomian troubles).[83] It is easy to see what the connection would be between prophesying and conversion narratives, for, as Geoffrey Nuttall tells us,

> "Prophesying," . . . was an activity of biblical exegesis, coupled with personal testimony and exhortation, after the preacher "had donn his stuff," and was open to all . . . The phrase used of those who were regarded as suited for the exercise, "gifted brethren," points to its essentially charismatic nature. Its possibility, . . . was dependent upon a conviction of the presence and activity of the Holy Spirit in men's hearts.[84]

This is very much like what Clap has described in Dorchester as the sharing of "the Workings of God's Spirit." But Clap is not the only one to raise the question of what sounds like prophesying in early New England. There is Richard Mather's statement that "such as are of more spirituall abilityes" were declaring their confessions of faith in their own words. It does not seem unlikely that such speakers might also be considered as "gifted brethren" who could carry on – "in a continued speech," as Mather wrote – an *ex tempore* exercise of a prophesying nature. Perhaps this is what Winthrop meant when he described the early Boston revival: Not only did many confess their sins, but, "Yea, the Lord gave witness to the exercise of prophecy, so as thereby some were converted, and others much edified."[85] Thomas Lechford noted that "the confessions or speeches made by members to be admitted, have been by some held prophesying."[86] One of the "some" was Richard Bernard, who, in his complaint of 1637, referred to New England's confessions of experience as prophesying. Bernard's remarks are revealing on two further counts: First, they too emphasize the two-stage penitential nature of the conversion story; second, they suggest that New England in the early years[87] was hearing conversion stories on a voluntary basis – that is, that "some" people were delivering them.

83 *Visible Saints,* p. 99.

84 Nuttall, *Holy Spirit,* pp. 75–6.

85 Winthrop, *History,* 1:121 ("December 5. 1633").

86 *Plain Dealing,* p. 42.

87 "Early" because it could take up to several years for a transatlantic response to any action. Writing in 1637, Bernard may be referring to the early 1630s.

Thus, Bernard wrote that he had heard that after the questions about doctrine were propounded to all the candidates,

> other some, it seemeth, of abilitie, make a brief confession, how God hath wrought in them, to bring them home to Christ, whether the Lawe hath convinced them of sin, howe the Lord hath won them to deny themselves, and their own righteousness, and to relye, only, on the righteousness of Christ. A. It were well if all God's people could prophesie; well it were if everie Christian could make such a confession, . . . but I aske, [whether such confessions and questions are warranted by Scripture].[88]

With all these hints that in the early 1630s confessions of experience were being given in the manner of prophesying, what might such discourses have been like? By its very nature, *ex tempore* speech resists preservation, and no such utterances have come down to us from New England.[89] But there is a confession of experience from the English congregational church at Rotterdam that seems to take the prophesying approach. In 1636 and 1637 three notable English Independents joined this church: They were William Bridge, Jeremiah Burroughs, and Sidrach Simpson, who, with Thomas Goodwin and Philip Nye, were to issue the famous *Apologeticall Narration* of Independent principles from the Westminster Assembly in 1643. Bridge became the pastor and shortly afterward, in 1637, Simpson was admitted to membership. (It is worth noting that Simpson later broke with Bridge over the issue of prophesying – Bridge disapproved of it – and formed a separate church, where prophesying was freely carried on, much to Robert Baillie's disgust.)[90] One of the saints who had been present at Simpson's admission wrote to friends in England about the event, noting that "two things were required of him, a profession of his faith, and a confession of his experience of the grace of God wrought in him."[91] Simpson, the

88 "Of the visible Church," fols. 16^{rv}, Bernard Papers.

89 For an unfavorable view of *ex tempore* discourse by the preachers at this time, see W. Fraser Mitchell, *English Pulpit Oratory from Andrewes to Tillotson: A Study of its Literary Aspects* (London: Society for Promoting Christian Knowledge, 1932), pp. 16–17, 371–2. A more impartial account of early prophesying is in Irvonwy Morgan, *The Godly Preachers of the Elizabethan Church* (London: Epworth Press, 1965), pp. 61–101.

90 Benjamin Brook, *The Lives of The Puritans,* 3 vols. (London, 1813), 3:312; Baillie, *Dissvasive,* pp. 174–5.

91 M.R., *Memoirs of the Life of Mr. Ambrose Barnes, Late Merchant and Sometime Alderman of Newcastle Upon Tyne,* ed. W. H. D. Longstaffe, *Publications of the Surtees Society,* vol. 50 (London, 1867), p. 131. This is the earliest indication of a required confession of experience in any congregation outside New England, but we do not know how the practice began at Rotterdam. It may be significant that the pastor there until 1635 was Hugh Peter, who next ministered at Salem, Massachusetts, for seven years (before his return to England

correspondent reported, "thus with flowing eyes [did] speak to the people":

> For my part, though I have reason to lay my hand upon my mouth, and cry, I am unclean, I am unclean, and deserve to be weighed in the small ballance, and to look for such a fann, as men might slight me who have so much dross, yet I beseech you do the work of an ordinance upon me. Thus it is with me. I go to Christ by faith because he hath commanded me; I must have grace from him, I can carry none to him. I would that deadly corruption were let out, though with the loss of pleasure, profit, yea of life too. If I be vanquished, I dare not lay down my arms. I make resistance; but how, if I be down? I fight and cry, and cry and fight. If temptations come, I dare not answer them, for there is strength alone in Christ. If Satan challenge me, I rather hold the conclusion than the dispute: and in this, whether I do well or no, judge ye. I dare seldom make vows, the forfeiture is so great, yet if I do, Christ is my counterbond. The duties I do, I do so infirmly, I have much cause to be humbled for them as my sin. But I believe the day is coming, when sin shall not domineer, nor Satan overcome, nor deadly corruption prevail, and I shall be more than a conqueror. All that I do is with incredible weakness. I go, but I stagger; I walk, but I faint; I look up to him, but mine eyes fail; I am dead, but am come to you to quicken me; I am empty, but am come to you who are Christ's fulness to fill me.[92]

This kind of rhetorical performance, with its dramatic flourishes, repetitions, rhetorical question, anaphora, chiasmus, parallelisms and metaphors, is partly attributable to the speaker's education: He was a trained preacher and a Cambridge University man. But it is not only more elaborate, it is also more exalted, more immediately, confidently (if artfully) emotional, and more frankly joyful than any of the surviving narratives by New England Puritans–even the earliest ones from

and his eventual execution in 1660 for high treason). Peter had already arrived when John Cotton delivered the famous sermon at Salem that is supposed to have inaugurated membership "tests" there (Morgan, *Visible Saints,* pp. 102–3); Peter became pastor six months later. His assistant from 1637 to 1640 was John Fiske, whose congregations at Wenham and Chelmsford produced twenty-three recorded conversion narratives, some of which were "second relations" by people who were already Salem church members. Could Peter have brought with him to New England the idea of church admissions by a relation of religious experience? He conducted a "drastic purging" of the Rotterdam membership in 1633 (Hall, *Faithful Shepherd,* p. 47) and, like his friend Thomas Hooker, opposed John Paget's views of church discipline. The other possibility is that Rotterdam began the practice with the arrival of Bridge and Burroughs, who, along with their three colleagues, favored "*the power of godlinesse* and the profession thereof" in the churches (Thomas Goodwin et al., *An Apologeticall Narration* . . . [London, 1643], p. 4).

92 *Memoirs of . . . Barnes,* p. 132.

Thomas Shepard's congregation, which are exactly contemporaneous with Simpson's. Though Simpson gives an account of his own sense of "deadly corruption" and sinfulness, it is the ecstasy of faith in Christ that claims the fullest resources of his imagination. If American conversion narratives did start out in this mode of prophesying, they quickly turned into something else and soon lost the impulse of freewheeling, dramatic, and joyous evangelism – assuming that they ever had it, and Winthrop's journal entry as well as Clap's memoir suggest that they did. For evangelism was the key element in prophesying, as Winthrop's remarks about the Boston revival indicate. Because prophesying was held to be inspired by the Holy Spirit, its "purpose . . . was not theological speculation" but (with the help of Scripture) "to persuade men to turn from a life of sin to a life of righteousness" – in short, to convert them.[93] And if the hearers were already converted, then they benefited by a growth in grace, or "edifying." Indeed, Simpson's confession elicited an effulgent response the like of which would scarcely be recorded across the Atlantic until Edward Taylor began to compose his poetry in the 1680s.

> The hearts of all there present were much affected, professing that this had been the fruit of prayers and tears, and many were upon the wing for heaven, saying, Now, Lord, lettest thou thy servants depart in peace, the glory of church-communion being so brightly discovered, and the state of gracious souls so sensibly anatomized . . . For a whole hour he poured out his soul into our bosoms, and we as heartily embraced him in the bosom of the church. Never saw I more beauty in the sanctuary, never did I think to have beheld it, till I had come amongst the just souls made perfect. O hasten under this safe covert and retreat. I thank the Lord he hath fitted me for this place, and so long as Hebr. 13. 5, 6, do last, I shall never lack.[94]

In the face of a response like this, the reader almost forgets that the confession of experience is supposed to have been a crucial "test" of the candidate's own spiritual qualifications; for in Simpson's case, it clearly had a much broader meaning for the audience itself. This kind of outgoing spiritual quickening seems in general to have been the effect hoped for in the churches abroad, where experiences, confessions, prophesyings, all seem to merge in one vast effort to gather in the saints, to comfort and reassure them, to glorify, and – not the least of

93 Irvonwy Morgan, *Godly Preachers,* p. 32.

94 *Memoirs of . . . Barnes,* pp. 131–2. Cf. John Canne's stress on the "love and joy" with which the candidate as "one that cometh to be married" was received in Continental churches. This open emotionalism appears to be characteristic of the reformed churches abroad and is seen again later in the Henry Walker and John Rogers congregations.

it–to herald "the perfect day" of the Second Coming.[95] Here, for example, in his prefatory epistle to Henry Walker's *Spirituall Experiences,* Vavasor Powell unequivocally stresses the spiritual supports they afford to others.

> And when Christ is with-drawne within the vaile, and the wings of faith clipped, and the flouds of temptation over-flow, and overwhelme the poor distressed, doubting, despairing, and drowning soule: this barke keepes, and holds up the soules-head above water, till the Arke return.
>
> That Christian beleeves strongest, that hath *Experience* to backe his faith, and that Saint speakes sweetest and homest, that speakes experimentally; for that which cometh from one spirituall heart, reacheth another spirituall heart.
>
> *Experience* is like steel to an edged tool, or like salt to fresh meat, it seasons brain-knowledge, and settles a shaking unsetled soule.
>
> What hath been Printed of this nature, hath both been acceptable and profitable, to many precious Christians.
>
> I hope that this is published for that end, . . . for herein you may see not only your owne hearts, but many hearts, and *heart-knowledge,* is both necessary and precious to sincere soules.[96]

When John Rogers published the confessions of his Dublin flock, he expressed his belief not only

> that the *variety* of the *flowers,* and of the *colors,* and of the *natures,* and of the *formalities* of them, *gathered together into one,* give a *glorious lustre,* and like the *Rain-bow* of *many colours,* signifie *fair weather for Ireland,*

but also that reading them would help people to "*perceive* the unparalleld *appearances* of Gods *love* and *light* as they *shine* more and more towards the *perfect day!*"[97]

Language like this is not found in early New England in the defense of conversion narratives. Thomas Shepard is often quoted as having said that professions of experience should be "such as may be of special use unto the people of God," but his aim was not to encourage soul-speech; he was criticizing those who would bend the ears of the saints with tiresome "revelations and groundless joys, [and] gather together the heap, and heap up all the particular passages of their lives."[98] And here is Allin and Shepard's restrained defense of "second relations": Another relation of religious experiences, they wrote, is to be expected

95 See Watkins, *Puritan Experience,* pp. 28–32.

96 Sigs. A3[rv].

97 Rogers, *Ohel,* pp. 417, 450.

98 *The Works of Thomas Shepard,* ed. John A. Albro, 3 vols. (Boston, 1853; rept. ed., New York: AMS, 1967), 3:631.

of a member when he moves from one church to another, on the grounds that the narrative might

> bee desired of the people of God, for the increase of their owne joy to see God glorified, and Christs name professed, and his vertues held forth, and for the increase of their love to those that joyne with them.[99]

This languid catalogue of spiritual advantages looks pallid indeed beside the bright effusions of the English ministers. Nor can we dismiss the contrast as a time difference, because the Rotterdam congregation appears to be in the same mood in 1637 as Rogers and Walker were in the early 1650s. Certainly by the time the English were able to take over and develop the practices begun in New England, they did so in a verbose and fluid way that was never matched in New England, except for those very early prophesyings of which we have heard some hints.

This English expansiveness is seen in another practice of the saints in Old England: the "experience meetings" or "conferences" in which the saints already admitted to church communion edified one another with further accounts of their experiences. The English narratives that have come down to us appear to be a combination of types: Thus, the Rogers and Walker collections contain the confessions of people explicitly "desiring to be admitted into this church,"[100] but the Walker group is also advertised as "held forth . . . at severall solemne meetings, and Conferences to that end . . . *wherein is wonderfully declared Gods severall workings in the various conditions of his chosen ones.*"[101] William York Tindall names the Walker collection as one of an "instructive literature [that] appears to have been influenced by the experience-meeting in which members of each congregation were accustomed to relate their conversions, openings, and lapses."[102] The relations offered for admission were apparently repeated and perhaps added to at these meetings and then published for an even wider audience. Owen C. Watkins notes that "a cohesive social life and a common culture are implied in all this activity, with free interplay between writers and readers, the published material being only a fraction of the ongoing dialogue."[103]

99 *A Defence of the Answer,* p. 194.

100 Walker, *Spirituall Experiences,* p. 368.

101 Ibid., title page.

102 *John Bunyan: Mechanick Preacher* (New York: Columbia University Press, 1934), p. 37.

103 *Puritan Experience,* p. 31. A glance at Watkins's bibliography impresses the reader with the great surge of English publications in this field. See also Geoffrey F. Nuttall, *Visible Saints: The Congregational Way 1640–1660* (Oxford: Basil Blackwell, 1957), pp. 111–14. By the starkest contrast, Shepard and Fiske did not see fit to rush into print the conversion experiences they had recorded so carefully in their notebooks.

Thomas Goodwin, perhaps the leading English Independent of this period, sharply distinguished between the saint's duty to be judged by a conversion story upon admission and his additional duty to continue communicating his experiences for the good of others in these meetings.

> This Duty of communion of Saints, doth not consist in giving an account of their Graces in that set way, as they gave an account of their conversion, when they were first admitted into the Church. But it is a communication of their experiences, as to the growth of their Graces, and as to the exercise of them. The Graces of a Believer, . . . may rather appear thus, by way of conference, than in a Set Narration. The Reason of it, is, because an account of the Person's Grace is not now given; for a Judgment to be made of his state thereupon, as it was at his Admission into the Church. There is not in this case any Autorative Act; for none have power to call for an account. But the Duty incumbent on the Person, is, to consider whether the Declaration of his Experiences may be for the edifying and comforting of others, and what good fruits may arise out of such a Manifestation, and accordingly to do it.[104]

Goodwin's characterization of the relation for church membership as a "Set Narration" or an "account," in contrast with the more free-wheeling, evangelical experience-meeting narrative, points up several often overlooked facts. First, though "Set Narration" may sound somewhat deprecatory, it also means that only the minimal stirrings of one's "first conversion," as Thomas Shepard called it, were expected, at least officially, to be exhibited by those who would join the gathered churches. First conversion involved "the least breathings" of the Holy Spirit, and applicants, at least in theory, were to be treated leniently. This was claimed on both sides of the Atlantic. "We refuse none for weaknesse, either knowledge or grace," wrote John Cotton, "if the whole be in them."[105] Thomas Weld insisted, "If they can give any evidence of Christ, now in them by the workings of his Spirit for present, though they know not how Christ came at first into them, its sufficient."[106]

But after the convert was already within church fellowship, it was assumed that he would experience the subsequent events known as growth in grace. Thomas Hooker preached that, after "these primitive and first impressions of the Lord upon the soul," there was "a principle of Grace received to renew and act over dayly these first Editions, and

104 Thomas Goodwin, *Of the Constitution, Right, Order, and Government of the Churches of Christ* (London, 1696), in *Works*, 4:302.

105 *A Coppy of a Letter of Mr. Cotton* of Boston, *in* New *England*, . . . ([London], 1641), p. 5.

106 See note 7, above.

Spiritual Dispositions imprinted upon the heart."[107] In their introductory epistle to this same sermon series, Goodwin and Philip Nye affirmed that the Holy Ghost, "the Author" of conversion, will "go over the whol of that Work again and again in the hearts of Christians," just as it did with the disciples.

> And the *coming of the Holy Ghost* upon them, at and after *Pentecost,* was as a *New Conversion* unto them, making them to differ as much *from themselves,* in *what* they were *afore,* as well-nigh they themselves (though afore truly wrought on) did then differ from other men. The Spirit of God himself goes over this Work afresh in all the parts of it: As to *humble* anew, to *draw to Christ,* to *change* and raise *the heart* to higher strains of *Holiness.*[108]

A person did not have to wait for all these events to occur before joining the church,[109] and one's conversion narrative was therefore geared to a specific place on the long scale of the saintly life. If it was "an account of the Person's Grace," it was not a full spiritual autobiography but a separate, special, and limited subgenre.

But more important, Goodwin's distinction between the kinds of narrative, and his less intense interest in the relation given for admission, also point up two crucial differences between the gathered churches of Old and those of New England. First, there was no chance that the English people on the whole would be deprived of a life in the church because of the "test" of a relation in some churches: There was neither compulsion nor uniformity in church practice between the Civil War and the Restoration.[110] Second, those who did feel moved to seek membership in the gathered churches by giving a testimony of experience had still further outlets for the expression of their spiritual feelings if they were so inclined. The fluidity of the situation for all religious temperaments (barring Papists and Laudians) diminished the importance of the single conversion narrative given for admission: There could never be the kind of pressure on it, the kind of burning focus of attention, that attended it in New England, where so much was at

107 *The Application of Redemption* (London, 1659) p. 377.

108 Ibid., sig. D^r^.

109 John Cotton made this clear in his famous Salem sermon. See Chapter 2.

110 Even among some Independents it was held that "confessions are good, and may be to edification, but are not absolutely necessary, therefore not insisted upon as the condition of admission" (J[ohn] S[later], *Flagellum Flagelli: or Doctor Bastwicks Quarters beaten up in two or three Pomeridian Exercises . . .* [London, 1645], p. 18). Cromwell's religious settlement of 1653 "imposed no set order of worship, no formal confession of faith, and no compulsory ecclesiastical discipline" (Austin Woolrych, "The English Revolution: an introduction," in E. W. Ives, ed., *The English Revolution: 1600–1660* [New York: Harper, Torchbook, 1971], p. 30).

stake; where no matter how lenient the churches claimed to be and no matter how diligent in searching out the "least breathings" of Christ in a prospective member, there were still no alternatives for participation in "church-estate"; and where whatever impulse there might have been toward an extended, regular practice of sharing joyful experiences was largely quashed after Anne Hutchinson's banishment. (Something akin to the experience meeting took place at the foundation of a new church, but we hear of no such activity afterward.)[111]

The sum of all this is that the conversion narrative in New England takes on a special, even mysterious importance, not only because New England was its birthplace, but also just because it was confined to that one cardinal moment when the believer sought union with the church. If New England Congregationalism was fundamentally "a speaking *Aristocracy* in the face of a silent *Democracy*,"[112] this was the one occasion in the colony's formative years when the democracy did speak, in its "own words and way," about its own experience, in the public arena.

There is a temptation to draw from these transatlantic contrasts the conclusion that New England was just that much more rigid, harshly imposing a single, all-or-nothing literary test on a helpless population of bewildered immigrants, "three parts" of whom, as Lechford's famous accusation held, "remaine out of the Church"[113] through fear, bashfulness, inarticulateness, insufficient self-mortification, or failure to memorize accurately the "morphology of conversion." Such an assumption would end the discussion right here, but it is not warranted by the evidence. We cannot blithely claim that the gathered churches of New England were "harsher" than those of England in the verbal requirements they set for membership; but in some way they were different. That difference is strangely heightened by the fact that the sternest criticism was always reserved for New England, even after English sectaries had begun testifying about their experiences in the

111 The purpose, however, was still – as Goodwin said – "for a Judgment to be made." The church gathering at New Haven in 1639 under John Davenport's direction was typical: "The towne being cast into seuerall priuate meetings wherein they thatt dwelt nearest together gaue their accounts one to another of Gods gracious worke vpon them, and prayed together and conferred to their mutuall edifficatiō, sundry of them had knowledg one of another and in euery meeting some one was more approued of all then any other; For this reason, and to prevent scandalls, the whole company was intreated to consider whom they found fittest to nominate for this [foundation] worke" (*Records of the Colony and Plantation of New Haven from 1638 to 1649* [Hartford, 1857], p. 15). See also Weld, *Brief Narration*, pp. 1–2; Lechford, *Plain Dealing*, p. 12.

112 Samuel Stone, Thomas Hooker's colleague at Hartford, so replied when asked to describe Congregational church-government (Mather, *Magnalia*, 1:437).

113 Lechford, *Plain Dealing*, p. 151.

home churches. Men like John Cotton and Thomas Shepard had strong ideas as to what the churches of New England might be; and it may be that their ideas did keep the level of church membership down.[114] But they also opened up a literary vista of peculiar importance, and of an apparently frightening novelty – if we may judge by the fearful bitterness with which New England was vilified for launching "this strange Practice."[115] These attacks were the first sign that right from the beginning, America was doing something – something "literary" – that England did not, and perhaps could not, understand.

114 On the still unsettled statistical question, most historians do agree, on the basis of figures for enfranchised males, that in the first two decades half or less of the population were church members. Morgan (*Visible Saints*, p. 137) says the statistics are not available, but Hall (*Faithful Shepherd*, pp. 99–100) briefly summarizes much of what is known, including the chief seventeenth-century reports. A recent estimate by Ralph J. Crandall and Ralph J. Coffman attributes an early, sharp decline in membership to Cotton's "test" ("From Emigrants to Rulers: The Charlestown Oligarchy in the Great Migration," *New England Historic Genealogical Register* 131 [January 1977]:12). Hall does not include Cotton's own arguments, which should be read in conjunction with Baillie's (Baillie, *Dissvasive*, pp. 59–60, 69; Cotton, "Way Cleared," in Ziff, *Cotton on the Churches*, pp. 263–6; Baillie, *The Disswasive From The Errors of the Time, Vindicated* . . . [London, 1655], pp. 38–41). The attacks on New England were based on numbers, but Cotton's defense stressed motivations: His consistent claim was that people forbore membership for reasons other than clerical strictness: "You come not more willingly to have communion with us, then we receive you, upon no harder terms then have been declared" (*A Coppy of a Letter of Mr. Cotton* . . . [(London), 1641], p. 5).

115 Baillie, *Disswasive . . . Vindicated*, p. 39.

2

CONTROVERSY

One of the Presbyterians' most persistent charges against their opponents was that they were unclear in explaining their views and practices. At first, the Congregationalists were accused of reticence. William Rathband complained that the *Apologeticall Narration* issued by the Independent minority in the Westminster Assembly in 1643 failed to tell the "full story" of the Independent way, and Robert Baillie accused the Independents of "coverings": Their "way lies yet in darknesse," he wrote in his *Dissvasive,* and at the same time, he said, they fear "their deniall might bring upon them the infamy of lying" about their "crimes."[1]

By 1646 this was hardly an accurate assessment of the case, and John Cotton effectively countered with a long bibliography of recent books on the subject.[2] Yet Baillie's lament was the product of a genuine feeling that something important was not being said, not being explained, or, at least, not being understood. As early as 1637, Cotton had been called upon to defend New England against accusations of "secret" church admissions procedures, even though, as he wrote in a letter to "a Friend" in England, questions about the candidates' experiences and knowledge were "all the secret we have among us, neither have we any more secret carriage, than this which no godly man that ever came over to us have ever disliked."[3] But by 1655, when the persistent Mr. Baillie published his *Disswasive . . . Vindicated,* the problem was no longer one of silence but of Babel. After years of debate, Baillie could only wearily conclude that Thomas Hooker and John Cotton (both now dead) had managed to sound both like the Brownists *and* like "their Opposites" whenever they had discussed the necessity of a demonstration of "reall sanctity and grace" for church membership.

1 Rathband, *Briefe Narration,* sig. A3^{r}; Baillie, *Dissvasive,* p. 59.

2 "Way Cleared," in Ziff, *Cotton on the Churches,* pp. 259–61.

3 *Coppy of a Letter,* p. 5. Everett H. Emerson estimates that this letter was composed in 1637 (*John Cotton* [New York: Twayne, 1965], p. 164).

> I do not satisfy my self for all that I have read or seen of their judgement in the state of this controversy. For sundry passages of their writings seem to import a full agreeance with us; but divers . . . seem as clearly to make them differ from us, . . . It were a pity but this matter were better cleared, and that for mistakes of expressions, there were no difference among brethren who professe oft an earnest desire of concord.[4]

Baillie was right, especially about the grounds of apparent "agreeance"; for on several fundamental points, there seemed to be little or no professed difference between the parties. From a theological standpoint, both sides said they accepted the ultimate unknowability (by mortal men) of the inward and invisible kingdom of Christ. From the standpoint of ecclesiology, both said that one hundred percent pure churches were impossible and that some of the chaff of hypocrisy must inevitably be mixed (albeit to differing degrees) with the wheat of true sainthood. And even from the psychological standpoint, they more or less agreed that conversion might be experienced in different ways, that even elect persons might not be able to tell "the time when, the place where, the occasion how they were converted," and that "many Christians may bee drawne to Christ, and have a seed of faith, yet may sometimes not know it, sometimes remember not the working of it."[5]

Yet the paradoxical effect of all this "agreeance" was to give the Presbyterians all the more reason to suspect that in their insistence on conversion narratives, their adversaries were either concealing something or deliberately confounding matters.

> The *Independents* would gladly dissemble their minde therein; to this day they have declined all solemn debate upon it [i.e., the requirement that new members show "convincing signes of their Regeneration"], they speake as if they were either fully or very neare accorded with us, . . . but I professe this hath alwayes seemed to me their capitall and fundamentall difference, the onely cause of their separation from us, and wherein if we could either agree or accommodate, there would be a faire possibility of accord in all things else, . . . but this difference, is the great partition wall.[6]

Thus, although the debate involved the entire question of the nature of the church and its polity, it always came down to the particular issue of admissions, and there the conversion narrative was the sticking point. Yet in the documents there is a sense that, even in the debate over such

4 Baillie, *Disswasive . . . Vindicated,* p. 52.

5 John Bastwick, *Independency Not God's Ordinance* (London, 1645), p. 99; Allin and Shepard, *Defence of the Answer,* p. 189. It should be noted that these two citations are themselves drawn from opposing sides of the debate.

6 Baillie, *Dissvasive,* p. 155.

a specific issue, something more is being argued or worked out – something perhaps not fully articulated by either party but nevertheless felt as palpably and dramatically as a "partition wall." And this sense is corroborated by the fact that even twentieth-century historians have not been able to agree about what was being said and what was being hidden (or left unsaid) in this 300-year-old dispute.

Two important studies of the conversion narrative illuminate this problem. The first – an answer to the Morgan thesis – has gone so far as to say that the whole question of a test of saving faith is "in a sense, . . . an artificial problem," since the institution of relations for church membership in New England was, after all, a difference not in kind but only in degree. Taking issue with Morgan's assessment of the practice as a genuine innovation that radically changed the character of Congregationalism, Raymond P. Stearns and David H. Brawner have called it rather a continuation, refinement, and "adaptation to new circumstances" of an already established concept of ecclesiastical purity, a concept that they claim had been worked out in proto-Congregationalist churches long before the settlement of New England, through the use of various criteria designed to identify the saints.

> Earlier Congregationalists may not have required candidates for Church membership to discuss the circumstances of their conversion, but we know that they did hold strict standards of admission; . . . we know that these standards were considered to be adequate criteria of saving faith . . . saints recognize[d] each other by virtue of that which Richard Baxter called "Connaturality of Spirit," or, less mystically, by a combination of common sense and intuition.
>
> The New England church relation supplied no serious deficiency in Congregational admission practices. By focusing on the process of regeneration, it more fully utilized the resources of Puritan pneumatology and gave additional grounds for judging the fitness of applicants.[7]

Stearns and Brawner further support their "continuity" argument by showing that the defenders of conversion narratives never claimed that the audience could exercise infallible ability to judge the human heart; they argue, quite accurately, that the churches' apologists always said they felt bound to take a professor on his word unless he was clearly ignorant or a hypocrite. But from this they draw the conclusion that the declaration of religious experience was "simply another form of outward profession," pointing out that even John Norton's *Answer to Apollonius* frankly admitted that "the inward side of the event [of con-

7 Raymond Phineas Stearns and David Holmes Brawner, "New England Church 'Relations' and Continuity in Early Congregational History," *Proceedings of the American Antiquarian Society* 75 (April 1965):13–45, especially 24–5.

version] in a person cannot be known by others."[8] In fact, they claim, the church relation may actually have been added to the requirements for admission "not in order to narrow but rather to widen the grounds upon which a candidate might declare, both for his own spiritual consolation and that of his auditors, 'the hope that was in him.' " This interpretation, they add, is confirmed by the ironic fact that a relation (just as the Presbyterians held) was *not* "a demonstrably more precise instrument for discerning qualified church members" than other methods.[9]

There is much to be said for this argument – especially as we have already seen in Chapter 1 that the profession of experience probably did grow out of the profession of doctrinal belief. There is even some evidence for the thesis that relations of religious experience could "widen" (or at least were not responsible for constricting) the base of admissions. For example, the records of John Allin's church at Dedham, Massachusetts, gathered in 1638, indicate that the business of testing members there was complex, repetitious, nervous, and picky: At least in the first few years, people were tested more than once, and there was considerable discussion, even hair-splitting, over the qualifications of this or that person.[10] Nevertheless, Kenneth A. Lockridge's study of Dedham shows that church membership there in the first twenty years was astonishingly high. By 1648, 70 percent of the adult men were members, and 80 percent of the children born between 1644 and 1653 were baptized – meaning that one or both parents were church members. Lockridge further claims that the membership was drawn from all classes, from servants to masters, and all personality types from the "tender-hearted" to the "stiff."[11] (These latter findings are paralleled in Thomas Shepard's group at Cambridge.) Clearly, then, the relation of religious experience meant something or did something for the people of Dedham, though just what, we have still to determine. It certainly does not seem to have kept people out of the church; but neither does the Dedham experience suggest business as usual. On the contrary, there was obviously something unusual, even upsetting, about the new practice of delivering relations.

8 Ibid., pp. 25–6; Norton, *Answer to Apollonius,* p. 33.

9 Stearns and Brawner, "Church 'Relations,' " p. 28.

10 Don G. Hill, ed., *The Record of Baptisms, Marriages and Deaths, and Admissions to the Church and Dismissals Therefrom, Transcribed from the Church Records in the Town of Dedham, Massachusetts, 1638–1845* (Dedham, 1888), pp. 1–15. Hereafter cited as *Dedham Church Records.*

11 Kenneth A. Lockridge, *A New England Town: The First Hundred Years:* Dedham, Massachusetts, 1636–1736 (New York: Norton, 1970), pp. 31–3. Membership figures for the second generation were dramatically lower. See pp. 33–4.

It is this part of the picture that does not jibe with the Stearns and Brawner thesis. If the relation of religious experience was a fairly innocuous step in the continuity of Congregationalism, it would have been much easier to assimilate into the life of the church than it apparently was. No matter what the ministers were claiming, the church records as well as the surviving narratives themselves show that the people of New England experienced some trauma when they were called upon to give a relation. They did it; they may even have liked doing it; but it was not, apparently, easy to do. To classify the test of saving faith as "an artificial problem" is thus to ignore the fact that it caused stir and confusion, not only among its enemies, but, even more significantly, among its advocates.

Nor can we take for granted the stir and confusion among those enemies. If the conversion narrative was "simply another *form* of outward profession" (emphasis added), rather than, so to speak, a whole new species, then why the alleged mystification on the part of the Presbyterians? They had seen outward professions before. They themselves demanded a declaration of faith for admission to their own churches,[12] and they had no trouble figuring out on the instant that the New England conversion narrative was not of the same ilk, that to them there *was* a sharp difference in kind. But beyond this, they kept claiming to find their adversaries' arguments inconsistent, contradictory, and confusing. Since they were not shy in expressing open anger and direct opposition to the New England way, and since they were not stupid, why should they claim to be confused, unless they really were? But the "continuity" theory claims that New England was taking a logical forward step in its church polity and explaining it simply and straightforwardly.

In his (partial) answer to Stearns and Brawner, Baird Tipson does work out a possible explanation not just for the Presbyterians' evident irritation over conversion narratives – this, as we have said, is understandable in light of their views of church polity – but also for their feeling that something about the matter was still "in darknesse." Tipson claims that where Stearns and Brawner find continuity there is instead "a flat contradiction" that exposes the New England test as altogether different in kind from previous church practices, just as Morgan stated. John Norton's supposedly reasonable admission to Apollonius that another person's conversion could not be understood from the inside just made matters worse: It "obviously compromised the internal-external distinction," argues Tipson, because a description of experience by its very nature could not be judged by its "outward side." No

12 Nuttall, *Visible Saints*, p. 112.

matter what they said about exercising the judgment of charity, the New England churches "had decisively broken with tradition in demanding internal evidence of grace."[13] Tipson concludes that the churches took this great risk of "abandoning the traditional restraints against judging the hearts of others" because of a much greater need: People wanted

> the church to "underwrite" the gracious experience of each communicant. By validating not only the visible but so far as possible the invisible sanctity of the sacramental community, the church was really confirming its members in their individual *certitudo salutis*.[14]

This need for assurance, Tipson explains, was always implicit in the doctrine of election's distinction between external and effectual calling. "By explicitly identifying membership in the church with a merely external calling," Puritan theologians since Elizabethan days had "pulled the rug out from under those who relied on church membership for assurance." But the need took on a new urgency in the new world, claims Tipson, because in Massachusetts, for the first time, "there was no persecuting state to defy," and therefore no way of "witnessing the work of the Holy Ghost" by performing, through courageous, communal resistance (as the separatist exiles had done by covenanting together), "the functional equivalent of a relation." As further evidence of this pattern, Tipson points out that "when similar political conditions arose in England, many Congregationalists there adopted a similar test."[15]

On the basis of this compelling analysis, Tipson offers a new reason for the transatlantic misunderstanding over the issue of conversion narratives. It is not that the churches were keeping people out, as Morgan's "exclusivist" view maintains; it is not that the churches were bringing people in, as the alternate "expansionist" hypothesis of Stearns and Brawner suggests. Rather, the tone of the debate is more comprehensible if the whole question is viewed in terms of this sudden surfacing of

13 Tipson, "Invisible Saints," especially pp. 465–6.

14 Ibid., p. 470.

15 Ibid., pp. 469, 470–1. In his remarks about the separatists, Tipson is citing and paraphrasing Stearns and Brawner, "Church 'Relations,' " p. 35. Cotton Mather reinforces the "persecution" argument in his discussion of the Cambridge Platform: "In the primitive times they made such a profession [of outward faith], at their being 'added unto the church;' and the profession had this justifying circumstance in it, when they endangered their very lives to make it. I make no doubt but, in such a time of persecution, the like profession ought to be esteemed sufficient. – But in places where the true religion is in *repute* and *fashion*, then to look for some other justifying circumstance of a profession [i.e., a relation of experience] is but a reasonable conformity to the custom and manner of the apostles" (*Magnalia*, 2:246).

an individual need of assurance – and of the churches' equally urgent need to meet it – and then to equivocate about it.

> Such an interpretation would explain the confused defenses of New England's admission policy. The apologists were not thinking primarily of straitening (or for that matter of broadening) the path into the church but rather of the assurance of those already within the church. But to offer a defense along these lines could only have constituted an admission that the critics' charges of sectarianism were fully justified.[16]

This is, as we have noted, a compelling argument, and we can see how it would largely account for both the heat and the confusion of the transatlantic dispute. As a matter of fact, there is confirmation for the Tipson theory in the conversion narrative as it developed in England, for as we have seen, it is the English form that stresses individual assurance, and especially the assurance that may be derived from the group: As John Megson typically testified in Dublin, "I *desire* to be of this Church, for God shall *adde such as shall be saved.*"[17] The American narrative, on the other hand, is very often tentative, anxious, and open-ended and reflects very little assurance. If the New England ministers were so bent on dispelling the people's doubts about their spiritual estate that they were willing to defy tradition, to compromise, and even to deceive in order to achieve it, it is sad indeed to see that their efforts produced such strange results.

But motives cannot be argued from results. There are other reasons why Tipson's theory does not entirely satisfy our inquiry as to what was causing the confusion in the transatlantic dispute. This theory holds (on the basis of an impressive amount of theological precedent) that the New England Puritans, in presuming "to encroach upon the divine prerogative of judging each other's invisible spiritual estate," had knowingly and willfully to cross over into territory that had hitherto been absolutely forbidden. The borderline of that territory – God's territory – was indelible, the distinction between inward and outward, invisible and visible unmistakably clear: "Inner evidence is incommunicable."[18]

Because of these sharp distinctions, of which the ministers were fully aware "despite their disclaimers" about charitable judgment, the conclusion is inevitable that John Cotton, Richard Mather, John Norton, and all their colleagues were engaging throughout the debate in a deliberate, if guilt-ridden, deception. Having "decisively broken with tradition," having made "a conscious decision" to judge, or to pretend to judge, the hearts of others, New England then made "repeated refer-

16 Tipson, "Invisible Saints," pp. 467–8, 470.

17 See Introduction, n. 33.

18 Tipson, "Invisible Saints," pp. 469, 466.

ences to the judgment of charity [in] a vain attempt to disguise the magnitude of the innovation."[19] This would mean that the transatlantic "agreeance" we have noted – as to the ultimate unknowability of the human heart – was, on the Americans' part, a deliberate misrepresentation of their opinion, or at least a refusal to reveal that they had changed their minds. If it was not – if the American Puritans still did agree with the English Presbyterians that only God truly knows the hearts of men – then their "test" of inward faith was sheer hypocrisy, just as the Presbyterians suspected. One way or the other, the New England apologists had to be consciously lying, albeit under the irresistible compulsion of the people's need to dispel "doubts as to [their] unworthiness to receive the sacraments,"[20] combined with the community's conflicting need to avoid looking sectarian.

Thus we are left with an uncomfortably final-sounding and somewhat partisan resolution: that Cotton and his friends were purposely, willfully obfuscating their true interest in the conversion narrative – even if for good, or psychologically understandable, reasons. Just as the Stearns and Brawner thesis takes the New England ministers entirely at their word as they ingenuously claim that there is nothing new or startling about their church practices, so the Tipson theory discounts their word on the grounds that they knew they could not afford to tell the shocking truth about what they were doing. On the underside of these propositions is the necessity to view the Presbyterian party, on the one hand, as inexplicably befuddled and, on the other, as not only factually but somehow morally justified in its indignation.

Such arguments, which are representative of much of the scholarship on this subject, leave no room for the possibility that both sides may have been telling the truth as straightforwardly, as clear-headedly, and as fully as they could – and may still have so seriously failed to communicate that at the height of the debate, in 1644, Thomas Weld could call William Rathband's ideas "as far from truth, as *Old-England* is from *New*."[21] At that more-than-geographical distance, admittedly, it is New England's arguments that sound, as Tipson says, the more "confused"; but perhaps we can make some sense of them.

John Norton's famous *Answer to Apollonius* offers one of the more striking examples of the apparent confusion or contradiction of New England's defenses, and for the very reason that Tipson noted: It is apparently caught on the horns of the inner–outer dilemma. Defining the four qualifications that a man must offer in order to be deemed "faithful to the church," Norton stipulates that such faithfulness can

19 Ibid., p. 468.
20 Ibid., p. 470.
21 *Answer to* W.R., p. 5.

only be visible: "He is faithful in the judgment of the church, even though he may not be so in the judgment of God."[22] Similarly, Richard Mather wrote to Richard Bernard that "as repentance from dead workes, and faith in Christ Jesus purgeth such persons, from all sinne in the sight of God: so the profession thereof in humble and holy manner, presenteth them cleane and pure in the sight of the church."[23] Thus the operations were at best analogous, never identical. Yet in trying to get a closer look at that profession of experience, Norton did not seem able to establish a definite connection between the two parts of the analogy. All he could say was that the person who is "faithful to the church" will give

> ii. A declaration of the work of experienced faith. In one way or another this involves the matter of conversion as an event even though the inward side of the event in a person cannot be known by others.[24]

To the unfriendly eye, this may look like double-talk, for the two main propositions seem locked in conflict. The introductory "in one way or another" is certainly not very enlightening. Then "the matter of conversion as an event": What can that be, if not the event as inwardly experienced by the convert? It is highly doubtful that by "matter of conversion" Norton meant that the convert simply states as a fact that he is converted. This would be rote recitation: anathema to the Puritans. Moreover, the candidate is speaking to other people – to "living stones" and not to blocks of wood. How are the hearers supposed to respond to this "matter"? We are hereupon told that the "inward side" cannot be known by others. Is there, then, an "outward side" to conversion that *can* reliably be known by others?

This, of course, is the crucial question. The first thing that springs to mind in considering a possible "outward side" to conversion is its visible effects, that is, some notion of behavior: the "godly conversation" that was one of the "fruits" of a work of grace; the sanctification that could be a man's evidence of justification – if and "only if he has first discerned the faith within him."[25] Here perhaps is an outward side that might be said to be glued, however precariously, to the inward side of the event.

But this cannot be Norton's meaning, because in defining the qualifications of church members, he includes outward behavior as a separate

22 Norton, *Answer to Apollonius,* p. 35.

23 "Apologie of the churches of New-England," p. 6.

24 Norton, *Answer to Apollonius,* p. 36. Norton supplies this proof-text: "And they . . . were baptized of him in Jordan, confessing their sins. Matthew 3:6 (Mark 1:5)." Again, the confession of sins is the "experimental" part of a profession.

25 Miller, *New England Mind: Seventeenth Century,* p. 51.

item on the list. In addition to knowledge of Christian doctrine and an experience of the work of grace, Norton writes, the candidate must exhibit "a life without scandal, that is, without any cause of offence in the sight of man uncorrected by repentance," as well as "a witnessing commitment to the Gospel of Christ and his kingdom."[26] The "outward side" implied in item ii must therefore be something other than behavior in the usual sense.

Norton's subsequent elucidation of the method of confession does not at first sight make things any clearer.

> Nothing is required in this confession which is not shared by all faithful men. There is no place here for private matters. Extraordinary beliefs are not sought after . . . It is enough if anything of Christ be made manifest in any way.[27]

If there is no place here for private, much less "extraordinary," matters, it is hard to imagine just what the convert would find to say about his religious experiences. But the qualifying phrase is: "shared by all faithful men," *commune omni fideli*. What is easy to forget so long after these events, and seeing them through the modern lens of individual isolation, is that the religious experiences that made men living stones in the temple or, even more to the point, members of the Body of Christ were (or were supposed to be) essentially known and understood and felt in common by all the other members.[28]

A great deal has been said of the incommunicability of religious experience – much of it by the very seventeenth-century figures we are discussing. Geoffrey F. Nuttall in his important study of the Holy Spirit shows how often "the inner certitude of the reality of the Holy Spirit's presence was accompanied by a sense of the difficulty of adequately describing the experience, in such a way that others might be convinced of its genuineness."[29] Daniel B. Shea, Jr. suggests that the cry "I know not how to express it" became entrenched as a convention in spiritual autobiography.[30] Many Puritan ministers emphasized the point to their flocks. Thomas Hooker was typical in his preachment that

> the soul . . . hath an inward work, which, though happily he cannot discover the manner and order thereof, nor expresse it to others, yet

26 Norton, *Answer to Apollonius*, p. 36. A similar list was given by Allin and Shepard, writing at about the same time (*Defence of the Answer*, p. 193).

27 Norton, *Answer to Apollonius*, pp. 42–3.

28 The most complete and illuminating study of Puritanism's commitment to "the unique communal nature of the Church" is John S. Coolidge's indispensable book *The Pauline Renaissance in England: Puritanism and the Bible* (Oxford: Clarendon Press, 1970), to which much of this chapter is indebted.

29 *Holy Spirit*, p. 138, and chap. 9 passim.

30 *Spiritual Autobiography*, p. 98.

> he knows more thereof than any man under heaven. Ask a child, How doe you know such a man is your father? Alas, he cannot tell you, yet he hath a strong affection toward him above all others, and feels in himself such a leaning in his affection towards him, as another feels not . . . So there is in a Saint of God an inward tenderness of affection, a leaning of his soul towards God which no man knowes but he that hath it.[31]

And yet, just as in spiritual autobiography the disclaimer about inexpressibility accompanies an intense verbal performance, so in the total context Hooker's acknowledgment of ineffability was not to discourage but to encourage communication – with oneself first, then with others. The fact is, as Nuttall reminds us, that such pronouncements were not to "lead to a quietistic self-centeredness in religion"; there was also a belief in "a 'fellowship of the Spirit,' the warmth and personal quality of which is a reflection of the spiritual experience shared by, and uniting, its members."[32] Thus the Welsh preacher Walter Cradock compared the way "a Saint follows the Holy Ghost with a kind of sagacity . . . as we see the Dog follow the Hare: . . . a man that hath the spirit may know the spirit in another by the spirit."[33] But radical Puritans like Cradock had no corner on this spiritual market: The moderate Richard Baxter, as Stearns and Brawner have pointed out, spoke feelingly of "a Connaturality of Spirit in the Saints that will work by Sympathy, . . . As a Load-Stone will exercise its attractive Force through a Stone Wall."[34] And Thomas Hooker went on to stress, in the sermon just cited, that even if "no man knowes but he that hath it," it is particularly the "naturall man" who cannot understand what it is to have a "spiritual frame of heart" – who cannot, that is, until "God is pleased to teach me this skill by the work of his Spirit within my self." But once that happens,

> when I finde my own heart wrought upon, then I can best discover it to another, then doe I know that which before I never understood; though happily I could discourse something concerning such things, and understand the outside as it were, yet that was all, I never knew the bottom, as I doe now.[35]

In short, genuineness of experience, expressiveness about it, and understanding of it in others all come together with the infusion of grace. If Hooker's syntax seems a little jumpy, it is because he moves from the

31 *Saints Dignitie,* p. 209.
32 *Holy Spirit,* p. 141.
33 *Divine Drops Distilled* (1650), cited ibid., p. 142.
34 *Reliquiae Baxterianae* (1696), cited ibid., p. 143.
35 *Saints Dignitie,* p. 210.

one to the other of these concepts so quickly – since for him they are all so closely related, the several verbal faculties part of one whole.

> It is not sufficient to salvation, for a man to be an often hearer, to have his heart now and then inlarged, to give assent to truths delivered, to conceive the grounds of them, or to be able happily to discourse of some points of religion. Oh look further, he that hath saving knowledge indeed, goes farre beyond all this.[36]

In sum, he that has saving knowledge, as Hooker said earlier, has been taught a "skill" – a skill in the combined faculties of hearing, understanding, and speaking that can only be exercised by the regenerate man. This is what the Holy Spirit teaches. In fact, skill of this sort may be a sign that a man actually does possess the Spirit. Thus Cotton defined the New Creature:

> He hath a new mind, and a new heart, new affections, new Language, and new employments that he was never wont to doe before; now he can read Gods Word, and conferre with Gods people about the things of God, and can instruct others, and fashion himselfe to a new mould, and all upon the renewall of the spirit of his minde; . . . By these causes you may clearly discerne whether God hath given you a new life or no.[37]

This is, of course, a skill "such as flesh and blood hath not revealed," not acquired at universities, not got, as Thomas Shepard warned, with a wet finger. And this is why it has nothing to do with the "froth of eloquence"[38] at which hypocrites so easily excel. In fact, the saint who has this skill may not be particularly clever with words or eloquent in worldly terms. He may even – on the oft-repeated Puritan ground that the man with most reason for comfort is the one who thinks himself furthest from it – he may even find himself sadly lacking the "power to expresse," especially if he is newly reborn.

> Of comfort to all those poore soules, as finde themselves looking up to Christ; they complaine they see little grace in themselves; it may be none at all as they thinke, . . . Well, you want grace, & you want praier, & you want Christ, you want all that which others comfortably attain unto, you want power to expresse your selves in company: Well, if your eyes be set upon Christ, & upon your failings in grace, and yet in Christ you see there is salvation, and you wait upon him for it, and all your owne parts are empty things in comparison of Christ; it is an evident signe God hath given you grace.[39]

36 Ibid., p. 212.

37 John Cotton, *Christ the Fountain of Life* (London, 1651), pp. 98–9.

38 John Preston, *A Pattern of Wholesome Words,* cited in Irvonwy Morgan, *Puritan Spirituality* (London: Epworth Press, 1973), p. 16.

39 John Cotton, *The Way of Life* (London, 1641), pp. 28–9.

Cotton is not being contradictory when he here describes the absence of "power to expresse" and elsewhere insists that the New Creature has "new Language," for – as he makes clear in his sermon at Salem – there is a distinction between the first conversion and the growth in grace that we discussed earlier.[40] In fact, the Salem sermon, which is taken as a sign of increased strictness in New England's idea of church admissions, may be interpreted equally well – along the lines of the Stearns and Brawner thesis – as the loosest and most wide-ranging approach to the definition of a saintly community within the church (assuming that such a definition needs to be made at all, which of course the Presbyterians dispute). For Cotton repeats here his idea that the least sign of true godliness is sufficient for admission; indeed, his sermon is almost a warning against the kind of "inquisitorial" procedure that Hooker later complained about.

> . . . Now then, doth the Lord draw you to Christ, when you are broken in the sense of your own sins, and of your own righteousness? When you look at duties you are not able to do them, not able to hear or pray aright. If the Lord do thus draw you by his everlasting arm, He will put a spirit into you, that will cause you to wait for Christ, and to wait for Him until He doth shew mercy upon you; . . . And whilst you do with patience and constancy wait, you are drawn with everlasting love; now you have Christ in you, though you do not feel Him; for as the earth is hanged upon nothing, Job xxvi, 7, so now there is a place for Christ in the heart, when it is emptied of everything besides; and such a man hath Christ, and is blessed, and the covenant of grace is his, *you may safely receive him into your church fellowship;* and though he do neither know Christ nor his covenant to be his, yet he will wait for Him, . . . And you shall find such meek in spirit and merciful, and mourning for sin: these kind of Christians will spring and grow.[41]

If this is a prescription for a relation of religious experience, it certainly is not a call for a rigid, codified, and elaborate morphology of conversion. In fact, it adheres closely to Cotton's earlier sermon from Old England, cited above, in emphasizing the possibility that the convert may not even have that verbal skill – may not "hear or pray aright" – and may yet have the true spirit within him.

Later, Shepard and Allin took the same approach, as had Weld in his *Brief Narration,* in assuring their English brethren:

> Let the profession of the worke of faith bee never so short, or so weake, let it be by their owne immediate relation or by question, yet if

40 See Chapter 1, n. 109.

41 "*Sermon at Salem,*" in Ziff, *Cotton on the Churches,* pp. 63–4. Emphasis added.

> it may but appeare to a regulated charity so as to hope that it is reall, it is to rest satisfied then, till God make discovery to the contrary.[42]

In English gathered churches, wrote William Bartlet, "broken language, and bad and low expressions" are no deterrent in a relation, so long as it "is accompanied with the power of Religion and godliness."[43] John Rogers gave many such assurances, and Thomas Goodwin and his four Independent colleagues wrote in a similar vein in their *Apologeticall Narration* about their church admission practices in Holland. (They do not explicitly state here that they are talking about professions of experience, but we know from Sidrach Simpson's relation that this was in fact the practice, as well as by the letter quoted hereafter.)

> Where as one great controversie of these times is about the *qualification of the Members* of Churches, and the promiscuous receiving and mixture of good and bad; Therein we chose the better part, and to be sure, received in none but such as all the Churches in the world would by the balance of the Sanctuary acknowledge faithful. And yet in this we are able to make this true and just profession also, That the Rules which we gave up our judgements unto, to judge those we received in amongst us by, were of that latitude as would take in any member of Christ, the meanest, in whom there may be supposed to be the *least of Christ,* and indeed such and no others as all the godly in this Kingdome carry in their bosomes to judge others by.[44]

This is the document that William Rathband found so inadequate in explaining the "full story" of the Independent way. The rule that every godly man carries in his bosom "to judge others by" was supposedly one of the puzzles, though it was clear that Goodwin was referring in part to Scripture, for example, Matt. 12:35–7 or Rom. 10:9–10. As he wrote in an earlier letter from Holland:

> We find Confession with the Mouth of the Work of Faith in the Heart, a Means among other sanctified by God to make any ones Grace evident and visible to others, and the Judgment we make hereupon to admit our Members, is no other, nor more rigorous, than what the Word holds forth as meet for us to judg of others by, and but such as I know your Conscience carries about with you, and which you can never lose, and which as occasion is given, you do use to judg of the Differences of Men by; and we know that in us it is righteous Judgment, being squared by the Rule given us, altho it is not infallible Judgment; for Men may deceive us in our Applications

42 *Defence of the Answer,* p. 191.

43 'Ιχνογραφία *or a Model of the Primitive Congregational Way* (1647), cited in Nuttall, *Visible Saints,* p. 110.

44 Goodwin et al., *Apologeticall Narration,* pp. 11–12.

> of it. Thus we do and have practised, . . . and that from the beginning.[45]

The ability to judge a man's confession, even that of "the meanest" member of Christ, was, of course, the reverse side of that special skill Hooker preached about. Goodwin was convinced that with the aid of the Word, the saints knew the "tast" of another saint's spirit despite that ultimate privacy of all experience that Norton acknowledges in his *Answer*.

> There is such a thing as a Manifestation of Spirits in a several way, whereby is not meant, that a person is obliged to lay open all that is in his heart, but that by a mutual conference concerning Spiritual things, there should be a tast given what is in one another's Spirits.[46]

Here is "the analogy of sense-perception" that Nuttail discusses (and that we saw in Cradock's dog-and-hare figure), which the Puritan extended "from the sphere of the soul's perception of God's Spirit in his own heart to its perception of the Spirit in other men."[47] Hence, the images of breath and breathing, "savour," and smell dominate these discussions. Back in England, Cotton's sermons on Canticles pictured the saints as a garden of flowers and spices, "of sweet and precious savour in the nostrils of Christ."[48] Thomas Weld speaks of the churches discerning "the least true breathing of Christ, though but as smoaking flax," and remarks that "those that are sound doe manifest the sweet smell of their graces."[49] Thomas Hooker describes the saints as those who either by their behavior and reputation or by "their expressions . . . savour so much, as though they had been with Jesus."[50] The Cambridge Platform speaks of "sincere members breathing after purity."[51] The saints of Cambridge under Thomas Shepard's leadership, reports Cotton Mather, were "a gracious, savoury-spirited people."[52] Jonathan Mitchel, still defending conversion narratives in 1664, wrote, "It cannot be imagined how a person can have had experience of a work of grace, . . . but that he can speak of it, in some way or other, after a savoury manner."[53] And as Cotton explained in *The Way of the Churches:*

45 "To the Reverend Mr. John Goodwin," in Goodwin, *Works,* 4:44.

46 *Of the Constitution,* ibid., pp. 302–3.

47 Nuttall, *Holy Spirit,* p. 142.

48 *A Brief Exposition Of the whole Book of Canticles, or, Song of* Solomon . . . (London, 1642), p. 157. This imagery, traditional in religious writing, is derived from Song of Sol. 4:12 and Isa. 51:3.

49 *Brief Narration,* p. 8, and see Matt. 12:20; *Answer to* W.R., p. 24.

50 *A Survey of the Summe of Church-Discipline* (London, 1648), pt. 1, p. 14.

51 Walker, *Creeds and Platforms,* p. 198.

52 *Magnalia,* 2:92.

53 "Propositions," in Mather, *Magnalia,* 2:103.

> Wee doe not exact eminent measure, either of knowledge, or holinesse, but doe willingly stretch out our hands to receive *the weake in faith,* such in whose spirits wee can discerne *the least measure of breathing and panting after Christ, in their sensible feeling of a lost estate;* for we had rather 99. hypocrites should perish through presumption, then one humble soul belonging to Christ, should sinke under discouragement or despaire.[54]

The sweet savour and the true breathing, faint and fragile though they might be, were the "outward side" of the event of conversion that could be known by others, as a mirror is held up to the nose and mouth to detect the breath of life. For as Thomas Shepard preached, "a dead man is a speechless man"–not in the sense that he is mute but in the sense that his verbal abilities are on a par with a parrot's: No matter what he says, "he is a breathless man."[55] Yet the signs of breath and life were not "extraordinary" or even, in an exclusive sense, "private," for they were shared by all godly people. They resided in, but did not constitute, behavior, not even the "behavior" of speech. Yet they were made manifest in words: not in an intricate arrangement of taffeta phrases and silken terms precise, but in a sometimes faltering account of what the believer simply and smartingly did feel. The crucial "test" of anything spoken was, for a man like Cotton, not the words but the music: "what Spirit breaths in such a speech." As he wrote to one captious adversary, "See what a vast difference there is betweene the Spirit of your language, and the language of the Spirit of Christ."[56] Such men thought it was perfectly clear what they wanted when they demanded, as did John Davenport, "such a publick profession of their *faith,* as . . . has blessedness annexed unto it, and such as flech and blood hath not revealed."[57] As Walter Cradock confidently said, "The greatest difference (that I know) in all the Book of God, between Saints and sinners is, that the one hath the Spirit, and the other hath not."[58]

This, at least, was the ideal–and to apparently rational, down-to-earth men like Baillie and Rathband, it was, if not exactly incomprehensible, certainly a dangerously murky proposition.[59] Even granted

54 P. 58.

55 *The Sincere Convert,* in *Works,* 1:27.

56 *The Grounds and Ends of the Baptisme of the Children of the Faithfull* (London, 1647), p. 160.

57 Mather, *Magnalia,* 1:328. After Peter testified his faith in Christ as the Son of God, Jesus replied that "flesh and blood hath not revealed *it* unto thee, but my Father which is in heaven" (Matt. 16:17).

58 *Divine Drops Distilled,* cited in Nuttall, *Holy Spirit,* p. 142.

59 Of course there were dangers in a "spiritist" approach to these matters, as the Antinomian controversy so vividly demonstrated. Even so, after the alleged errors of the enthusiasts were revealed, church relations continued, and Thom-

that the Spirit breathes in all the godly, and even granted, as Richard Bernard had, that "it were well if all God's people could prophesie" and reveal thereby their fitness for membership, there was still simply no way of achieving certainty in any of these matters, and therefore there was no earthly reason to add a compulsory verbal test to the other already established tests of behavior and knowledge that at least weeded out the scandalous and the ignorant. Indeed, such a test might even be a hindrance to church fellowship.

> Seeing if the party to be admitted be not discovered unsound by any of the other trials, then either he is sound indeed, or else a subtle hypocrite, which if he be, then he will deceive the Church present as well as he hath done others absent, and by his golden words, (wherein hypocrites usually excell) as well or much more then by his deeds and conversation: unlesse we should imagine (as some of that way here doe) that the Church hath in it ever *such a spirit of discerning, as that it cannot be deceived* by any.[60]

This view sounds reasonable, but woven through it there is a markedly negative approach toward the use of language. It is easy to read the literature of this debate as a confrontation between sweet reason and practical common sense, on the one hand, and a kind of fearful, high-handed rigidity, on the other (New English) hand. But the closer the reading, the more it becomes apparent that the English arguments are grounded in a genuine apprehensiveness of their own. It is not just that an additional test would be superfluous, unproductive, or even obstructive; nor even, as Tipson claims, that a test of inner experience is a sacrilegious invasion of God's territory. There is also the fear that any plan that hinges on the exhibition *through words* of signs of regeneration in church members is particularly liable to abuse. And this is the factor – in effect, a "literary" judgment – that demands some further attention.

This underlying sense of the potential dangers of popular verbal activity in the churches takes two major forms: first, that ordinary people cannot be trusted to express themselves on such an abstruse subject as conversion – even their own; and second, that the evaluation of such

as Shepard, notwithstanding his opposition to the Hutchinsonians, could write in 1645 that "so long as the rule [of charity] bee attended wee leave every one to the wisedome of Christ" (*Defence of the Answer,* p. 192). In fact, his and Allin's *Defence* stood for the extension of the charity which Hutchinson was felt to have violated: "To account any unfit for the Church, because their hearts cannot close with them, or because they like not their spirits, speake not with favour or any such like principles, and yet can give no rule or convicting argument from the word, why thus they doe, we thinke is rigour" (ibid., p. 189).

60 Rathband, *Briefe Narration,* p. 8, n. 1.

expression cannot safely be left up to ordinary people, especially *en masse*. The objections to a test of religious experience may therefore be read not only in terms of the indisputably difficult and age-old problem of getting from the inward side to the outward side of *any* experience; they are also, and sometimes heatedly, argued as a problem in particular of the limited expressive and cognitive capacities of the "multitude."

To this extent, the issue *is* the broader question of church polity that deals with the power of the keys; the question that fundamentally divides Congregationalist from Presbyterian and that emerges in all sorts of disputes about the technical details of church discipline and especially about the necessity for explicit covenants. This broader question is thought of as a question of where power resides; but beyond that, it is a question of "gifts" and abilities – of human capacities, insofar as these are given by God. The Presbyterians argued that those

> who have a right from God to the acts of Jurisdiction, they have a promise of gifts needfull for the performance of these acts. For a divine right and calling to any worke is backed with a promise of Gods presence, gifts and assistance in doing of that worke; but, the people have no promise of any such gifts. For besides that daily experience declare numbers among the people to be altogether destitute of such knowledge, wisedome and other gifts which are necessary for the performance of these acts of Jurisdicton: The Apostle himselfe teaches that such gifts are not given to all, but to some onely.[61]

Given these assumptions, the critics of conversion narratives did not concentrate on the fact that "this declaration is made first in private before either some of the officers, or other persons betrusted with the examination." That was bad enough; but that it was given "after also in publike before all the Church (though never so many) and that so as to the conviction and satisfaction of them all" was especially galling.[62] Yet this is a rather odd distinction. Considering their distaste for the whole idea of a conversion narrative, why did the critics bother to distinguish between the "all" and the "some" when it came to hearing those narratives? Why did they find it unpalatable, not just that a man must declare his experiences at all but that he must "declare publikely in the face of the Congregation," and give "full satisfaction, not onely to the Minis-

61 Baillie, *Dissvasive*, pp. 184–5.

62 Rathband, *Briefe Narration*, p. 9. There has been considerable discussion even up to the present day as to whether the acceptance of a new member had to be unanimous or only by a majority. As Tipson points out, church practices seem to have differed from place to place. Lechford reports that in Mr. Cotton's Boston, admissions and other matters went "most an-end, by unanimous consent," whereas in Salem "they rule by the major part of the Church: You that are so minded hold up your hands; you that are otherwise minded, hold up yours" (*Plain Dealing*, p. 38). See also ibid., pp. 21–2, n. 12 and pp. 38–40, n. 37.

ters and Elders, and many of the people, but to all and every one, or at least, the major part of the Church"?[63] The only possible answer is that "such gifts [of hearing and understanding] are not given to all, but to some onely." And this, too, is a literary judgment.

It is here for the first time that we glimpse some real inconsistency in the Presbyterian position. For by their own argument, if a thing is wrong, it is wrong; conversion narratives are unacceptable, they maintain, because a *degree* of certainty (which is all that the Congregationalists could claim) is worse than useless. Yet here they may be found claiming that there are degrees of *un*certainty in the matter: And conversion narratives are somehow especially uncertain when subjected to the scrutiny of the ungifted multitude.

It was this aspect of the procedure, in fact, that supposedly turned Thomas Hooker away from it. Hooker did not object to private examination; it was the "curious inquisitions and niceties" that emerged in the public forum and "which the pride and wantonnesse of mens spirits hath brought into the Church" that he wanted to nip in the bud.[64] Hooker's complaint was in line with the Presbyterian claim that people were being kept out of the churches: For one thing, as Perry Miller has pointed out, he had a "preoccupation" with "the evangelical element,"[65] and questioning by the congregation was a "trouble," the removal of which "would mervailously facilitate the work of *Admission*." Indeed, nothing should be allowed to "disturb the peace . . . and to prejudice the progresse of God's Ordinances," even if it meant having more hypocrites inside the church.[66]

The Dedham experience already mentioned does suggest that Hooker was not exaggerating about the "trouble" caused by public examination: Yet curiously enough, as we have seen in Lockridge's study, church membership boomed in Dedham, Hooker's "inquisitions and niceties" notwithstanding. This may also be so in the case of Shepard's Cambridge congregation. The reader will note that some confessions from this group include close and painful questioning;[67] yet all the

63 Baillie, *Dissvasive*, p. 22.

64 *Survey*, pt. 3, p. 6.

65 *Errand into the Wilderness* (New York: Harper, Torchbook, 1956), p. 28.

66 *Survey*, pt. 3, p. 6; Miller, *Errand*, p. 32. Miller also points out that Hooker had "a decided aversion to strife" within the churches (p. 28).

67 I assume that the elders asked most of the questions at Cambridge. (Selement and Woolley's notes propose the names of various church members, but Shepard recorded initials only, most of which could belong to known elders of the church.) This conflicts with Hooker's complaint but conforms to John Norton's claim in the *Answer* that if the brethren wish to ask a question, they must do so "indirectly" through the elders, to preserve "the dignity of the candidate" (p. 42).

people whose confessions Shepard recorded "were entertayned [i.e., received] as members." A number of their relations seem rather pallid, even lame; others seem confused; often the questions seem to make things worse; yet all the "propounded" members were accepted, and many more besides, whose confessions, for reasons unknown, Shepard did not record.[68]

This kind of evidence suggests that John S. Coolidge is correct in his rejection of Morgan's theory of "jealous exclusivism" and correct in his speculation that candidates were not generally turned away for delivering an inadequate narrative.[69] In fact, one of the most perversely fascinating arguments against New England was that the churches were *too* lenient.

> Notwithstanding all this rigour and strictnesse, sometimes . . . the Churches use great indulgence in their triall, . . . *W.T.* to Mr *B.* saith, If a man be humble, and have an earnest desire, though he be but in a waiting condition, if in other things he make conscience of his wayes, he knowes no man of wit will denie him to become a member. The same man to *P.H.* If your ministers were here, they would not think us too strict, but too remisse in Discipline. I think in time we shall grow like old *England*.[70]

Of course we still have Lechford's parenthetical remark that "(. . . often some members doe)" take exception to "the parties expressions" and thereby hold up the admissions process (though for Lechford, this is a very mild observation).[71] And we still have all those arguments by the English critics, on solid, practical grounds, that the system was just unworkable. Very much like Hooker, they spoke of "the inconvenience of bringing all things to the examination of the multitude,"[72] and they said that the turmoil in New England's churches, especially the Antinomian controversy, proved just how inconvenient it could be. This was, in fact, a very effective argument. Baillie used it against prophesying as well and especially against the practice whereby "any member of the

68 A few names, all women's, are crossed out in the manuscript, but we do not know why. At least two of these women were definitely listed as members in the church records; there is no sure information about the others. The quoted phrases are from Shepard's own title at the beginning of his diary: "The Confessions of diverse propounded to be received & were entertayned as members."

69 Coolidge, *Pauline Renaissance,* p. 65, n. 33. Note especially Coolidge's incisive treatment of the allegedly harsh rejection of the Dorchester group in 1636.

70 Rathband, *Briefe Narration,* pp. 10–11. W.T., Mr. B., and P.H. are the unidentified writers of private letters that Rathband claimed to have had at his disposal.

71 See Chapter 1, n. 7.

72 Rathband, *Briefe Narration,* p. 9, n. marked "m."

congregation" might publicly question the preacher "about any point of the Doctrine" – an obvious parallel to the questioning of candidates for admission. Such practices "proved so unhappy in *New-England,* that gladly there they would be quit" of them – and he had evidence from Richard Mather's own pen to prove it.[73]

But the sifting and resifting of these factual claims is an endless pursuit that can only leave us as confused as the participants. In the end, it is probably impossible to decide once and for all on the basis of actual effects whether the Presbyterians were "right" or "wrong" in their objections to the delivery of religious experiences before a "multitude." What is more important to our examination of the problem is feeling, not statistics. For beyond all their facts and evidences from actual events, the critics felt, justifiably or not, that to expect comprehension and judgment from the brethren was just somehow wrong; they were not capable of it.

It was really on the same grounds that they rejected the assumption that every member could be expected to talk persuasively about his experience to his fellows. This is so despite the Presbyterians' frequent stress not on the people's incapacities but on their plight as victims of injustice. It was "unjust scrupulosity to require satisfaction of the true grace of every *Church-Member.*"[74] It was absurdly precise to exclude

> many thousands who in old *England* had lived without all scandal, and who had been reputed there good Christians, alwayes partaking of Church ordinances without any impediment, yet could not be admitted to any Church fellowship in *New-England.*

These people had not just been "fair professors." They had given

> this addition as a proofe of reallitie, a leaving of their native country, a undertaking a dangerous voyage even to a new world . . . [Yet] all this would not suffice.[75]

This, too, was an effective, reasonable, not to say heartrending, argument, well corroborated, according to the critics, not only by the ministers' official statements (such as Richard Mather's heavily quoted answer to the first of the famous thirty-two questions that "many also there are who are not yet admitted") and not only by Lechford's reports but also by many "Letters between friend and friend" across the ocean.[76]

73 Baillie, *Dissvasive,* p. 118.

74 Ibid., p. 154.

75 Baillie, *Disswasive . . . Vindicated,* p. 39.

76 Mather, *Church-Government,* p. 7; Rathband, *Briefe Narration,* Preface, p. 4[r]. J. Hammond Trumbull provides a brief summary of this aspect of the dispute in his edition of Lechford, *Plain Dealing,* p. 151, n. 252.

All this hard evidence allowed the critics virtually to hang New England by its own rope, while themselves seeming to remain in the unexceptionable position of defending the rights of the people. What makes the matter so delicate is that there are two sides, a positive and a negative, to these "rights." The positive right that New England's critics insisted was being denied – and certainly this was their most compelling argument – was the right of the godly, brave, well-behaved people who had traveled so far for "libertie and purity of Church ordinances"[77] finally to have those privileges extended to them in deed. But the negative right that they were defending is one that equally concerns us here, and it is harder to detect – being negative. It was sometimes rather appealingly put as the right of people not to be kept out "till they could speak of the mysteries of Christianity feelingly";[78] not to be subjected to a system that was "taking a very few that can talk more than the rest, and making them the Church."[79] It was, in short, the right *not* to have to speak, not to have to stand up before one's fellows and give an account of one's inner self – not just by behavior or reputation but by one's own words and expressions. It was the right not to enter into a communal literary relation, either because it was "a thing impossible for many good soules (fit for church-Societie, and who have right to Church-ordinances) to render such an account";[80] or because, even if they were capable of doing it, they might, like Bartleby, prefer not to. "Sundry [professors] may bee the elect children of God, and really most gracious in his eyes, *how unable or unwilling soever* they be to make this much appeare to the world."[81]

Such statements reflect more than a reasonable doubt about the ordinary person's communicative ability or interest. They are part of a broader attitude of suspicion, even animosity, toward the possibilities of language itself. Words must be handled very gingerly – like live explosives, they are not for amateurs to meddle with and can go off in unexpected, dangerous ways. William Rathband actually suggested that "if there must needs be such an account given both of mens knowledge and grace, were it not better *and safer* that a set and standing Rule were by common agreement made according to Gods Word, for triall of both[?]" Such a formula, he assured his readers, could be made "one and the same (for substance at least) in all the Churches, durable, and to continue the same without variation." If only the language of individual saints could be kept absolutely under control by

77 Baillie, *Disswasive . . . Vindicated,* p. 39.

78 "Of the visible Church," fol. 13^r, Bernard Papers.

79 Baxter, *Reliquiae Baxterianae,* cited in Watkins, *Puritan Experience,* p. 30.

80 Rathband, *Briefe Narration,* p. 9.

81 Baillie, *Dissvasive,* p. 171. Emphasis added.

such a rule of measure all might yet be well. But "for want of such a Rule," see what social and psychological havoc (Rathband calls it "inconveniences") may follow,

> as in the stronger that can speake better, may grow spirituall pride of their own abilities, and contempt of others that are weaker. In the weaker, envie at those that doe better then themselves, and discouragement, being afraid to offer themselves to triall, because they know not whether they shall be judged fit or no, or having offered themselves, and repulsed, they will hardly offer themselves againe, but rather live they and theirs out of the Church all their dayes: or being accepted and admitted, yet the remembrance of their own weaknesse, perhaps absurdnesse, in delivering themselves before such a multitude, when others have done so farre better, and with more acceptance then themselves, sticking by them may much rebate the edge of that little goodnesse that is in them.[82]

Thus human nature sinks beneath the pressures of expression. Indeed, there was no end to the foreseeable anguish if the saints were going to be forced to deliver a relation "both publike, and *ex tempore* too: Not knowing what will be asked them before it be asked."[83]

In view of the common assumption that New England imposed a rigid code for conversion narratives, it is important to note Thomas Weld's shocked reaction to Rathband's anxieties.

> Would he have us make a *New-England* Primer, a set forme? this were a way indeede to bring all to a formall course, and to teach every one (though no grace or experience at all of Christ in his heart) to learn (by rote) this forme, and then all were well.
>
> *W.R.* was . . . first, for common praiers, and then for Overtures and shewes, and now you have him for standing formes; You shall see him goe further anon, are not your fingers singed enough yet with such formalities? Its time to cease.[84]

On the contrary, Weld, Cotton, and the other New England spokesmen maintained a faith in the individual's capacity – and willingness – to speak for himself and to do it before friend or foe – but especially before friend.

> If it seemes so impossible for some Christians to give an account of the worke of Grace in them, what meant *Peter* to direct *all believers to bee alwaies ready to give an answer to every man of the hope that is in them?* If they must give this answer to all (even to persecutors themselves,) (as the Text intends) of the grounds of their hope, is it impossible that

82 Rathband, *Briefe Narration,* p. 9. Emphasis added.

83 Ibid., p. 8, n. 1.

84 Weld, *Answer to* W.R., p. 24.

> these good soules should render account to their godly brethren, who in a loving way demande it, and for their owne good too?[85]

The opposition's answer to this last question could only be that it was improperly framed. Perhaps it was not "impossible" – but the point was, it was not certain, either. Besides, the opposition did not distinguish between the unsympathetic and the sympathetic, the persecutor and the brother, in matters of communication. Men were "hid" away inside of themselves, there was no certainty anywhere in the process, and attempts to break through could only "breed" confusion, even among "understanding men."

> It requires a great deale of more ability in every member in every Church, then can be found in any mortall man: . . . how is it possible to attaine unto any grounded certainty of true grace in the heart of any other man? for the hid man of the heart, and the new name, are not certainly known to any but to such as have them. The grounds of a mans own certain perswasion, the act of his faith either direct or reflex, the witnesse of his conscience, or the seale of the spirit, cannot goe without his own breast: all the demonstrations which can be made to another, are so oft found false, that in understanding men they can breed at most but a fallible opinion, or a charitable hope, which is farre from any certainty either of sense or science, much more of faith or immediate revelation.[86]

Baillie's continual return to the concept of "certainty" demands that we pause here to clear up one of the most misunderstood elements in this long dispute. This is the mistaken idea that John Cotton, Baillie's chief adversary, insisted upon a demonstration of "infallible signs" of regeneration by church members. Baillie perpetuated this misunderstanding by remarks like those above and by his repetition in the *Disswasive . . . Vindicated* that

> M. *Cotton* lets fall there behoved to be farther a positive affirmation of true grace; . . . certain [i.e., sure] signes, satisfying the body, at least the pluralitie of the people, . . . This being, the rule of admission, what marvell the half of any societie and many more should be for ever excluded?[87]

In his important study of preparation for conversion, Norman Pettit supports this view of Cotton and quotes him as stating that new members could not be admitted "till we be convinced in our consciences of the certain and infallible signs of their regeneration."[88] But Cotton's

85 Ibid.

86 Baillie, *Dissvasive,* pp. 160–1.

87 Idem, *Disswasive . . . Vindicated,* p. 39.

88 *The Heart Prepared,* p. 134. Pettit repeats this as Cotton's view on p. 195.

full statement in *Of the Holinesse of Church Members* was exactly to the contrary. Listing nine points that are "consented to on both sides," Cotton gave as point number five:

> . . . That though it be comfortable, and desireable in the admission of members into the Church, when the whole Church and all the members thereof are satisfied in the sincerity of the regeneration of such who are to be received, (especially in the first gathering and plantation of a Church:) yet neither in judgment, nor practice do we suspend their admission, till we be convinced in our consciences, of the certain and infallible signes of their regeneration.[89]

To drive home this point, Cotton later stressed again and again the difference between de facto and de jure membership: what members are and what they ought to be. Ultimately, he implied, the burden is on the member, who "is not onely in profession, but in sincerity and truth *to be* a Saint, and faithfull"[90] – and to express it so that it may be conceived to be so by others.

> But Mr. *Baily* carrieth it, as if I had said, We receive none into the Church, But such as we are certain to be regenerate. But there is a broad difference between these two: *We receive none but such as (according to the judgement of charitable Christians) may be conceived to be regenerate:* And this, we receive none, but such as we are certain to be regenerate.[91]

The emphasis on Cotton's nonexistent certainty principle and in general on his supposed strictness and rigidity in the matter of admissions have kept the debate somewhat out of focus, both then and now.[92] On the New England side, the central question is not really one of infallibility or certainty on the part of the church, but it *is* important to the opposing side insofar as they manifest anxiety and distrustfulness both toward human potential and toward language itself as a specific means of discernment. To the opponents of conversion testimonies, language is generally divisive and suspect, a threat to "that little goodnesse" that is in the saints; to the advocates of the narratives, language can be a force – if in some ways a mysterious one – for cohesion among "these good soules," despite its externality and imprecision. The reason that it

89 Cotton, *Of the Holinesse*, pp. 1–2.

90 Ibid., p. 45. Emphasis added. The complete sentence is italicized in the original but is romanized here to clarify emphasis.

91 Ibid., p. 43.

92 Larzer Ziff's work on John Cotton provides the most understanding approach to his ideas (*Cotton on the Churches, Career of John Cotton*). See also Jesper Rosenmeier, " 'Clearing the Medium': A Reevaluation of the Puritan Plain Style in Light of John Cotton's *A Practicall Commentary Upon the First Epistle Generall of John*," *William and Mary Quarterly* 37:4 (October 1980): 577–91.

can work for cohesion is that God so arranged it: There being a "*neare relation between Christ Jesus, and the Church,*" Christ himself "maketh the profession of the faith of his name, and such a profession as *flesh and bloud hath not revealed* to a man, . . . to be the rocke on which his visible Church is built."[93] To Baillie, the individual's situation is not only an unfit analogue to this scriptural one (in Matt. 16:17–18): "Shall no man be a member of a Church, till the holy Ghost dictate unto him such a confession of Faith as he did unto *Peter?*" The analogy is also, again, a dangerous one: "If none but the Elect and those who are filled with the holy Ghost, may be members of Churches, the *Anabaptists* have won the field."[94] Here again, Baillie's skepticism about men's "skills" makes him see things in terms of separations. But Cotton's answer is his most complete and deeply felt statement during the debate of what church *society* is and of the vital connection between the visible and the invisible churches.

> . . . And whence is all that spirituall power and life, which the people of God do ordinarily finde in all the visible Churches of the Saints, . . . if the holy Ghost dwell not in them? Mr. *Baily* may speak long enough of our leading men towards Anabaptisme, and Socinianisme: but . . . if I should intend to drive men to Enthusiasme, and Familisme . . . I should take no other course, but these principles chiefly; why do men stand so much upon visible Churches, and their purity? They are neither temples of the holy Ghost, nor members of Christ, nor children of God almighty: these glorious stiles belong not to them, but to an hidden invisible company of Saints scattered universally, and invisibly all the world over. And will not this strengthen the hands of Seekers and Familists, to seek Christ (where he is found in true spirituall life) in deserts and secret chambers? *Math.* 24. 26. what stand we upon visible Churches, or ordained Elders, or censures? These are husks, and shels: the kernel, and Spirit of life lyeth in an hidden society. But surely it is neither good nor safe, to pluck away from the visible Churches of Saints, I say not, their ornaments, and vails: but their very vitals, and cordials, which is the fellowship of the Father, Son and holy Ghost breathing amongst them.[95]

The invisible church and the visible church must be kept in constant relation, not in an impossibly exact and perfect alignment but in the "neare relation" Christ established for them. This can be so only if events in the visible church are patterned on events in the invisible church; and the visible pattern of the spirit "breathing" among men is the speaking, hearing, and understanding that Thomas Hooker preached about. This was seen in apostolic times, when

93 Cotton, *Way of the Churches,* pp. 56, 57.

94 Baillie, *Dissvasive,* p. 169.

95 Cotton, *Of the Holinesse,* pp. 48–9.

> the Lords act in adding daily to the Church such as should be saved, was not onely by giving them faith, and thereby adding them to the invisible Church: but by giving them an heart to offer themselves to the fellowship of the visible Church, and to professe their faith before them, and by opening the hearts of the Apostles and brethren to receive them.[96]

Cotton makes it clear here that he is describing a relationship and a process, not a scientific proof. "Offer . . . professe . . . opening . . . receive": These linked actions produce a whole relation that we murder to dissect.[97] Earlier in the century, John Robinson had tried to explain the same process to Richard Bernard, arguing that in gathering "the true materials for a church" it was not the bare act of recitation that brought the member into fellowship.

> It is not for the profession of faith, *ex opere operato,* or because the party professing utters so many words, that he is to be admitted into the church; but because the church by this his profession, and other outward appearances, doth probably, and in the judgment of charity, . . . deem him faithful and holy in deed, as in show he pretendeth.[98]

Robinson was probably referring to a doctrinal profession, but his statement about the relationship between the member and the church body holds for any verbal profession, whether of doctrine or experience. In effect he affirms what Cotton suggests decades later, that something significant happens *between* the speaker and the hearers that validates a profession. Robinson uses the term *ex opere operato* (i.e., "from the work wrought" or "in virtue of the action"), a phrase applied by theologians to the sacraments, which asserts their merit independently both of the minister and the recipients (hence, the Lord's Supper is sacrosanct even if the participants are unworthy). Such is *not* the case with a confession, Robinson argues, nor is it wholly a matter of the action of the "party professing." In the end, the value and efficacy of a profession are not in the speech nor even in the speaker but in the joint action of speaker and audience – that is, in the words being spoken, heard, *and believed.* A simple, perhaps obvious assertion; yet on this fragile web of literary relation – of literary faith, really – rests the whole weighty issue of the conversion narrative.

This is not the same as Tipson's argument that the churches had to "underwrite" the gracious experience of each communicant. Tipson's

96 Ibid., p. 53.

97 On the gathered church as an "organic" body, see Coolidge, *Pauline Renaissance,* pp. 35–41, 47–52, 69, 75, 146–8.

98 Robinson, *Works,* 2:285.

stress is on the need of the isolated individual struggling for assurance of his election and hoping that the church will validate or bolster his own inner personal experience. Cotton's ecclesiology makes it very clear that at least in theory it is the other way around. Public profession of faith (growing out of the prior faith of the individual) is not necessary to the individual but to the church – that is, it is necessary to link up the two halves of that living analogy, the invisible–visible church relation. Thus he tells his Presbyterian opponent Samuel Rutherford in the second part of "The Way Cleared" that the church keys are given to believers not because they believe but because, believing, they *then* make "public confession of their faith before the Lord, and their brethren," as Peter did before Christ gave him the keys. And those in whose name Peter received the keys are in turn

> not [understood] as keeping their faith to themselves, but as making profession of their faith publicly; so as they come to be received into the society of the visible church. Faith giveth a man fellowship in the invisible church, and in all the inward spiritual blessings of the church. But it is profession of faith, that giveth a man fellowship in the visible church.[99]

It is not profession, then, that makes a man a believer, but it is profession that makes a church a church. And this means, among other things, that the unique communal nature of the congregational way as John S. Coolidge describes it depends upon a complex verbal process. The language "skills" of believers knit church society together: a church society whose nature is dictated by the single most important fact of history, namely, that these are the days of the New Testament. And this is why the words that knit the church together must arise in part from the inner experience of regeneration.

> And we think any Christian Man may blush to name (now under the New Testament, when Types and Shadows are fled away, and the Body of the Truth is come) a Body, and Church, and Members of Christ our Head, and not mean Saints, and by Saints understand at least such as by the Rules of the Word given by God himself, to judg others by, are visible Saints. And we find Confession with the Mouth of the Work of Faith in the Heart, a Means among other sanctified by God to make any ones Grace evident and visible to others.[100]

The opponents of such "New Testament" views often took strikingly "Old Testament" positions. Thus John Ball states (in answer to John Canne's *Necessity*) that at the present time, "in the degenerate state, the

99 Cotton, "Way Cleared," in Ziff, *Cotton on the Churches,* p. 357.

100 Thomas Goodwin, "To the Reverend Mr. John Goodwin," in *Works,* 4:44.

Church doth not ever consist of such as you confesse [i.e., true saints]."[101] And Richard Bernard also argues against a test of religious experience by harking back to Old Testament times – when church members did not have to have "skills" or regenerate perceptions.

> The church is to be of a motherly affection, to embrace little babes and weaklinges, which desire her milke for nourishment & growth, and to catechise her young children in the groundes of Christianitie, their skill being small, in the first entrance into the Church, and school of Christ, not being able to answere to many of these questions.
>
> . . . Let me remember to them, here, the tender mercie of God to Israell, to enter into covenant with them [Deut. 29. 10. 13] when Moses saith, that God had not given them an heart to perceive, nor eyes to see, nor eares to heare [v. 4] yet the same Moses saith, they were the children of God. [Deut. 14. 1][102]

We saw earlier that English conversion narratives, when they finally did blossom and were written down, seemed often to take a more childlike, needy, helpless tone, reflecting an attitude similar to this one of Bernard's (even though he is opposed to such narratives). The English context of war and upheaval and the years of vitriolic contention undoubtedly promoted among New England's critics the same apprehensive feelings that we found in the Rogers and Walker congregations. The "Old Testament" attitudes of the critics and their conservative view of the ordinary man's communicative powers grew partly out of their own need for stability, order, and peace. They saw the divisiveness that plagued the country being repeated in microcosm in churches that demanded obedience to "new-born lawes and traditions," in which testimonies of religious experience and judgment by the massed congregation were symptomatic of a dangerous new release of individual inclination in religious matters.

> They are to be abominated as vaine traditions, and such as by which they break the lawes of God, making devisions in the Church and Kingdome, and through all the families, and houses of the same, so that neither masters of families nor parents have any rule over their wives, children or servants, their husbands goe out one way, the wife another, their children to this assembly, their servants to that congregation, . . . and so they flutter about like a company of chickings without either heads or wit, and none will be under obedience . . . and if ever there was a pantheon of all Religions in the world, it is now in *England,* by reason of these new teachers, to the great dishon-

101 *An Answer to Two Treatises of M^r. Iohn Can, The Leader of the English Brownists in Amsterdam* (London, 1642), p. 72.

102 "Of the visible Church," fol. 17^r, Bernard Papers. The brackets are Bernard's.

> our of God, the hinderance of Reformation, and the allienating of the affections one from another of those that are joyned together in nighest relations.[103]

This is a broader-ranging expression of the "aversion to strife" that disenchanted Thomas Hooker with tests of saving faith, and it shows up repeatedly in the English arguments against the practice. When Baillie, the great debater, bewailed the "difference among brethren" engendered by the "mistakes of expressions" in the very matter he was debating, he was also reflecting a feeling that unbridled discussion and spontaneous expression had produced too much discord in England or at least had accompanied and exacerbated it. Why should the churches encourage more of the same, especially when "experimental evidences of . . . dejections, convictions, terrours, exaltation, consolations, and soul-pacifying assurances, &c" were "works of super-erogation at the best"? – as Zachary Crofton wrote in response to John Rogers's publication of the Dublin confessions. It was not just that "terrible convictions, trembling dejections, and dreadful despondencie of spirit," on the one hand, and "joy and future consolations," on the other, were no signs of saving grace. The Presbyterian Crofton's most vehement point, and one that made him sound much like Milton's "Old Priest writ Large," was that the church was a place for assent and submission, not for self-expression and "experience."

> Christians are not baptized nor admitted into the Church as experienced, but convinced; not as dejected, and exalted, but perswaded of the truth of the Doctrine of Jesus Christ; not as assured of Gods favour to their soules, but as beleeving Christ to be the Son of God, and subjecting to him as the Sovereigne, by whom they will be guided and guarded.[104]

It was society's right to control and order (the same felt need that permeates the general aversion to expression), and not the people's "rights" to admission, that was really being threatened by the new system. Robert Stansby's well-known letter to John Wilson in 1637 suggested as much.

> [We hear] that you are so strict in admission of members to your church, that more then one halfe are out of your church in all your congregations, and that Mr. Hooker before he went away preached against yt (as one report who hard hym) (and he saith) now although I knowe all must not be admytted yet this may do much hurt, yf one

103 Bastwick, *Independency*, pp. 115–16. See also pp. 143–4 for a similar description of conditions in New England.

104 Zachary Crofton, *Bethshemesh Clouded, or Some Animadversions on the Rabbinical Talmud of Rabbi* John Rogers . . . (London, 1653), pp. 172, 184.

> come amongst you of another minde, and they should ioyne with hym.[105]

Coming as it did in the midst of the Antinomian troubles, this letter must have hit a nerve. And the ironic fact is that many of the fears that New England's critics expressed did come true. John Cotton himself provides one of the greatest ironies. While still in Old England, Cotton was well aware of the need for quiet and discretion, and he advised "the children of God" within his Boston congregation "to take heed of disturbing their peace." This was because "young commers on in Religion, are soone scared away by dangers and troubles arising against the Church";[106] and he warned that

> fearefull Christians, . . . they will start away; many are willing to come into the Church, but if the profession of Christ be troublesome and hot, they will not abide it: therefore . . . walke holily, that Christ be not stirred up.[107]

Cotton's fearful Christians presumably had nothing to fear in the new world; yet all the same, his warning at St. Botolph's came true in Massachusetts Bay. The new kind of profession was in its way as "troublesome and hot" as the old one was under the conditions of persecution; many, though how many is still unknown, stayed out of the church; and the community that saw itself as the Body of Christ was "stirred up." Despite Cotton's vision of holy unity, the system that required testimonies of spiritual experience involved a certain amount of commotion and even some of the "devisions" that Bastwick deplored.

But what the English observers and critics could have no way of knowing was that in the new situation stability, order, and serenity were not necessarily synonymous, or even consistent, with social cohesion. Instead, what was evidently called for, and certainly obtained, was ferment; and yet it was a ferment whose inevitability even the participants could not fully recognize.

For an example, let us return to Dedham. A crucial fact about this community is that its thirty original families had gathered in 1637 "from se'rall pts of England: few of them knowne to one an other

105 "Robert Stansby to John Wilson," *Winthrop Papers,* 3:390. Stansby was the uncle of John Stansby, a member of Shepard's congregation whose testimony appears in the "*Confessions.*" On Presbyterian objections to the Independents' "mutability," see Nuttall, *Visible Saints,* p. 117.

106 Cotton, *Canticles,* p. 64. Cotton was one of the nonconformists who gathered a special covenanted group within the congregation. He told about it in "Way Cleared" (Ziff, *Cotton on the Churches,* p. 198). See also Chapter 1, n. 15.

107 Cotton, *Canticles,* p. 95.

before."[108] In their immediate effort "to stablish a peaceable society" from these disparate folk, they decided that

> it is requisite that p'fessours being strangers to one an other before, meeting fro' many parts should be well acquainted with the harts and states of one an other–joyne by way of confession & p'fession of ther faith & that this be publikely testified for the better union of the harts of other churches unto the'.[109]

It took over a year for this effort to produce a church "foundation" of eight "stones." The original meetings consisted of ten men, but four were challenged, "ther cases being scanned" within the group. Two of the four were subsequently found suitable, but Joseph Kingsbury, "remaining stiffe & unhumbled," was rejected for foundation work; and Thomas Morse "was thought by the company to be so darke & unsatisfying in respect of the worke of grace that though his life was innocent in respect of men yet they had not grounds to imbrace him."[110] (It took Morse three years to gain admission, and when in 1640 he finally did, it was partly because of "the spiritt of prayer observed in him by his inocent conversation & some testimony of the godly that knew him in England.")[111]

But the two who had been questioned and then accepted, Edward Allin and Antony Fisher, were again challenged when shortly afterward the entire process was begun anew. This was partly because a delegation from Watertown "objected some greivances & offences" against Allin, a former resident there, and partly because of the late arrival of still another prospective foundation man, John Hunting. As a result, everyone had to deliver "a new relation of the dealings of god with them," the group

> desyring to scann & seeke satisfaction in any offences discove[re]d by any since we were approved partly to give satisfaction to Jo. Hunting newly co'e to us & partly for our more clere p'ceedings in this worke. In this way of tryall I say some new objections were made against Edw: Allin which yet at last were satisfied & he still joyned to the company. And further offences arising against Antony Fisher which could not be clered to the satisfaction of the p'ties offended not [nor?] to the co'pany * * * scruples arising in diverse minds of the co'pany

108 *Dedham Church Records,* p. 1.

109 Ibid., pp. 1, 3. In citations from this work, some words abbreviated in the original have been extended.

110 Ibid., pp. 6–7. According to the church book, "p'ticular p'fessions of the most" of the early members, "with notes of the churches p'ceedings with them remaine in private notes" (p. 14), but I have not been able to determine whether they survive.

111 Ibid., p. 23.

we were generally so unsatisfied concerning him that we wholy left him out of the worke for the present & desired him to be content to waite till the Church gathered & then to give further satisfaction.

The rest of the company (some few scruples except which arose about one or 2) were continued with the same approbation of all as before.[112]

When regular members began to be admitted, this kind of worried wrangling continued. Out of an early group of ten admissions, for example, four were subjected to objections or "scruples" and had to be "clered"; but one member, it was noted, was "easily and gladly received" after "divers of the Church that had long knowne him testified."[113] In fact, being known and being able to "clere" one's antisocial behavior or "cariage" were by far the decisive factors. David D. Hall has called attention to the "agonies and scuffling associated with the test of a 'relation' " at Dedham,[114] but the curious fact is that, excepting Thomas Morse, there is no mention of "scruples" in regard to the verbal testimonies of candidates. It seems as if the test of a spiritual relation was not in itself the stumbling block in the sifting of potential church members.

Of course, New England's critics disliked the "testing" of behavior just as much. To them it was a plain injustice to demand "triall by a long conversation of the sociable and complying disposition of the person to be admitted with the spirits of the whole Church whereof he is to be a member."[115] Equally distasteful was the rule that "such as live farre off, and altogether unknown to any of the Church," must bring "letters testimoniall," and it was especially galling to the English (as it had been to Cotton before he emigrated) to hear that such letters were required only "*from the congregations in Old-England,*" not from "*these Churches in New England,*" which were "*better knowne to us then the other.*"[116] But the English critic was not in a position to understand that something about being in the new place required affirmation and reaffirmation of ties in these particular ways, and that such rules were not so much signs of provincialism or semiseparatism as they were of new and peculiar needs. Roger Clap gave eloquent if inadvertent expression to those needs when he recorded that in the first years of the colony,

the Lord Jesus Christ was so plainly held out in the Preaching of the Gospel unto poor lost Sinners, and the absolute Necessity of the *New*

112 Ibid., pp. 8–9.
113 Ibid., pp. 14–15.
114 *Faithful Shepherd*, p. 99, n. 21.
115 Baillie, *Dissvasive*, p. 106.
116 Weld, *Answer to* W.R., pp. 21–2. Weld is citing Richard Mather's *Answer . . . To two and thirty Questions*, in *Church-Government*, pp. 29–30.

> *Birth,* and God's holy Spirit in those Days was pleased to accompany the Word with such Efficacy upon the Hearts of many; that our Hearts were taken off from *Old-England* and set upon *Heaven.* The Discourse, not only of the Aged, but of the Youth also, was not, *How shall we go to* England? (tho' some few did not only so Discourse, but also went back again) but *How shall we go to Heaven? Have I true Grace wrought in my Heart? Have I* Christ *or no?* O how did Men and Women, young and old, Pray for Grace, beg for *Christ* in those Days.[117]

Beneath the surface rapture, there is pain in this passage, as there is in the Dedham church records. It is a pain tied to the notion of place, to both the New England and the Old, and to a sense that the "poor lost Sinners" are also literally lost and therefore struggling toward a rebirth felt more sharply than ever as an "absolute Necessity." There is a sense, too, in which shared turmoil, even though it cannot be directly expressed, is felt as capable of producing good. But to take hearts "off from" England and set them upon heaven required more than a "nursinge mother" church teaching her "little ones." If New England seemed to seek as church members "only such as can feed on stronge meate" rather than "very babes to suckle them, and to feed them with milke,"[118] it must be remembered that "very babes" are literally *infantes,* that is "not speaking": They cannot articulate who they are or what is happening to them.

This is the crucial point. Under the circumstances, as Clap's memoir suggests, turmoil and pain could best be dealt with through language: through the Word, through preaching, "Discourse," prayer – and through the personal testimony of spiritual experience: "Many were Converted, . . . confessing their Faith publickly, and sharing before all the Assembly their Experiences of God's Spirit in their Hearts to bring them to *Christ.*"[119] But the New England system that sought to establish such public verbal sharing was not, as Baillie thought, "the onely cause of their separation," for it was not in fact a cause. It was a symptom, and at the same time a hopeful remedy: "Our Hearts were taken off from *Old-England* and set upon *Heaven.*" Stearns and Brawner have said that "if the New England Way was a mutant," as Edmund S. Morgan holds, "the mutation must be sought elsewhere" than in high standards of admission to the churches.[120] They are right. The real mutation was a literary one: It was in the half-unconscious attempt to evolve a collective expression, and it was new because the experience was new, because the "errand" demanded it. This is not to say that the results were very grand; many of these voices were not so much crying

117 Clap, *Memoirs,* pp. 20–1.
118 "Of the visible Church," fol. 17r, Bernard Papers.
119 Clap, *Memoirs,* p. 21.
120 "Church 'Relations,' " p. 21.

in the wilderness as they were stammering to themselves in the dark. But they did talk, because they had to.

Louis Hartz has developed a theory of migration that illuminates these events. The theory holds that a "fragment" is struck off from the whole of a society, moves onto new territory, and there evolves according to its own unobstructed "interior drama" until eventually it produces a "new nationalism" that "buries" but still contains the old fragment.[121] In a small way, we are witnessing one of the very first steps in this unfolding – a step that involves the articulation of part of that interior drama and struggle as the Puritan fragment breaks away from English society. And Hartz's theory accounts for the apparent confusion of our transatlantic debaters, for he points out that "separated perspectives" are inherent in the process.

> It is in the nature of fragmentation, perhaps its greatest irony, that it prevents both the European who stays and the European who leaves from understanding the pattern involved. The European who stays is bound to think of national histories in terms of the revolutionary process which it is the genius of the fragment to escape. He can understand an England in which the bourgeoisie carries the aristocracy along with it, . . . But how is he to understand a North America where the bourgeoisie, having escaped both past and future, unfolds according to interior laws? . . . the men of the fragment are in no better position: they are the European in reverse.[122]

For "bourgeoisie" put "Puritan" and for "aristocracy" put "established church" and this description applies to our problem. The English resentment toward tests of saving faith is inflamed by the very multiplicity and complexity of the English context from which American Puritanism broke away: a context where "being English means sharing a community in which there are not only Calvinists but Anglicans,"[123] and where a "literary" phenomenon like a test of saving faith is possible for the sects but unthinkable on a society-wide basis. What looks like New English rigor and extremism arises from its very removal, both actually and imaginatively, from the constrictions of that old world context. And if these differing perspectives are "unconscious" as Hartz claims – though "each side could find out the secret of the other if it wanted to"[124] – it is no wonder that the respective parties did not even understand the conflict, much less resolve it.

121 Louis Hartz, *The Founding of New Societies: Studies in the History of the United States, Latin America, South Africa, Canada, and Australia* (New York: Harcourt, Brace & World, 1964), pp. 3–15.

122 Ibid., pp. 9–10.

123 Ibid., p. 11.

124 Ibid., p. 10.

Certainly New England, the broken-off fragment, was in no position to explain what it was doing or to acknowledge its own pain. When we read Thomas Shepard's insistence in 1645 that "the churches are here in peace; the commonwealth in peace; the ministry in most sweet peace; the magistrates (I should have named first) in peace,"[125] the only thing we can be sure of is not that "Shepard had ample cause to rejoice in New England's serenity"[126] – Shepard is not giving a statistical report – but that he and his comrades needed to believe these things. And the fact that such statements were issuing from the bridge while clearly there was trouble down below makes New England's apologists not dissemblers but prisoners of their own perspectives. If the vision for which John Cotton was the chief spokesman – a vision of community, of wholeness, and of communion by joyous communication – was not quite working out that way, it was because, as always, between the idea and the reality had fallen the shadow of experience. It was not the kind of experience for which the "relation of religious experience" had been intended, but by the force of a greater necessity, it was there that it found its expression.

125 *New Englands Lamentations for Old Englands present errours* (London, 1645), p. 4, cited in *God's Plot: The Paradoxes of Puritan Piety, Being the Autobiography & Journal of Thomas Shepard,* ed. with an Introduction by Michael McGiffert (Amherst: University of Massachusetts Press, 1972), p. 9.
126 McGiffert, ibid.

PART II

SEA CHANGE: THE CONVERSION NARRATIVE IN THE NEW WORLD

But I say unto you, That every idle word that men shall speak, they shall give account thereof in the day of judgment.

For by thy words thou shalt be justified, and by thy words thou shalt be condemned.

Matt. 12:36–7

3

DISAPPOINTMENT

One of the most famous first impressions of America is the memory poet Anne Bradstreet preserved for her children: how she

> came into this Covntry, where I fovnd a new world and new manners, at which my heart rose. But after I was convinced it was the way of God, I submitted to it and joined to the church at Boston.[1]

In this stark fragment from her "Religious Experiences," Anne Bradstreet quietly spoke the feelings of many of her fellow settlers. For of all the contemporary reports about the new land – from William Bradford's "hideous and desolate wilderness, full of wild beasts and wild men," to Francis Higginson's delight in the "fat black earth," "dainty springs," and "extraordinary clear and dry air" of Massachusetts[2] – Bradstreet's somehow captures, in its swift, pained understatement, the emotional tenor of most of the accounts that ordinary people gave of their experiences in the early churches of New England.[3]

It is no discovery that the emigration to America promised a change in people's spiritual and emotional lives, nor even that the new land proved disturbingly different from their expectations. Indeed, Alan

1 *The Works of Anne Bradstreet in Prose and Verse,* ed. John Harvard Ellis (Charlestown, Mass., 1867; rpt. ed., Gloucester, Mass.: Peter Smith, 1962), p. 5.

2 William Bradford, *Of Plymouth Plantation 1620–1647,* ed. Samuel Eliot Morison (New York: Modern Library, 1952), p. 62; "Francis Higginson's New-England's Plantation," in Young, *Chronicles,* pp. 243, 250, 251.

3 Robert Daly intriguingly suggests that Bradstreet's "heart rose" not at general conditions in New England but at the stringency that required a confession for church membership. (Sister Collins of the Shepard group voices a similar complaint a few years later [p. 131].) Although there is little evidence for mandatory confessions in 1630, when Bradstreet arrived, Daly's argument is compelling. See *God's Altar: The World and the Flesh in Puritan Poetry* (Berkeley: University of California Press, 1978), p. 238.

Heimert has shown how the colonizing experience so crucially modified Puritan attitudes toward the meaning of the physical setting that it was imaginatively transformed from a promised land into a wilderness.[4] But the immediacy with which the shock is internalized and begins to struggle for expression in religious testimonies is striking. Even more so is that the kind of reaction people choose to talk about quickly accumulates at one end of the emotional spectrum, to be voiced in a haunting tone of muted, almost imperceptible anguish. Like Mrs. Bradstreet's, the experience is always one of the heart and of feelings; yet the feelings emerge not in colorful verbal effusions like those of many of the Rogers congregation in Dublin (who are also, in a sense, exiles), and still less in the smooth, conventional prose of Henry Walker's London saints, but most often in an intense, cryptic, emotional shorthand that tells not of high drama but of deep hurt and disappointment – not of the outward adventure or even so much of the severe hardship that we know were experienced, but of the struggle against inward sadness, bewilderment, depression, and especially spiritual paralysis, or "deadness" of heart.

It is as if, for most of the people, there is an unexpected deadlock between their experiences of the migration and the fulfillment of their religious hopes. As Anne Bradstreet's heart "rose," then "submitted," the hearts of her fellows were sinking into an even deeper mire of exhausting inner turmoil. "Since I came hither" went the refrain at Cambridge, the heart was not only "discontented" but "hard," "stubborn," "estranged," and "overwhelmed"; it was "not a heart so much as to desire help from the Lord"; it "found no rest," "went after the world and vanities," and even "called all into question"; it felt "more enmity . . . against the Lord than ever before."[5] Such things were common enough, admittedly, in Christian experience, but now for the first time they were linked to an actual place. In case after case, the hearts of New England's saints were afflicted most intensely *after* their possessors arrived in the New World – even if the trouble began before or during the ocean voyage. Barbary Cutter, for example, was one of many who

> embraced the motion to New England. Though she went through with many miseries and stumbling blocks at last removed and sad passages by sea. And after I came hither I saw my condition more miserable than ever. [I] knew not what to do. (pp. 89–90)

4 Hall, *Faithful Shepherd*, pp. 156–66; Alan Heimert, "Puritanism, the Wilderness, and the Frontier," *New England Quarterly* 26 (September 1953):361–82.
5 *Shepard's "Confessions,"* pp. 183, 66, 179, 183, 123, 185, 51, 123, 34. Except where clarity may be impaired, subsequent references to the Shepard document appear in the text by page number.

Of course, in most such accounts the speaker manages to survive the disappointments and eventually to experience, or to claim to have experienced, conversion. Yet the voice continues to vibrate with doubt and anxiety, and the final resolution is, as often as not, lukewarm and pallid. Barbary Cutter's confession proceeds in such a fashion – halting, jagged, and, on occasion, genuinely confused. Sometimes the confusion emerges as mere vagueness, as when "hearing the excellency of person of Christ in five particulars," she only gives four, or of "four cautions in laying hold," only gives two (pp. 90, 92). Sometimes it is more serious, as when she recalls, "hearing because it felt not what it would, denied what it had yet discouraged" (p. 91) – a statement that, although not incomprehensible, is a close marriage of anxious style with anxious content. Like most converts, including Mrs. Elizabeth White, she rides a relentless seesaw of hope and despair:

> Cleaved to Him, then questioned whether grace or no.
>
> So found sweetness. But I lost that which I found in the Lord. Sweetness lost.
>
> Lord then stayed her heart, yet lost that. (pp. 90, 91, 92)

But unlike the Elizabeth Whites of the world, she does not realize radical change even after "I saw and was convinced of my sin" in New England (p. 92). Instead, Barbary Cutter's culminating experience is this:

> And since, Lord hath let me see more of Himself as in doubtings. That Lord did leave saints doubting as to remove lightness and frothiness, hence doubtings, and to cause for fresh evidence and by this means kept them from falling. Lord made these suitable to Lord and to draw my heart nearer to Himself. And so answered all doubts from Christ I saw; somewhat more: and this day in forenoon. (p. 92)

Even though there is a genuine if distant gleam of light at the end, the real energy of this passage is in its nervous, repeated invocation of doubt and in its almost defensive insistence that doubt, in fact, must be equivalent to hope, the thing that keeps one from falling. Even when "all doubts" are answered, the most positive thing one can see is only "somewhat more." For Barbary Cutter and for many people like her, all that the "motion to New England" had apparently produced was the revelation and the cold comfort of "doubtings."

It must be acknowledged that such feelings are normally to be found in many accounts of Christian and certainly of Puritan experience. The question here is one of degree and proportion, of tone and of structure. What is notable in a majority of New England conversion stories is the sense of strain, the meagerness of genuine, fulfilling relief, the contrast between the long, painful tales of struggle and fear, and their endings, so often perfunctory or desperately capped with limp, bland, or hasty resolutions. Above all, there is an unmistakable sense that the root of these problems is not just in the gospel way of things but in the specific shift to America, in the "motion to New England," where, as Goodman Foster admitted in the Wenham church, one "was left a more flat condition than before";[6] where, as John Stedman's wife Alice testified at Cambridge, one of her neighbors came "asking what such a one should do that did think they had grace but since they came here could not see it" (p. 104); and where, as for John Sill,

> upon my first coming I thought that then my heart was in a pretty frame. But being here some little time . . . my heart began to be troubled and so lost that frame I had. (p. 48)

Indeed, in about half these stories, the new world is not just a disappointment; it is, as for Mrs. Stedman and John Sill, a positive setback, and one from which many people scarcely recover – all the more so because the expectations were so high to begin with, the desire to be "drawn" so strong, and the will so great to "answer the end for which He sent me" (pp. 191, 84). As Alan Heimert has pointed out,

> America was to be "the good Land," . . . a veritable Canaan. The Atlantic, if not the Red, was their "vast Sea," and the successful conclusion of their voyage, the end of their tribulations, their emergence from the "wilderness."[7]

From Goodman With (Nicholas Wyeth) hoping "to come hither where we might enjoy more Freedom" (p. 194) to William Hamlet "seeing the sweet people that came hither and seeing sins and sorrows of the [old] land, I desired to come" (p. 127; interpolation mine), the literature is pervaded with that yearning for an "end of . . . tribulations." The end, of course, would be accomplished in the churches and in church fellowship: Widow Arrington (Ann Errington), "feeling not the means work" in England, "desired hither to come thinking one sermon might do me more good than a hundred there" (p. 185), and Joan White, in the Wenham church, felt "her heart being drawn to New England because good people came hither."[8] Golding (Golden) Moore recalled that

> means being taken away and fearing my condition and feeling my ignorance of Christ and hence I set myself to seek Christ and to get more acquainted with Christ and hence used means to come hither. Hence [I] did think to enjoy more of the Lord. (p. 123)

6 Fiske, *Notebook,* p. 89.

7 Heimert, "Puritanism, the Wilderness, and the Frontier," pp. 361–2.

8 Fiske, *Notebook,* p. 30.

Mr. Sparhawk confessed that

> the Lord let me see that I looked to men too much and that the old score was not crossed. And hence I had no rest but desired to come to New England to enjoy them [the ordinances] in purity and helped me to be contented though in a prosperous way. Yet I thought the superstitions clouded God in ordinances and had thought to find power and thought to prize means here. (p. 64; interpolation mine)

Many others echoed these sentiments: "Though in a prosperous way" at home, they came to New England for pure ordinances. Since they were expected to say exactly this, the frequency with which they mentioned "the means" is not surprising; for John Cotton had made it plain that the gatherers of a church should profess that "it was the principal end of their coming to enjoy the presence of the Lord in the liberty and purity of his ordinances."[9] But they also said, with an urgency and sincerity that are not to be doubted, that they harbored the more significant and pervasive hope: Like Mr. Sparhawk, they wanted to cross the "old score" of Adam, and to find a new "power" within themselves. It was this power that Goodwife Willows (Jane Palfrey) defined with simple eloquence when she said, "I had a mind for New England and I thought I should know more of my own heart" (p. 151), and that Mrs. (Alice) Stedman desired when, feeling "lost" in New England, she pondered the case of another wanderer:

> I considered of Abram that the Lord did not need to know what was in his heart but that he [Abram] might know it.* So I had need to know what was in my own heart. (p. 104)
>
> * Gen. 22:1–18.

Ultimately, it was the power that Goodwife (Jane) Holmes confessed that she needed: "Yet hearing a sermon that feeling follows faith of saints and I labored to feel it and Lord making way for New England I thought I should find feelings" (p. 78). Even the most reluctant pilgrim (and there were a few who admitted they did not want to make the journey) still hoped, like Mrs. Sparhawk (Mary Angier), "to get good . . . hoped to be better here than worse than ever before" (p. 66).

We are not surprised by these spiritual longings, for we are used to the idea that the first generation of settlers to Massachusetts Bay counted among its numbers a spiritually dedicated, determined, pious band who, if nothing else, derived energy and courage from their belief in their own special mission as an elect people. Puritanism, we are told, taught these elect folk

9 Cotton, *Way of the Churches*, pp. 6–7.

> that they had brought all necessary for the church when they brought themselves and their Bible, and evaporated anxieties that other men felt when they sensed that by their physical removal they were also removing themselves from the sustenance of traditional institutions.[10]

The contemporary reports were not quite so sanguine; yet they too promoted the fundamental assumption that "cheerfulnesse and constant resolutions" bolstered the "weak and tender" emigrant through the "straits, wants, and tryalls" that admittedly were to be found in "this Countrey." That is what John Allin and Thomas Shepard wrote to John Ball and other critics at home in England, exclaiming,

> What shall wee say of the Worke it selfe of the kingdome of Christ? . . . That the Lord hath carryed the spirits of so many of his people through all their toylsome labour, wants, difficulties, losses, &c. with such a measure of chearfulnesse and contentation?[11]

All these beliefs, both then and now, about the spiritual ardor and strength of the first generation are rooted in the assumption that the people who journeyed across the ocean "to enjoy the presence of the Lord in the liberty and purity of his ordinances" were convinced that they *were* "his people," were in fact already saved (or, like Mrs. Stedman's neighbor, "did think they had grace"), and were coming to the new land to work out their salvation, to actualize it in the world. Of course it had to be done with the requisite fear and trembling, but their strength was in their salvation nonetheless for that. It was the second generation that had qualms about its election, not the first; for without the faith, how could they have come? How could they

> leave our accommodations and comforts, . . . forsake our dearest relations, Parents, brethren, Sisters, Christian friends, and acquaintances, overlooke all the dangers and difficulties of the vast Seas, the thought whereof was a terrour to many, and all this to go to a wildernesse, where wee could forecast nothing but care and temptations, onely in hopes of enjoying Christ in his Ordinances, in the fellowship of his people?[12]

This, indeed, is one of the questions that throbs beneath the stories of conversion in Shepard's own congregation – and the answer, on the surface of it, is disconcerting: For we do find people talking about the "toylsome labour, wants, difficulties, losses, &c." that Shepard acknowledged, but without any compensating measure of saintlike "chearfulnesse and contentation." We can see this discrepancy in a

10 Larzer Ziff, *Puritanism in America: New Culture in a New World* (New York: Viking, 1973), p. 26.

11 *Defence of the Answer,* pp. 7, 8.

12 Ibid., p. 7.

simple calculation. Of forty-eight completed narratives in the Shepard group, forty-two mention the migration to New England – as we would expect. Yet only nine of the saints indicate that they have actually had the joyful experience that Shepard calls "first conversion"[13] *before* their voyage to the new world. Of the remaining thirty-three, all of whom must be presumed to have experienced conversion some time between their arrival and their church testimonies,[14] only twelve, in the present writer's judgment, describe what can be characterized as a strong, positive spiritual experience. This leaves twenty-one people (half of all those who mention the migration) who supposedly had a saving experience in New England, but whose narratives are notably perfunctory, lukewarm, anxious, or confused in their spiritual claims.[15]

Among the nine members who seem to have been converted before the migration, there is another peculiar pattern. In seven of their narratives, the experience of America is felt as a numbing blow from which the narrator never quite revives. We saw this earlier in the case of Mr. Sparhawk; and John Sill, who "so lost that frame I had," is one of these. Thus, only two already converted souls seem to have encountered America in a completely positive way. One is Mr. (William) Andrews, a shipmaster, who, having realized his election through suffering a shipwreck,

> came hither, God making way, and when I saw the people my heart was knit to them much and thought I should be happy if I should be joined and united to them. And when I came, God made way both in removing the minister and also in selling off all that I had . . . Afterward my wife in my absence came hither, which I bless God for. (p. 113)

The other is Mr. Dunster, whose narrative is unique in this group. He is the Henry Dunster whom Shepard admired as "a man pious, painful, and fit to teach,"[16] and who was the second president of Harvard College, replacing the scandalous Mr. Nathaniel Eaton, whose vivid confession is also in the Shepard document. Clearly one of the elite, Dunster is the only member whose profession of doctrinal faith Shep-

13 "Why is grace so precious at first conversion, that heaven and earth are too little to hold praises enough for it?" (*Works,* 2:105).

14 The *Ten Virgins* sermon series is full of Shepard's preachments about people's feelings that they had lost their "first conversion" (*Works,* 2:53–60, 86, 93–105, 632, et passim), and this may be the case with many of the thirty-three. But technicalities aside, it is clear that New England represented some kind of stumbling block, either to the perception of one's calling or to making one's calling sure.

15 This is not intended as a literary evaluation, still less a theological one. It is an observation of the substance or content of stories people told about themselves. Some of them are, in fact, among the most affecting narratives.

16 *God's Plot,* p. 68.

ard saw fit to preserve. This long, fervent near-sermon, undoubtedly delivered upon Dunster's arrival in 1640, towers in the midst of the manuscript and marks something of a turning point in both the style and substance of the subsequent narratives.[17] And well it might, for in those post-Antinomian days it sternly warns the "Dear Brethren and sisters" that "every persuasion is not Christ," that "some erring ones cast off the word of faith to receive suggestions and revelations without the word . . . which is provoking God to take away all the spirit," and that the church must "give not ear to them that look only to be fed by heaven, casting off ordinances" (p. 158). Lest anyone should miss his point, Dunster repeats in his "personal" relation the necessity for submitting to the Word:

> The greatest thing which separated my soul from God was inordinate love of human learning. Take heed of this lest desiring to be as gods we becomes as devils.* (p. 162)
>
> * See Ps. 85:8.

And in his conclusion he makes it clear that if Old England is a place of trouble, New England is the place for order.

> So after ten years troubles I came hither and the Lord gives much peace to see the order of His people. And I bless God for keeping one out[18] but I desire you to be careful what scholars enter to your churches and pray for humility of spirit. (p. 164)

As different as Andrews the shipmaster and Dunster the teacher are, they share an important interest that helps to explain their presence in the "positive" (and extreme minority) camp. Both assign all their suffering to the old country and focus on the visible effects of God's grace in the new, especially as manifested in the communal life of the new land. This makes them virtually the only ones who are telling the kind of American success story that the elders were apparently hoping to hear in the churches. That hope, at least, is conveyed in Goodman (Robert) Daniel's confession, for when Daniel fails to weave the migration into his story, the elders attempt to lead him to that end by means of a series of questions.

17 Several of the remaining thirteen narratives are more polished, more verbose, and yet less ardent than earlier ones, though this may be because they are from younger, more educated members like Sizar Jones and young William Ames. Still, there is a sense that some of the speakers, especially the men, are being careful.

18 The phrase *keeping one out* is my reading. Selement and Woolley give "keeping me out," but Dunster is not being kept out of the church. He is almost certainly referring to Anne Hutchinson.

> (1) How did the Lord bring you out of that estate of security into a state of fear and spirit of bondage? . . . (2) How hath the Lord brought you out of this estate unto the Lord Jesus? . . . (3) Question. How came you to assurance? . . . (4) How have you walked with God and what effect have you found of mercy in this land? (p. 61)

It will be seen that the four questions neatly conform to cardinal points in William Perkins's ten-stage morphology of conversion: The first question pertains to the "preparatory" stages; the second to the "kindling" of saving faith; the third to " 'assurance' and persuasion of mercy"; and the fourth to the very last stage, in which "God gave a man 'grace to endeavour to obey his Commandments by a new obedience.' "[19] The sequence suggests that on the scale of the morphology of conversion, "this land" is to be associated not so much with the first stirrings of true faith but with the ultimate earthly experience of grace, namely, sanctification: As we have already mentioned, this is the place where salvation will be worked out with fear and trembling. Yet Goodman Daniel does not have much to say on the subject.

> Faith hath been wrought more and Christ more revealed more savingly unto me. I fall short in that obedience that should be, which is my burden when I see how the Lord hath led me.[20] (p. 61)

This is the sort of answer that Edmund S. Morgan might characterize as "faith in its proper imperfection," for he accurately points out that a too-perfect assurance would after all only have led to suspicions that the speaker was "on shaky ground."[21] Nevertheless, the people in London and Dublin did not hesitate to articulate in great detail just how they walked with God and what effects they found of mercy: Over and over again, they could point to their delight and satisfaction in God, their thirsting after the ordinances, their joy in duties, their desire to serve, their peaceful consciences, their cheerful spirits, and, above all, their longing, like Mr. Andrews's, to join the congregation of the people of God. These were the "effects" of grace, and they could be described verbally for all to hear.

All this may have been so in England, but it was not the American way of conversion. To judge by both the Shepard and Fiske groups, "effects" were either scarcely thought of, despite the elders' prodding,

19 Morgan, *Visible Saints,* pp. 68–9.

20 In Shepard's notebook the word *which* is written over a virgule, indicating that it may have been hurriedly added after the apparent end of the testimony. There is a sense here that the speaker is faltering or groping for something to say.

21 *Visible Saints,* pp. 91–2.

or else deemed so unsatisfying that they were not worth mentioning.[22] It was the earlier stages of conversion, and not the effects, that still (or again) preoccupied the speakers, the problem of their identity, of knowing their own hearts. This, of course, was an age-old religious problem, but now it was suddenly and fiercely entangled with a new and secular one, namely, the problem of place. People needed to settle the question of who they were by understanding and articulating where they were, and it is just because the two were irrevocably merged that the conversion narrative marks a crucial, albeit embryonic stage in American expression. The usual "effects" might or might not be found, but what did they mean in the new place if, as with John Sill's wife Joanna, "the Lord absented Himself from her so that she thought God had brought her hither on purpose to discover her" (p. 51)? Of course, it was not always thus: For Mr. (Edward) Collins, the outer "motion" to a new land triggered an equivalent inner "motion" so that "at the first coming seeing the great change from this and that place did much transport my heart" (p. 84). But with suffering souls like Mrs. Sill's, it was frightening to find that the motions could also reverse themselves, so that "she could not believe indeed and she knew not where she was" (p. 52).

The Puritans, however, knew how to visualize problems as opportunities. If the migration brought disappointment, it also afforded a test of that very inner heart that it was so vitally important to get to know. The test would be the feeling engendered by the land itself: "Considering that when I was farthest from God then my heart was scared from coming" but that "when it was nearest to God then I did desire to come" (p. 127), the saint from the very start had a mark by which to gauge his reactions. If after coming he felt disappointment, he could be sure that an alarm was being sounded; thus Thomas Shepard explained such feelings to his Cambridge flock.

> Before you came to this land, you thought Christ and persecution, Christ and the meanest condition, nay, Christ and death, would be sweet. The Lord, it may be, doth or will try your love; and here you find Christ and losses in estate, Christ and crosses in your family, Christ and many fears and toils and cares. Do you love him now as well as ever you did for all this?[23]

The true saint's answer to this rhetorical question had to be yes, for "a discerning Christian" would see that estates, family troubles, toils and cares were not the issue at all. He would see that the real trouble was in

22 The only extensive testimony at Cambridge about "effects" is by William Hamlet (pp. 128–9). He seems to use a set of conventions similar to those seen in the English narratives, where virtually every one concludes with a numbered list of "evidences."

23 *Works,* 2:90.

> the hearts and spirits of his own friends declining, that there is not that life of Christ, that presence and savor and power of Christ in hearts, in prayers, in lives, and no complaints of this. Now is the fittest time of love, when no eye sees, when no heart loves him or cares for him, . . . if any love it will appear now.[24]

In short, there were illusory troubles and real troubles, and the true saint could tell the difference between them. In doing so, in "discerning" what was worth "complaints" and what wasn't, he could still achieve what he had come to New England for: He could "know what was in my own heart" in the very act of confronting, acknowledging, and transcending the "toylsome labour, wants, difficulties, losses, &c." of the new land. He could "find feelings," as Goodwife Holmes wanted to do, by discovering, or rediscovering, the only thing that was worth having feelings about.

And this is exactly what a number of the saints did testify to in their conversion narratives. Mr. Collins, for example, whose heart was "transported" by his "first coming," told the common story of having suffered a subsequent relapse: "Yet after this his frame was quickly lost by distractions and thoughts and cares which deadened my spirits." (Mr. Collins was a substantial member of the community, eventually a large planter and a member of the General Court. His distractions and cares would undoubtedly have been "worldly" ones.) But "God seasonably took care to cure" him "by a heavy hand," whereupon he

> saw and was convinced of unthankfulness and discontent . . . And I blessed God that He would not let me lie still but to show me my unthankfulness. And so at last I came to see need of all God's ordinances, watchfulness that I might answer the end for which He sent me. And I saw His hand to bring me to the same ministry that first Lord did me good by and to beget me to Himself. (p. 84)

His false disappointment thus having been dispelled by a recognition of his own ingratitude (especially his ingratitude for communal benefits like the ordinances and the ministry), Mr. Collins could know that he was a true New England saint. If there was anything close to assurance in New England, it was manifested in such an exemplary expression of the "test" – and its resolution in the public arena.

In this way, an extra element began to seep into the American conversion narrative that obviously could never be present in the English one. For added to the list of chastisements that God might send to any of his elect was the experience of coming to America itself. The chastisement, as Shepard explained, was not to be construed as the "toylsome labour, wants, difficulties, losses, &c." of the voyage or of the

24 Ibid.

new world but as the danger of succumbing to private preoccupations about them. Thus America itself, by being perceived in the proper way, or by kindling the proper feelings, or, above all, by deflecting the wrong feelings, offered to clarify one's spiritual condition; and one's reaction to the whole experience – stumbling blocks, sad passages by sea, "frames" lost and found, hard hearts, distractions and all – could be turned into one huge "evidence" or "effect" of grace.

But there were drastic side effects to this ingenious remedy. It irrevocably entangled the internal heart questions with the external questions of the physical place; it gave an awesome, divine power to the country itself; and it left no way out for the people who could neither neatly tie up the knot of feelings, like Mr. Collins, nor untangle it, like Sister Norton in John Fiske's congregation, who was perhaps the only emigrant besides Roger Williams to see that

> because God had emptied her of herself she would have it other ways by coming to N.E., by a husband, by ordinances; but they could not do it and rest came when depending on God only.[25]

Lacking her perspective and her readiness to let go, to accept the condition of being "emptied," almost everyone else had become locked to the idea that "coming to N.E." would "do it," and that if they were disappointed in the outcome, they must be horribly betraying the God who brought them there. In short, to feel disappointment in America was a sin. Even to think, as Goodman (William) Manning did during the voyage, that "I had not done well in doing this [which] I had done" – and knowing that "they were but carnal thoughts and would if possible returned [*sic*] again" – even so, "it was a sin so to wish or think" (p. 97).

And yet they were the people of God; they were saved. Therefore, they had to attempt in their conversion narratives to resolve these bad feelings, to explain the disappointment of the saints by means of a "since-I-came-hither-dead-hearted-but-I-have-been-revived" convention that unfortunately, for many people, neither reflected their actual condition nor produced the desired purgative effect. Hence the words of the narratives say that hearts have been cured of their disappointment in New England, but the music says that hearts are disappointed in themselves for still being disappointed in New England. This double disappointment is often what is really being "confessed" in the relation of religious experience, which, as we saw in the first chapter, is probably a direct extension of the confession of sin. And it is indeed construed as a sin, a very special kind of American sin – perhaps the first,

25 Fiske, *Notebook,* p. 52.

the primal stain on life in the new world and all the more corrosive because it is not quite able to achieve full expression.

One of the most poignant examples of the way this new sense of sin clogged the narrative is the confession of Goodman Nicholas With, who

> went through many difficulties before and when I came to sea. Yet I went on and God took away my son, some telling me the Lord was displeased for going on . . . I had many things to call me back, my wife all the time going through many afflictions . . . *but I did not look as coming to New England was the cause*. (p. 194; emphasis added)

This wan protest is much belied by the Goodman's subsequent litany of woes, his repetition that "the Lord's hand hath been much out against me," and, above all, his obvious bewilderment as to the meaning of his experience. Surely all losses must be his own fault – or must they? Of course he is unable to pose this dangerous, unutterable question, and the verbal result can only be a tangled mass of contradictions.

> And yet God's hand hath been much against me since I came hither and I know not but it hath been for my carelessness in not watching over my child in regard of the sin of the family . . .* Though I have been much drawn away unto new plantations though I could never see a clear way to go away for I saw so much of love of God's people here that I thought I should bring much evil on me if I did remove. But for that sin which broke out it had been good for me if I had never come hither to this place. The Lord's hand hath been much out against me and is so still. He gave me a child after my own heart and God hath taken it from me and 'tis so just for I have gone on so formally and coldly since I came here. Though I have enjoyed much in public yet I have been very unfruitful and unchristianlike. (p. 195)
>
> * Exod. 20:5; Deut. 5:9.

The reader who continues to follow the convolutions of Goodman With's entire testimony will quickly see that in his case the "since-I-came-hither-dead-hearted" convention never really works. It never helps him to resolve either the actual or the rhetorical problem. His narrative falters, he is unable to satisfy the questions of the elders, and, above all, he is unable to express his feelings to himself or to others in an active, direct way that might produce some sort of resolution. Obviously a man who suffers deeply, he protests, "I am shallow"; obviously impatient and angry with his lot, he protests, "I have comforted myself in waiting upon the Lord"; obviously very confused, disheartened, and conflicted about the quality and meaning of his experience, he can only resort to a self-deprecation that he does not wholly feel. Thus, though he can admit, "I have been very unprofitable," he must hurry to add, "and so it appears yet I desired to enjoy society of God's people." Thus he confesses that "I have heard of [people continuing as] unprofitably after hearing [the Word] as before,"[26] yet there is a hint of defensiveness: "though I went with much expectation." The elders are sensitive to that tone: Is he saying, then, that the Lord would "deny"? Of course the only answer available to him is the proper one: "No want in Him but in myself" (pp. 195–6). This man who walked four miles, then sixteen miles, then twenty miles to hear God's word in Old England, then traveled three thousand to hear it in the New, now gropes for some advantage to having made the trip, some "truths I heard not in old." About the best he can come up with is, "as how to observe Sabbath and prepare for it and others which I cannot speak." True, "I have here much of Christ's love," but somehow in the new world he "cannot remember." "Why," the elders persist, "do you forget things, brother?" Again, the only reply available to him is the proper one:

> I see cause enough in my own heart why Lord should deny me. I know many things in my practice. I have not so meditated on the word. (p. 197)

Yet mixed with the requisite humility, is there not some agitation, even a timid resentment here, turned back upon the speaker at least partly for lack of a clearer object?

This obliquely anguished tone, which we noticed at the start and which pervades so many of these stories, reflects, more than anything "factually" claimed by the speakers, a sadness, an injured bewilderment, and even a stifled anger that would seem to have scant place in a conversion narrative. Even if these emotions are also in much of the other literature of the time and place, what makes this particular situation unique is the very fact that this is supposedly a literature of *conversion*. These narratives are not like other literature, not like histories, diaries, or letters, not even like full-fledged autobiographies. They are supposed to be true stories about vital and absolutely transforming spiritual experience, spoken with solemn public purpose. In the words of Sister Geere, who made her relation at Wenham in 1644, "this practice of relation submitted to privately for example's sake, the safety of this church, and this [publicly] to the honor of God."[27] In view of such a formidable trinity of beneficiaries – the brethren, the church, and God – the mixed confusion, sadness, urgency, and sense of unresolved sin in a narrative like Nicholas With's takes on a special poignancy – a poignancy heightened by the ironic fact that the heart of the experience,

26 Interpolations mine.

27 Fiske, *Notebook*, p. 9. Interpolation mine.

New England itself, proves also to be the very thing that deters, or defers, the transformation of the heart.

To this extent the New England conversion narrative does not perform with the same rhetorical success that has been claimed for allied forms of literature by Sacvan Bercovitch in his noted study of the complex ways in which "the spiritual uniqueness of the locale" affected early American expression and fed the concept of American selfhood. Bercovitch has heavily emphasized what he construes as the positive implications of the intermeshing of identities between elect individuals and an elect land whose history is seen as "a case of conversion" initiated by the "ocean-crossing as a spiritual rebirth."[28] Necessarily confining his investigation to the kind of biographical-historical "rhetoric" that emanated from the official spokesmen for the culture, Bercovitch finds even in their earliest efforts clear signs of success: He claims that the rhetoric of the first generation's notions of an "American Jerusalem" really did work – that "somehow through all the difficulties of the young plantation, the orthodoxy upheld, and was upheld by, their vision." Despite innumerable crises, he asserts, "their energy and conviction continued unabated, and there is every reason to suppose that they exerted a considerable influence upon the populace at large."[29]

The primary pattern in Bercovitch's analysis is the American tendency to "invert" traditional figuralism by imputing "to state and country alike" the experience of grace as given to the individual soul; and as part of this pattern, Bercovitch finds that in the biographical literature "the migration to America displaces conversion as the crucial event."[30] On the latter point, the documents agree: Such a displacement occurs in virtually all the conversion stories of the first generation, wherein over and over again, as we have seen, "hither I came" (sometimes marked by a switch from personal to "national" imagery) is meant to mark some kind of spiritual pivot in the narrative. But the implications of success attendant upon Bercovitch's findings are not borne out by most of these testimonies. His assumption, for example, about Thomas Shepard's famous memoir, that its "equation of new life with New World, and of baptism with the Atlantic as a greater Red Sea, became a staple of early colonial autobiography,"[31] is joyfully corroborated by only a few conversion stories, like that of Katherine, Mrs. Russell's maid, which we saw in the Introduction. But the greater number of conversion stories are unable to complete the equation. In-

28 Sacvan Bercovitch, *The Puritan Origins of the American Self* (New Haven: Yale University Press, 1975), pp. 109, 115, and Chapter 4, passim.

29 Ibid., p. 98.

30 Ibid., p. 118.

31 Ibid.

stead, many of them evince a different and unexpected kind of "inversion," namely, that the failure of New England, of "state and country alike," to meet the spiritual expectations of the individual who is trying to articulate his experiences devolves back upon that person and presses him into a doubtful limbo of semiconversion or even nonconversion. The speaker is, of course, unable to confront the problem directly, since his ostensible reason for testifying at all is to manifest his gracious condition, and since, should he openly "blame" New England for the dilemma, he would have to blame God. The "rhetoric" of the saints must therefore emerge more in sorrow than in triumph, more in muffled anguish than in "self-assertion" – especially in a self-assertion that would depend on the alleged Puritan habit of attributing to "America the status of visible sainthood."[32] If the "non-separating emigrant . . . had to justify himself by justifying America,"[33] as Bercovitch claims, it is no wonder that the first members of the New England churches had so much trouble finding themselves. For the fact is that the America in the forefront of their minds (at least as reflected in their "rhetoric") as they rose to deliver their relations was not the America celebrated by Cotton Mather or Edward Johnson. For most, it was an America neither of joyous fulfillment nor, on the other hand, of fearsome, howling hideousness, but a strange, foggy limbo of broken promises, where the human heart was felt to be "dead and dull . . . dead and senseless . . . so dead . . . dead." If in fact it was not a place but some kind of national "person," the America encountered by these yearning souls was no visible saint but an invisible, ever-receding, unloving god. And as this feeling struggled to be articulated in the stories people told about themselves, the struggle may even have begun to take on a life of its own and to exert a reflexive, intensifying influence on the nature of the experience itself – in short, to become a new literary convention that marks no "highpoint"[34] of early American rhetorical effort but rather the aphelion of an ever-expanding orbit of expression around the heart of religious experience.

32 Ibid., pp. 103, 108.

33 Ibid., p. 103.

34 "The Puritans' image of America marks the highpoint of their effort to find a rhetoric adequate to their sense of mission" (ibid., p. 109).

4

THE PROBLEM OF EXPRESSION

Every reader of *The Pilgrim's Progress* must have noticed that as Christian and Hopeful approached the Celestial City the promise of free and true communication became more and more imminent. Having reached Beulah Land, they rested in the King's Vineyard and "they talked more in their sleep at this time, than ever they did in all their Journey"; for they had eaten of the fruit whose nature it was "to go down so sweetly, as to cause the lips of them that are asleep to speak." When they got over the river, they "went up through the Regions of the Air, sweetly talking as they went." And when they asked the Shining Ones what heaven would be like, they were told that they would "serve him continually with praise, with shouting and thanksgiving, . . . your eyes shall be delighted with seeing, and your ears with hearing, the pleasant voice of the mighty One."[1] Yet there were two crucial moments when either the senses or language itself seemed to fail. The worst crisis was in crossing the river, where "a great darkness and horror fell upon *Christian,*" and

> he in great measure lost his senses, so that he could neither remember nor orderly talk of any of those sweet refreshments that he had met with in the way of his Pilgrimage. But all the words that he spake, still tended to discover that he had horror of mind, and hearty fears that he should die in that River, and never obtain entrance in at the Gate.[2]

The other crisis belongs to the narrator himself, who, having brought the pilgrims to the gate of the city, is unable to do full justice to their feeling: "Oh! by what tongue or pen can their glorious joy be expressed."[3] Thus at the very moment of death and at the very moment

1 John Bunyan, *The Pilgrim's Progress* (London, 1678; facsimile rpt. ed., Menston, England: Scolar Press, 1970), pp. 262–3, 268, 270.

2 Ibid., p. 265.

3 Ibid., p. 273.

of life, the human faculties are stilled by what Richard Baxter called the "unexpressible weight of things Eternal."[4]

The weight pressed especially hard upon New England's saints, who, to judge by their conversion narratives, responded to the Atlantic crossing far more like Christian in "*conflict at the hour of death*"[5] than like the Israelites being delivered through the Red Sea. The Red Sea crossing, Owen C. Watkins reminds us, was to all Puritans "a prefiguring of the release of man from bondage to sin," whereby the blood of Christ could itself figure as a red sea in which old sins were "dead and drowned";[6] and as we have seen, both Alan Heimert and Sacvan Bercovitch have suggested the almost inevitable literalization of that figure for the Puritans who migrated to America. And yet the figure scarcely shows up in conversion testimonies. For example, in the Shepard manuscript, Exodus is the eighth most frequently cited book of the Bible, but most of the references concern the Commandments, the building of the sanctuary, or other matters from the Sinai portion of the book, and only two testimonies explicitly call up Exod. 14:13, which is one of the verses treating of the crossing through the Red Sea waters. Similarly, in John Fiske's congregation, Sister Moulton is the only one to cite Exodus 14.[7] The sparseness of these references is especially surprising when we recall how many people mention the migration – for example, four-fifths of Shepard's congregation.

What *is* associated with the migration is not the washing away of sin but the increased, almost overwhelming awareness of sin – an awareness so painful and fearsome that it produces a short circuit of the verbal faculties, exactly like the affliction Christian suffers as he plunges into the water. The tendency "neither [to] remember nor orderly talk" of the "sweet refreshments" of the saintly life, and the concomitant tendency to apply such words as are left to "horror" and "hearty fears," are so common among New England's converts that the Atlantic Ocean does begin to look like the River Lethe. Of course we know that Christian, supported by Hopeful, reaches the other side of the river. But New Englanders are not so sure they have done so, and furthermore, they do not have a Bunyan to tell their story. They must speak for themselves, and many of them have such difficulty doing it that the reader suspects that in some sense they still feel themselves to be in mid-passage.

This problem of expression is actually a series of problems, because

4 *Works,* 1:3, cited in Watkins, *Puritan Experience,* p. 223.

5 Bunyan, *Pilgrim's Progress,* p. 265 (marginal note).

6 *Puritan Experience,* p. 210.

7 See Katherine and Goodman Shepard, pp. 100 and 174; Fiske, *Notebook,* p. 9.

the association of expressive power with spiritual power takes several successive forms in conversion stories. At the bottom of the ladder there is the frequent complaint that the sin-oppressed soul has been ashamed to speak to others of his or her condition. This is supposed to be something of a convention for all Puritan confessions, one of the ways to signify the pre-enlightened state. And yet it is a convention far more frequently used in American conversion stories than in the English ones: The English saints, when doubting their condition, tend to complain that they cannot pray to God;[8] the American saints are as likely to complain that they cannot speak to their neighbors. Even more important, the communication problem almost always arises *after* the arrival in New England. Thus Barbary Cutter, "after I came hither," found not only her "condition more miserable than ever" but that she "spoke to none as knowing none like me" (p. 90). Sister (Mary) Parish "could not speak of my condition" at the peak of her postmigration troubles (p. 137). Goodwife Willows "could not resolve to speak to any" (p. 151), Richard Cutter, Barbary's brother, "could not speak to any" (p. 179), Goodwife Champney "would not speak and hence in straits" (p. 191), Sizar Jones was "loath . . . to make my state known to any that might have helped me" (p. 200); and for all these people, the silent suffering descended after they were "brought hither." This suffering, being a social one, went two ways: for Mr. Haynes, "loath I was to speak, or others to me" (p. 168); Mrs. Sparhawk, who "could not desire to be here," found that "she could not speak to anybody and thought also that they would not be plain with her" (p. 66). On the other hand, when Barbary Cutter's condition did begin to ease, "I discovered my estate to some," who then "spake to me as that it . . . was a mercy" (p. 92). The sinfulness of all this antisocial, noncommunicating behavior consisted in its being an act of self-will and a willful deception. Thus the Puritans knew "of fears if they carried to Lord they were good," whereas people "that kept their conditions that some were in hell lamenting it" (p. 66). But the New England Puritans seemed to make a special point of equating openness toward the brethren with that openness that was required toward God himself. Thus "God suffered Satan to assault me with many temptations as from speaking to others so from opening my mind to God" (p. 206). The refusal of interpersonal speech, especially in the new land, had cosmic ramifications.

But there was a second and worse verbal problem in New England: the general "loss of expressions and affections" (p. 127) that came with

8 E.g., "I could not name God, or Christ nor speake a word to God for the present" ("*Experiences of* E.C.," in Walker, *Spirituall Experiences,* p. 82).

the American territory of sin and dead-heartedness, a condition so paralyzing that "I have not had a word sometime to speak" (p. 104) or "I could not understand anything was said, I was so blind" (p. 183). That this was not just an empty claim, that there was a genuine sea change from receptiveness to deadness and inarticulateness is demonstrated by Mr. Sparhawk, who, as we saw earlier, experienced a revelation of the Lord at Dedham (England) so sweet that it "made me to break out to weeping and hardly could I refrain from speaking to others to let them see what Lord had done" (p. 63). Yet "since I came hither," he confesses, "the assurance of Lord's love I have not found," and there is an obvious verbal sign of that: The only thing Mr. Sparhawk can find to cheer him is his vaguely synesthetic perception that "the Lord hath lately let me hear His voice in His hand in my family," a claim immediately followed by his final, sorry admission, "I cannot remember many things which I cannot now express myself" (p. 64). Others, too, cannot remember things since they sailed the Atlantic: Trying to express "the promises that did stay me formerly" in Old England, John Sill finds that "there was more than I can now remember or call to mind" (p. 48), and Goodwife Willows's bad memory forces her to conclude her testimony with an odd emotional letdown: Having "had a fellow feeling of Christ's sufferings," she thereupon "had many objections and doubts answered which I forget" (p. 152). We have already witnessed the painful testimony of Goodman With, who "cannot speak" and "cannot remember," and who, when asked to explain "why do you forget things," can only reply, "I see cause enough in my own heart why Lord should deny me" (p. 197). The Goodman's answer is ironically to the point, for with all his hesitation and self-deprecation, he is the one to articulate the heart of the problem: Language and expressiveness are felt to be gifts of God and their denial a withholding of divine love – perhaps even of conversion itself. It may be for this reason, and not explicitly for fear of more Antinomian troubles, that early in the series God's own voice ceases to be mentioned by the converts; for after the testimonies of the Sparhawks and the Stedmans, no longer do we hear that "God spoke to me" or "many times since the Lord hath spoken to me to help me" (pp. 75, 105). It is tempting to assume that people are merely afraid to say such things after the controversy of the late 1630s, but the problem of God's silence goes beyond that, since it permeates the overall tone and feeling of the narratives themselves, even in the absence of any specific reference. In New England God's silence seems in the larger sense to have muted the very expressiveness and confidence of the voices of "his people."

Scholars on both sides of the Atlantic have tended to dismiss the Puritans' claims to difficulties of expression. Either the speakers were acknowledging "essentially a limitation in literary competence,"[9] or they were mouthing a complaint "more than familiar; . . . so conventional in the literature of spiritual experience that distinction becomes possible only for . . . singular expressions of inadequacy."[10] Yet when it comes to the public performance of conversion narratives in the churches (rather than spiritual autobiography in general), there is a marked skew to the American side that clearly calls for attention. In English church testimonies, inexpressibility just does not seem to be the matter for deep, nagging concern that it is on the other side of the ocean. Several people in the Rogers and Walker groups do protest that they can't express themselves or "can speake but little of Jesus Christ,"[11] and Elizabeth White mentions once, with Bunyanesque fervor, that "I was filled with inexpressible Joy," though she is just as quick to point out that her "Deliverance . . . filled my Heart and Mouth with Praises to the LORD."[12] But more significant than any conscious disclaimer, complaint, or even disingenuous remark on the subject is the fact that the texture of the English narrative as a whole simply does not convey the sense of language being weighed and found wanting that comes through in New England's church relations. There is always that assurance, that finished quality, that we noticed earlier in Mrs. White's *Experiences*. Here, for example, is the entire relation of Mary Barker, given before the Dublin congregation of John Rogers.

> I have great *experiences* of God, though at present I am not able to *expresse* them. I have been much *afflicted* for many years together in my *relations,* which for my *sins* have been taken from me; but the *Lord* who hath laid his *hand* heavy upon me, hath made me very *sensible* of my *sins,* and I have long layn under the *burthen* of them; but the *evidence* of my *pardon* is, that the *Lord* hath *removed* the *burthen,* and brought in the *roome* his *grace,* and given me a *heart* to *him-ward,* and I have *received* much *benefit* by *preaching,* and *praying,* and *reading* in *private* and *publique,* and by the *preaching* of Mr. *Rogers* I have received infinite good, and found great *comforts* by his *showing* how we might *know Christ is in us of a truth;* and by *prayer* which the Lord brought me earnestly into; the *Lord* made those *means* so *usefull* to me, that I am much *satisfied* in the *love of God* to me, in *Christ* in me, who is *all in all,* and I doe rest alone on *Jesus Christ,* for *pardon* and *Salvation* by *his blood.*[13]

Even the most perfunctory glance at this narrative tells us that Mary Barker has a method of dealing with her self-proclaimed problem of expression. First, she skims over the inexpressible "great experiences of

9 Watkins, *Puritan Experience,* p. 209.

10 Shea, *Spiritual Autobiography,* p. 98.

11 "*Experiences of* E.R.," in Walker, *Spirituall Experiences,* p. 367.

12 *Experiences,* pp. 13, 10.

13 Rogers, *Ohel,* pp. 413–14.

God" and scarcely even lingers over the "sins" from which she has been redeemed. Instead, she concentrates on the happy "effects" of grace, which are capable of description and which, not surprisingly, take up two-thirds of the story. Second, she is willing to rely on many verbal conventions in describing those effects, from "brought in the *roome* his *grace*" to "*Christ* in me, who is *all in all*." The result is not ineffective, if somewhat stylized and incantatory. In fact, the reader who goes through the entire Rogers document may feel that he is present at a continuing and rather comforting ritual that is not the less valid for being couched in familiar, reassuring repetitions of phrases and images that obviously pulsate with meaning for both speakers and hearers. If there was a "safer" method of church testimony that might satisfy William Rathband's desire for "a set and standing Rule," Dublin and London would seem to have been practicing it.

But we know that this kind of communal assurance and verbal solidarity were not possible in New England, because the identification of conversion with the migration itself had created a pressure cooker in which the "effects" or "evidences" of conversion could only be located in individual responses to the entire experience of crossing, with all its inner conflict of expectation with reality, of hope with disappointment, and of acknowledged guilt with unacknowledged anger. We have seen that many of the saints felt half-consciously thwarted by these conflicts, unable to complete the experience or to understand the contradictory "effects" in them of their actual spiritual–secular "change." They suddenly found themselves standing up in the churches to talk about their combined conversion–migration, armed only with the old, safe, and inappropriate language of joyous religious rebirth, and with no new language available for embodying and explaining the new, complex, double experience. The one sure element in this dilemma was that a conversion narrative must be given: not because the churches insisted on it but because, as we have seen in previous chapters, the entire experience (especially the feelings of guilt and sinfulness over the inexplicable dilemma itself) demanded expression or "confession." There was, however, one portion of the old vocabulary still somewhat appropriate to the problem, and that was the negative language of "deadness." The New England saints therefore latched on to this formula; but they used it not so much to provide a literal description of their emotions (for they could evince very strong feelings over their alleged deadness) as to symbolize the inner deadlock over the problem of expression itself.[14] Thus the attempt to "find feelings" in the new place *became* the attempt to find an adequate expression for them.

14 For a different interpretation of the "deadness" problem, see Hall, *Faithful Shepherd*, p. 157.

This is not to say that there is no glad feeling, no successful expression, indeed, no conversion in New England's conversion narratives. As we shall see in the next chapter, a number of the saints eventually overcome Bunyan's narrative "problem" and do find tongue or pen to express "their glorious joy"; in effect, they find the feelings by finding the expression for them. Others at least partially succeed. But when problems of expression remain unresolved they tend to form around the painful parts. It is the pain that can be neither fully expressed nor suppressed, neither exorcised nor denied, and that constitutes the core of the real expressive challenge. And yet, it is an odd sort of problem, considering that the Puritans were accustomed to hearing and using a highly developed vocabulary of sin and pain – much of which, as Watkins demonstrates in his study of English spiritual autobiography, needed only to be taken directly from the Bible, which provided a limited but useful range of such expressions for the English saints.

> Paul's description of spiritual conflict was diffused into more general terms, and they too found themselves sorely buffeted by Satan or met him disguised as an angel of light. The comparatively narrow range which was drawn on is emphasized by the continual recurrence of certain phrases. Not one but many of them had a heart like a cage of unclean birds, turned with the dog to their vomit, watered their bed with tears, or had been plucked like a brand from burning.[15]

All the more surprising, then, is the absence of such images from American conversion stories. In fact, not one of this particular series shows up in the Shepard group and only one in the Fiske group: George Norton testified at Wenham in 1645 that he had tried to overcome his repeated flirtations with Arminianism by remembering "that scripture, the dog returned to his vomit &c."[16] – and even here the words were directly quoted from the Bible and not incorporated into the speaker's own idiom. Nor in the succeeding generation did this kind of colorful (if conventional) language become part of the tradition for ordinary people to the extent that it did in England. At the gathering of Edward Taylor's congregation at Westfield, Massachusetts, in 1679, a typical convert spoke in the usual way of his "Sins, as Pride, Worldliness, & the Lust of the flesh," lamented "the hardness of my heart & Strength of Sin," and recalled (in terms all too familiar to the sons of the founders) "hearing that New England Sinners should have

15 Watkins, *Puritan Experience,* p. 210.

16 Fiske, *Notebook,* p. 36. The scriptural reference is 2 Pet. 2:22.

their place in hell."[17] But his small lexicon of misery was no match for that of his pastor, Taylor himself, who, in his own conversion narrative before the church, cried:

> Oh the sight of [it,] oh a lost State, oh a deceitfull heart, a vile heart, a [har]d heart, a formall heart, neglect of Christ, deadness in duty, [lov]e of vanity, and the like . . . an universall weriness of myselfe, disqui[etude w]ith myselfe, judging of myselfe . . . all things of mine [are] dung & dogs meat.[18]

Daniel B. Shea, Jr., points out that Taylor's "Spiritual Relation" is not readily identifiable as that of a great poet, insofar as "any number of Puritan preachers might also have mined scripture for figurative vehicles" like Taylor's "dung and dogs meat" and the like.[19] This may be so of the preachers,[20] but Taylor's relation is certainly different from those of lay Puritans, who evidently did not pursue such mining expeditions to fuel their conversion stories; at least, there is little sign in their narratives that they tried to imitate the more colorful effusions of preachers like Taylor, or, in the earlier generations, the rhetorical flourishes and tropes of Shepard's or Hooker's exhortations. This is in part symptomatic of the fact that American conversion stories were not primarily devoted to evangelical purposes, as were many of the English narratives, in which certain conventionally dramatic figures do appear quite frequently. For example, in the Rogers group there is a continual refrain about "the bruised reed" and "the smoaking flax" and in the Walker congregation about the "Throne of Grace" and the "footstoole of God's mercy." There is also a near-obsession with "the sin against the holy ghost," along with a great deal of explicit material about Satan or the Devil. Indeed, many people seem to have shared Mrs. Elizabeth White's bedside vision: For example, E.C. (a woman in the Walker congregation) was not untypical in reporting that, after "strange temp-

17 "The Relation of Lt. John Mawdsley," in *The Unpublished Writings of Edward Taylor,* 3 vols., ed. Thomas M. Davis and Virginia L. Davis (Boston; Twayne, 1981), vol. 1: *Edward Taylor's "Church Records" and Related Sermons,* pp. 105, 106.

18 "The Relation [of Edward Taylor]," ibid., p. 101.

19 *Spiritual Autobiography,* p. 98.

20 Personal spiritual testimonies by ministers, delivered like Taylor's before an entire congregation, are rare, because complete records of church foundings are rare. Thus John Winthrop records that "Mr. Shepherd" declared "what work of grace the Lord had wrought" in him at the first church gathering in Cambridge (*History of New England,* 1:180), but this testimony has not come down to us. A collection of experiences almost exclusively by ministers, but probably not given for church membership, is F. W. B. Bullock, *Evangelical Conversion in Great Britain: 1516–1695* (St. Leonards On Sea: Budd & Gillatt, 1966). John Rogers includes his own church testimony in *Ohel,* pp. 419–39.

tations" to put God out of her mind, "Satan then appeared to mee in a most ugly shape, laughing and jeering at me," and another woman, E.R., "boldly . . . sate up in my Bed, and told Satan, That he was a Lyer, and that I would rather be damned then to deny Jesus Christ."[21] Here are many people, as Watkins points out, who are just like St. Paul in being "sorely buffeted by the Devil"; more than that, they are terrified, hounded, "assaulted . . . so that I had scarce time to fetch my breath," and "repulsed in all duties," even to the point

> that when in the bitternesse of my soule I was groping after Jesus Christ, and had named God, he would put into my minde the objects of bruite creatures; even whilst I was powring out my soule to the creatour, and was pleading a promise, he brought a curse to my thoughts.[22]

Extreme contrasts, tussles with the Devil, cursed thoughts – none of these show up to any great extent in the utterance of Thomas Shepard's flock, despite his own dramatic, intense preaching. At the same time, New England's saints are just as unlikely to fall back on the more lifeless, mechanical, stock phrases of sin and misery that Watkins describes as typical of the English Baptists (but also frequently seen in the Rogers and Walker church relations):

> Having been brought up under the means, [the convert] sooner or later found . . . his miserable state by nature; he then became burdened and pressed down by his sin, and lived in legal bands and slavish fears. He was exposed to waves or floods of temptations, and only delivered when Christ was presented to him so that he could cast himself upon Him . . . thus rolling his soul on his Redeemer.[23]

Watkins points out that the antisectarians had short patience with such a "*Jargon* of empty, senseless Metaphors";[24] yet this language seems to have been in constant use by many English converts and seems to have satisfied their particular need to describe whatever in their experience was felt to be indescribable. The question is, why didn't the New England saints take a leaf from the same comforting and readily available – if not very imaginative – book?

Part of the answer can be found by looking at the ministers of these respective congregations, for they were without question the major literary exemplars (save for the Bible itself) in the lives of their auditors. We can see by reading their conversion stories that ordinary Puritans

21 Walker, *Spirituall Experiences,* pp. 82, 366. For Mrs. White, see Introduction, above.

22 "*Experiences of* M.W.," ibid., pp. 144–5.

23 Watkins, *Puritan Experience,* pp. 212–13.

24 Robert South, *Sermons* (1727), 3:165, cited ibid., p. 213.

did not try to emulate the style of what they heard from the pulpit in terms of architectural arrangement, use of tropes or other rhetorical techniques, and we can also see that they placed little, if any, emphasis on a complicated or sophisticated theology or "morphology." These were not the major *formal* ministerial influences on conversion narratives. What did evidently make an impression, and what had real literary consequences, was the overall set of attitudes and values that the ministers managed to convey, in all that they said, about the possibilities of human expression – and, in this case, about the possibility of expressing the experience of saving grace. We saw in Chapter 2 how John Cotton, for example, imparted his confidence in the ability of the new creature to speak "a new Language," to "read Gods Word, and conferre with Gods people about the things of God" – a confidence at least partially justified by the documents before us, since several of the more affecting experiences seem to owe their emergence, in one way or another, to "Mr. Cotton."[25] Thomas Shepard, however, did not have so much to say about the literary advantages of a gracious condition; on the contrary, he seems to have exuded a vigilance and caution about the use of words that cannot have had an imaginatively or rhetorically liberating effect. Shepard, after all, was instrumental in the banishment of the voluble Antinomians and was one of the most vehement critics of Anne Hutchinson's use of language: He was horrified by "her fluent Tounge and forwardnes in Expressions to seduce and draw away many," and he was "wholy unsatisfied in her Expressions" at the church trial, arguing angrily with her definitions of words[26] and conveying by his own expressions the violent agitation he felt in the face of an apparent verbal anarchy that was as dangerous and "infectious" as sexual libertinism.

> But seeinge the Flewentness of her Tonge and her Willingness to open herselfe and to divulge her Opinions and to sowe her seed in us that are but highway side and Strayngers to her and therefore would doe much more to her owne . . . I account her a verye dayngerous Woman to sowe her corrupt opinions to the infection of many and therefore the more neede you have to looke to her.[27]

25 See John and Alice Stedman and Robert Ho[l]mes, pp. 74–5, 105, 143; and Mrs. Farwel in Fiske, *Notebook,* p. 146. Unfortunately, no conversion narratives survive from Cotton's own congregation in Boston, except for Anne Hutchinson's autobiographical outburst during her examination at Newtown (David D. Hall, ed., *The Antinomian Controversy, 1636–1638: A Documentary History* [Middletown, Conn.: Wesleyan University Press], 1968, pp. 336–8).

26 Hall, *Antinomian Controversy,* pp. 365, 377, 378.

27 Ibid., p. 353. Shepard's language echoes the parable of the sower (Matt. 13, Mark 4, Luke 8), but the imagery of infection is his own. For further

Shepard was genuinely distressed by what he considered the antisocial effects of the sinful distortion of language during the Antinomian troubles, especially in the new land where so many were "but highway side and Strayngers." Complaining to John Winthrop at the height of the difficulties that "they . . . abolish the very forme of wholsom woords of truth which the apostle exhorts Timothy to keepe as well as the truth itselfe,"[28] he must have been mindful of St. Paul's additional warning that "doting about questions and strifes of words" brings "envy, strife, railings, evil surmisings,/Perverse disputings of men of corrupt minds" (1 Tim. 6:4–5). But his horror took such a worried, suspicious form in terms of the possibilities of language itself that he anxiously urged Winthrop not to argue "by woord or pen" at all about sticky theological questions.

> Yet its a great scruple in my thoughts . . . whether it will be most safe for yow to enter into the conflict with your pen (though the Lord hath made yow very able and fit for it) or if yow doe, whether then so largely; it being an easy thing for a subtill adversary to take aduantages at woords, or if yow doe wright . . . ,whether yow do not think it most meet to leaue them to the view of some of your freinds, before you send them . . . if yow shoulde thinke it fit in your wisdom to forbeare wrighting for a while, I perceiue it would be most safe for yow.[29]

If it was not "safe" for Winthrop (albeit so "able and fit," according to Shepard's diplomatic protest) to be trusted with word or pen, what of the average churchgoer? In his sermon *Of Ineffectual Hearing the Word,* Shepard conveyed scant hope that even the saints could consistently use their faculties "aright." Saved or no, they were subject to constant fluctuations in their auditory skills, "sometimes their hearts . . . quickened, fed and cherished, healed and comforted, relieved and visited" by the Word; "sometimes again dead and senseless, heavy and hardened." This constant interference between the ear and the heart was necessary "to make us ashamed of our own darkness, that when he speaks yet we can not hear, there is so much power of spiritual death and Satan yet within us." This was far indeed from Cotton's confidence in the regenerate perceptions, even considering his admission (intended as encouragement) that some "poore soules" who do have grace may think they "want power to expresse . . . in company." And it was far from the general Puritan view that grace was "an elevation of reason, a freshening and quickening of the understanding; . . . an imparting to man of

discussion of New England's language problems during the controversy, see Caldwell, "Antinomian Language Controversy."

28 Thomas Shepard to John Winthrop, Dec. 1636, *Winthrop Papers,* 3:327.

29 Ibid.

that spark of imagination and that breadth of insight whereby he can at least perceive in part" the divine order.[30] Yet Shepard was just as self-deprecating, just as uncompromisingly hard-eyed about his own abilities (and those of the clergy in general) as he was about the capacities of his auditors, both for true understanding and – an ever-present danger – for complacency or self-deception about it.

> I do not speak that the soul should take every thing that ministers speak as the word of God, but that which is the word of God, take it as God speaking. I am not able to express the infinite unknown sweetness, and mercy, and presence of God, that you shall find thus coming. I know it is a common truth, but I am not ashamed to tell you, I have not for many a year understood this truth, and I see but little of it yet; ye have heard of it, but ye do not understand what it is to hear God speaking.[31]

This is the wary shepherd whose sheep gathered in Cambridge to witness to their personal conviction that God had been speaking truly and clearly to their souls – and speaking of his infinite love and salvation. How were they to filter out "that which is the word of God" amid so much peril and deception as Shepard warned them to beware of? How were they to recognize the "sweetness" that even their own teacher was "not able to express"? Even worse, once having heard and seen it, how were they themselves to speak about that "infinite unknown" thing?

Shepard's own answer was as paradoxical as the man himself sometimes seemed to be. In one of his sermons on the parable of the ten virgins, he revealed the aspect of his personality that Andrew Delbanco has called "an impulse . . . to disdain the rustle of pages, to play the raw, untutored enthusiast," and even to echo "momentarily . . . the anti-intellectualism that flirted with Hutchinson's movement";[32] for here he told the saints that their faculties not only could perceive "aright" but could actually transcend language.

> Saints do not only see things in letters and syllables and words, but see things as they are in themselves. The wicked see the word, sin, and Christ, and heaven, (and in seeing see not,) but not the things themselves . . . So this is the happiness of saints, that though they see things darkly, yet they see things truly, the Spirit creating glorious impressions on the mind of things as they are.[33]

30 Shepard, *Works,* 3:367–8; Cotton, *Way of Life,* pp. 28, 29; Perry Miller and Thomas H. Johnson, eds., *The Puritans: A Sourcebook of Their Writings,* rev. ed., 2 vols. (New York: Harper, Torchbook, 1963), 1:39.

31 *Of Ineffectual Hearing, Works,* 3:381.

32 Andrew Delbanco, "Thomas Shepard's America: The Biography of an Idea," in *Studies in Biography,* ed. Daniel Aaron, Harvard English Studies 8 (Cambridge, Mass.: Harvard University Press, 1978), pp. 171, 170.

33 *Works,* 2:144–5.

But the translation of those private "glorious impressions" back into publicly shared speech was another matter. If Shepard's heart really did contain the Antinomian impulse at dramatic odds with his deep-set need for psychological and social order,[34] it is all the more understandable that he might feel, on the one hand, the painful limitations of language and, on the other, a willingness, if not an eagerness, to settle for a minimal, socially cohesive, "useful" public utterance. It is as if Shepard picked up his pen and with a sigh of moral resignation drew a thick black line between private experience and public expression – the same line that runs through so much of seventeenth-century literature and that manifests itself to any reader of Shepard's own published writings and unpublished journal.[35] Thus, to the question of confessing one's inmost religious experiences, Shepard could address himself in a completely down-to-earth manner without seeming to contradict himself. Despite whatever doubts he had about the human faculties even under grace, he was committed to the examination of church members as a necessary preliminary to Christ's "very strict search and examination of wise and foolish when he comes."[36] At the same time, considering those doubts, as well as the inevitable separation between private and public matters, he felt compelled to warn against "relations of this odd thing and the other . . . revelations and groundless joys," and even "scriptures and sermons" indiscriminately or too enthusiastically cited. The proper confession consisted in

> such [things] as may be of special use unto the people of God, such things as tend to show, Thus was I humbled, then thus I was called, then thus I have walked, though with many weaknesses since; and such special providences of God I have seen, temptations gone through; and thus the Lord hath delivered me, blessed be his name, etc.[37]

Nothing could be plainer than this simple blueprint for a conversion narrative, which Shepard provided for his Cambridge congregation at the end of the *Ten Virgins* sermon series around 1640 – in perfectly good time for the majority of confessors to adapt their testimonies to this pattern if they wished to do so. The same holds true for John Fiske's congregation, for even though Fiske's general opinions are not so well known today (he never published any sermons or treatises), it is highly

34 Delbanco, "Thomas Shepard's America," pp. 171–2.

35 Daniel B. Shea, Jr., discusses this discrepancy in the writings of Jonathan Edwards. See *Spiritual Autobiography*, pp. 190–4, and "The Art and Instruction of Jonathan Edwards's *Personal Narrative*," *American Literature* 36 (March 1965):19–21.

36 *Works*, 2:626.

37 Ibid., p. 631.

unlikely that he kept his flock in the dark as to what was expected in a conversion narrative. He even commended the literary talent of one (but only one) of his church members in the church records: "Respecting Mrs. Farwel her relation was brief, clear, and full as respecting the manner of God's drawing her soul unto Himself."[38]

Whatever their other differences may have been, Shepard and Fiske thus shared one central conception of the relation of religious experience: They obviously felt that the accent should be on the positive. They wanted to hear (congenital Puritan anxiety notwithstanding) what can only be characterized as a success story, both in manner and in matter – brief, clear and full, free of oddities or subjective irrelevancies; a story of God's drawing the soul, with special providences and temptations – but those, "gone through," so that "thus the Lord hath delivered me, blessed be his name." In their conscious pronouncements on the subject the ministers were not, therefore, calling for a manifestation of the endless (and time-consuming) anxieties and insecurities that are said to have been so crucial to Puritan piety and so integral to the preaching of the day, especially to Shepard's. Shepard is, in fact, probably better known today for his anxiety-ridden sermons than for any other factor, despite his earlier unbroken reputation of three hundred years' standing as "the holy heavenly, sweet-affecting, and soul-ravishing Minister"[39] and "one of the best loved men" among the founders.[40] Samuel Eliot Morison's view half a century ago was that "Shepard preaches a gospel of love, of infinite compassion,"[41] but later, more detailed analyses turned up a larger measure of anguish in bittersweet mixture with the love. Thus Michael McGiffert finds in Shepard the most vivid illustration of "the central paradox of Puritan piety," namely, "the deeper the doubt, the higher the hope: . . . Making despair do the office of delight, Shepard . . . grounded assurance on anxiety itself."[42] Similarly, Phyllis M. Jones and Nicholas R. Jones stress the tentativeness and uncertainty that shadowed Shepard's American sermon series on the parable of the ten virgins, his insistence on "how unstable are both the assurance and the sanctification of

38 Fiske, *Notebook,* p. 146. Perhaps it is more than coincidental that the admirable Mrs. Farwel "found stay to her soul in Christ" while "living under Mr. Cotton's ministry."

39 *Johnson's Wonder-Working Providence,* p. 252. The most critical contemporary view of Shepard is that of Giles Firmin in his *The Real Christian, Or A Treatise of Effectual Calling* (London, 1670). See also Norman Pettit, *The Heart Prepared,* pp. 185–9.

40 Samuel Eliot Morison, "Master Thomas Shepard," in *Builders of the Bay Colony* (Boston: Houghton, 1930), p. 106.

41 Ibid., p. 128.

42 *God's Plot,* p. 20.

the converted."[43] No reader of these sermons will deny that such ideas are present in abundance.[44] And yet, when Shepard concluded the series by reminding church members to "be always converting, and be always converted," not to "lay all by, and so live on old scraps," he explained: "Not that a Christian should be always pulling up foundations, and ever doubting; but to make sure, be always converting, more humble, more sensible of sin, more near to Christ Jesus."[45] If this is anxiety, it is also the "high-pitched fervor" of an "intense desire to hear and obey God"[46] and especially an intense desire to feel the true "spring," the "principle within," lacking which men are "like some dead cattle, there is nothing good but their skin."[47] Yet there is a special irony in the fact that the complacency and hypocrisy against which Shepard was striving to marshal so much vigilance was very likely to show up in

> a long story of conversion, and a hundred to one if some lie or other slip not out with it. Why, the secret meaning is, I pray admire me; hence complain of wants and weaknesses; pray, think what a broken-hearted Christian I am; and hence, if comforted, they complain, if not they will comfort themselves; hence many lift up eyes and hands, and fetch deep sighs in prayer, remember and note sermons, look now what a gift I have; hence, if you come to their company, they will have so many good words as may make you think well of them.[48]

Thus, with one further twist of irony, anxiety itself could be feigned, "wants and weaknesses" overdone, broken hearts displayed in a fever of exhibitionism, and all because of "an outward, but no inward principle . . . Those whose principle is nothing but external applause and praise of men." With threats of infinitely varied and seductive verbal deceptions looming on every side and fed by human pride, it is no wonder that Shepard, like Fiske, looked for a brief, clear, no-nonsense

43 *Salvation in New England: Selections from the Sermons of the First Preachers* (Austin: University of Texas Press, 1977), p. 133. For a comprehensive discussion of this sermon series, see Delbanco, "Thomas Shepard's America," pp. 169–74.

44 But for the more reassuring side of Shepard, see also Chapters 9, 10, 11, 19, and 22 (*Works*, vol. 2). A telling assessment of Shepard is reported by Giles Firmin: "I remember my Father [in-law Nathaniel] *Ward* made this observation upon him to me, *When Mr.* Shepard *comes to deal with Hypocrites, he cuts so desperately, that we know not how to bear him, made them all afraid, that they were all Hypocrites: when he came to deal with a tender humble Soul, he gives comfort so largely, that we are afraid to take it*" (*Real Christian*, p. 215).

45 *Works*, 2:632.

46 Morison, "Master Thomas Shepard," in *Builders*, p. 129.

47 Shepard, *Works*, 2:284.

48 Ibid., pp. 284–5.

conversion narrative, one through which the inward principle would emerge in a low and modest murmur: "A Pharisee's trumpet shall be heard to the town's end, while simplicity walks through the town unseen."[49]

All this exceeds the familiar Puritan distrust of false eloquence. It arises from an attitude that Andrew Delbanco calls, in his discussion of Shepard's politics, "a high conservatism, . . . a truly personal disenchantment with unfettered man,"[50] here turned upon man's very capacity for managing his own ears and tongue and imagination. From a literary standpoint, this anxiety – fiercely entwined with more strictly theological fears about the state of the soul – was the decisive anxiety that Thomas Shepard broadcast from his pulpit; this was the fountain of rhetorical doubt and insecurity that could not but dampen the full expression of inexpressible feeling among his listeners. If speech itself was so terrible a breeding ground for sin, then anxiety about conversion was bound to merge into anxiety about the expression of it, and there was always the chance that the convert, even while telling his story, might find the words turning to toads or pebbles in his mouth. On the other hand, people were evidently unwilling – or unable – to settle for Shepard's safe, compact, "useful" prescription for a conversion narrative, and we can only assume that this was because it did not suit their actual experiences. Therefore, unless they were to remain silent, their only alternative was to try to make their own literary way. Unguided but not "unfettered," they would not find the way to be easy.

The case was far different in Old England, where the literary guidance provided by the ministers was much more closely attuned to the expressive needs of their prospective church members. If we take as fairly representative the pronouncements on this subject by Henry Walker and John Rogers, we find that the keynote is always encouragement. Just as the end of the spiritual relation in England was assurance, the ministerial attitude toward it as a form was grounded in reassurance. Where Thomas Shepard was casting a cold eye on the hypocrite's "long story of conversion," full of fake prayers and "good words," John Rogers was delivering a holy pep talk, painting an exuberant picture of the saint whose transformation by grace steadied both hand and eye and improved "performances" through an assurance that was virtually superhuman.

> Now do but minde these men, how much they differ from what they were before their assurance of *Gods favour* and love: before, whilst they were *doubting,* they did but *stagger* at best, if not tumble; and now

49 Ibid., p. 284.

50 "Thomas Shepard's America," p. 181.

> being *assured,* they stand fast; before they did but *smoake,* now they *flame;* before full of *faintings,* palenesse, and shiverings, now full of *faith,* of *ruddy* complexions, lively and *vigorous;* before but *tossed* about, but now at *anchor;* before afraid to lift up their *quivering* hands, and *trembling* eyes, but now boldly *wrastling* with *Omnipotency* its selfe; before durst not *draw nigh* the Lord, but now durst *run* into his armes, and *leap* into his *lap;* before came but behinde to touch the *hem* of his *garment* (Scriptures and Ordinances;) but now, O they can look him on the *face!* and flye into his *bosome* with embraces! . . . before their *performances* were *green* and unfit, but now *mellowed* with the hot *Sun-beams,* and are sweet *mature* fruits.[51]

In the end, Rogers insisted, men with such powers were obligated to exercise them in communion with others, "nothing *ashamed* to shew our assurance, as much as we can expresse it by our *experiences.*"[52] In fact, the combined power of all those expressed experiences would actually change the world.

> Every *Church of Christ* which is *full of experience,* must needs be *ful of Faith,* & have *provision* laid up for *many years,* wch being so *advantagious* as hath bin said, should exceedingly oblige others to bring forth out of their *treasures, new and old;* & I would have every *Church* . . . take up all the *experiences* which the *members* declare, and to bring the *best & choicest* of them into *publique light,* Oh how *beautifull* would they be abroad! and how *sensibly* and forcibly should we *perceive* the unparalleld *appearances* of Gods *love* and *light* as they *shine* more and more towards the *perfect day!* and oh how *obvious* to every *eye* would the *work* which God is about be in this *age!* and then we should see how far these *experiences* surpasse the *former,* or the *Saints* in *former ages;* and how *far* our *childrens* will be *before* us.[53]

If there is little in the confessions printed by Rogers to suggest the fulfillment of this exalted function, there is enough confidence, solace, and even joy in the document taken as a whole, with its incantatory, almost ritualized language, to suggest at least a positive relation between the supportive attitude of the minister and the satisfactions afforded the people by their use of this literary form. Whatever his "essential limitation in literary competence," the Dublin saint had the comfort of being told that the communication of his experiences was an important contribution to a providential scheme that was being realized with an ever-accelerating power and that was reflected in the experience of the individual believer who felt "the Lord leads me on, *higher* and

51 Rogers, *Ohel,* pp. 376–7.
52 Ibid., p. 379.
53 Ibid., p. 450.

higher in himself."[54] Such persons could at least believe that they really did "have something to say," despite their human sinfulness, because an ever-growing grace "emboldned" them to speak.

> I have something to say, and I desire that the *grace of God* may appear more in me every day. I am *convinced* of this *way of Christ, for believers to walk in;* and I have nothing to *plead,* but my *own unworthiness,* yet *fully assured in Christ,* I am *emboldned* to bring my *desires* here like *smoaking flax.*[55]

Henry Walker's congregation was also used to active encouragement of their expressive capabilities. Mindful of that principle of reform, advocated from the sixteenth century, that held that every applicant for communion must be able to "say [how] he holdeth and how he serveth God,"[56] Walker, like many Puritan preachers, continually exhorted his hearers to test their hearts by asking what they could "truly say" (always "by Faith," of course) about their condition. But he went even further by making two very decisive points: first, that the kinds of things people ought to be able to say were very conceivably within their capacities; and second, that being able to say them was at least a "claime" to being in a gracious state.

> When a man (by Faith) can truly say to God; *I am thine, and thou art mine, and Christ is glorified in me.* Ioh. 17. This layes claime to salvation, this layes hold on the merits of Christ as a mans owne, and assures him of the pardon of all his sinnes.[57]

Moreover, there was no place on the scale of grace that was not subject to a verbal measurement.

> And hee that knowes himselfe to be in God, knowes himselfe to be safe from all evill and that nothing can take him out of Gods hands, such a man will dye before he will *renounce* God, and give himselfe over to a sinfull course of life. But alas what misery is the *Swearer* in, he cannot *say,* God is my God, what misery is the Sabboth breaker in; God is ashamed to be *called* the God of such as pollute his holy Sabboth.[58]

It must be admitted that Walker at times seemed to court Arminianism: He was capable of urging his listeners "to do what God requireth, that themselves may attain salvation"[59] or of posing the startling ques-

54 "*Experience of* Elizabeth Avery," ibid., p. 406.

55 "*Experience of* Hugh Leeson," ibid., p. 412[10].

56 Cited in Hall, *Faithful Shepherd,* p. 24.

57 Henry Walker, *A Gad of Steele* (London, 1641), p. 3.

58 Ibid., pp. 3–4. Emphasis added.

59 *The Sermon of Henry Walker, Ironmonger* (London 1642), p. 2^r. This sermon was evidently printed at the behest of Walker's opponents and should be used

tion "How shall I doe to lead my life so as it may please God, and my soule may be saved."[60] But it should also be noted that in answering this question, he stressed not good works or any outward behavior but rather the inseparable involvement of genuine inner change with *words* flowing between the believer and God.

> If we expect to profit we must fix our hearts on God; and daily call upon his name, for prayer is a mighty prevailing thing with Almighty God, where fervent and hearty prayer is put up to God, God cannot depart till he leave a blessing behind him, it binds the hands of God that hee becomes a petitioner himself as he did to *Moses;* let me alone saith God. Oh Gracious God: how great is thy mercy, oh how pitifull a God have wee.[61]

It would be a mistake to conclude that Walker is telling his flock that "saying it makes it so," for he is very severe with mere "outward professors." But he obviously conceives of the relationship with God as an intensely verbal one or at least one that is fully subject to the active verbal interchange implicit in covenant theology: The God he envisions, who "will not *own* the Drunkerd, the Adulterer, the Idolater,"[62] is the Hebrew God who promises, bargains, argues, listens, debates, urges, warns, and so condescends to the level of human communication that he even "petitions" his people. Such a God actually makes his invisible grace discoverable by a "clear" visible means: Namely, he enables the faithful to *say* that they are his. Thus, in presenting *Tragimata, Sweet-Meats. Or, Resolves in all Cases who are Beleevers,* Walker assures his readers:

> Here is a rich Banquet for Beleevers, and a clear distinction who are such; as by the grace of faith can truly say to the Lord, Thou art my Father, my God, and my Saviour, and I am thine in the precious bloud of Jesus Christ; and this distinction is not made by Forms, Professions, and Notions, but real discoveries.[63]

In his customary encouraging style, Walker hereupon invites his readers to match their "experiences" to the "Divine Delicates . . . spread before them," again noting that God's children "may be distinguished by these following marks, so that whosoever hath any of them really upon his Soul, may truly say, The Lord is my Father, my God, my Re-

with caution. The epithet is not friendly: George Thomason, himself a Presbyterian, was in the habit of crossing out the word *pastor* or *minister* next to Walker's name and inking in the word *Ironmonger* on the title pages of works he included in his famous collection (now in the British Library).

60 *Gad of Steele,* p. 7.

61 Ibid. The scriptural reference is to Exod. 32:10.

62 Ibid., p. 4. Emphasis added.

63 (London, 1654), "To the Reader," p. 1^{r}.

deemer, and my Saviour."[64] Then follow 216 numbered conditions, each one in *its* turn introduced by the same words: "If I can truly say . . ." In sum, in "truly" saying "any" of the 216 statements, one knows oneself to be a child of God; "truly" saying is a truly gracious act, indistinguishable from (or another stage of) being. If this is a heavy burden to put upon language, it is also a comfort and hope to believers, a human way of having "their warrants made plaine to have a right to that glory which dazels their eys."[65] Thus, though some of the 216 items are long and complex, many are of the briefest and plainest nature.

> 203. If I can truly say, I do truly beleeve in God; then am I called the Friend of God.
>
> 208. If I can truly say, I lay out my self sincerely to do the will of God; then shall I abide for ever.
>
> 212. If I can truly say, I walk after Gods Commandements; this is love.[66]

With such a list of conditions, "any" of which are a sign of grace, and the permission to "passe those by" that are either inapplicable or incomprehensible,[67] Walker offers a guide in which few earnest Christians could fail to find some satisfaction. But above all, it is a guide that perforce instills the confidence to speak. The pattern holds throughout Walker's preaching: Over and over again, he affirms the positive linguistic connection between human beings and divinity, from the "cheerfull echo answering in the Holy Ghost" a believer's knowledge of the truth,[68] all the way back to Abraham's continual and personal conversations with God.

> Not that God, (who is spirit) hath a corporall being as men hath, and so spak by a mouth, but *Jehovah made it forth* to *Abrams* sence to understand [covenant]: *The Lord discovered his mind,* for so the Hebrew word 'âmar signifies, any way of making forth to another to understand what is in ones mind, or thoughts.[69]

There was a particular consolation in the contemplation of such an intimacy between God and Abraham, a consolation felt to be badly

64 Ibid., p. 1, and title page.

65 Ibid., title page.

66 Ibid., pp. 91, 93, 94.

67 Ibid., "To the Reader," p. 1r.

68 *A Sermon, preached In the Kings Chappell at Whitehall . . .* July *15, 1649* ([London], 1649), p. 14.

69 *A* SERMON *Preached in the Chappell at* Sommerset-*House in the* Strand, . . . *the* 27 day of June *1650* (London, 1650), p. 5. In the original text, the Hebrew word appears in Hebrew script, here transliterated. The scriptural reference is Gen. 13:14, 15.

needed at the time Walker delivered this sermon in June 1650. It was the eve of Cromwell's campaign to subdue Scotland, and "*our wives, children, estates, and lives are in danger to be ravisht, beaten, plundered, and taken away, . . . if God not inable you* [Cromwell] *to suppresse them that rise up against us.*" In such straits, with England/Israel in peril of "Ægyptian *Kirk bondage,*"[70] it was comforting to remember that the promise had not been made to all the Jews; that even though Abraham and Lot ("godly Christians" and "Antichristian Presbyters")[71] had once acted together for God, they, too, had later gone their separate ways; and above all that, come what might, those who walked and talked with God, like Abraham, had a heavenly bond that could more than compensate for the "parties and factions" here below.

> . . . Let what come can come, concerning the Parliament, Army, People, Nations, Friends, Estates, Externalls, Internalls; they can still say with the Apostle *Paul.* Rom. 8.28. *And wee know that all things worke together for good, to them that love God, to them who are the called according to his purpose.*
>
> Those that are only outward professors, they may be often startled at transactions of Affaires by the Parliament, or by the Army, or persons, or actings of men, but this is because their hearts are not found with God.
>
> But those that are true believers, that live not by carnall sence, but by the spirit of God, . . . they have this comfort, which is the highest of all comforts, that they have union with God in Christ, and that God will take care of them.[72]

This is one of the major reasons why the English saints were compelled to believe in their own verbal and communicative powers, and why they focused those powers directly on God and, unlike New England's saints, less upon their neighbors. In a world of party and faction, it was absolutely imperative to affirm the other kind of communion; as the gulfs among "People, Nations, Friends" widened in all directions throughout the Civil War years, it was ever more urgent to be able to

> say, I know that my Redeemer liveth, and I doe know that *God* is my *God,* and that the *Holy Ghost* hath set a seale upon my heart, and I doe know that I am the Child of *God.*[73]

It was equally important not to use the gift of speech to be what Walker called a "caviller," not to be like those "captious, and contradictory

70 Ibid., p. 1^{v}.
71 Ibid.
72 Ibid., pp. 22–3.
73 *Sermon . . . at Whitehall,* p. 13.

spirits" who "speak also the very language of Atheisme, bewraying by their tongues, their spite, and deepe dislike against the truth of Christ, revealed in his Word."[74] Rather, what was required was simply

> *to repent, and beleeve the Gospel, to walk circumspectly,* as by a line, *abandoning the fashions* and courses *of this present World, and taking heed unto* [one's] *waies, according to the Word.*[75]

Beyond this, there was no need for "questionings and reasonings" and "cursed speakings."

Thus a common, familiar, shared, noneccentric language both could and should hold together the "invisible union" of the people of God against the vagaries of "Parliament, Army, People, Nations, Friends, Estates." It is very important to note that all of these were "Externalls" – visible things, upon which the saints could fix their angry, bitter, confused, or sad emotions. This, in fact, is the second crucial point about the problem of expression in conversion narratives. Not only did the ministers convey different attitudes and assumptions about language; but life itself offered different visible "expressions," a different "language" to represent experience and especially the sense of sin. In England, sin and guilt were likely to be perceived in and through the "Externalls": If "sin . . . be the cause of all our crosses," the crosses were there to be seen and suffered, the facts were clear in the "outward wants"[76] of everyday life, and for the members of gathered churches, the sin could therefore be articulated and even exorcised in the rituals of public testimony and covenanting by means of a shared, readily available language directly describing real things. Far more than in New England, trouble in England was externalized, "translated," and *explained* in concrete terms.

> The Enemy took *Liverpoole,* and killed my Husband, and a childe, both before my face, and stript, and wounded me, and a childe of five yeares old; and it was thought I could not live. And this was a strong tryall; and I was much tempted, my senses me thought were going from me, and my heart I thought would have melted in pieces, yet I prayed, and the Lord heard me, I thought it was too much for me to beare: but I remembred my Saviours words, *He that will not forsake Father, or Mother, or Sister, or Brother, or Husband, or Childe for Christ, is not worthy of him,* and I desired to give glory to his name. I considered that I must part with all for Christ, I strove hard against my own weaknesse; and my heart said, that God was just in all his dealings with me.[77]

74 *Sermon of Henry Walker,* pp. 1^{rv}.

75 Ibid., p. 1^{v}.

76 "*Experiences of* I.I.," in Walker, *Spirituall Experiences,* p. 19.

77 "*Experiences of* M.W.," ibid., pp. 11–12.

This is the good Christian soul who naturally "thought, when I had considered of it, that I did but suffer as an evill doer my selfe"; yet she could work out this insight because there was a real, external enemy as well.

> But our cause was Gods, and our Enemies Popish Rebels; *Paul* was ready not only to suffer, but to dye at *Jerusalem* for the name of Christ; so I took it patiently, giving glory to God, and beleeving that God, who was come so neare me, would not forsake me.
>
> I was assured with much joy, that the Lord would bring me to himselfe, and in this confidence did rejoyce with my wounded Childe, and a little daughter, in a Barn where we were put, having gotten a peece of an old Bible; and then and since I have found much setlednesse in my faith from severall Promises of the Lord, revealed in his holy Word.[78]

Thus conversion took place directly through affliction – affliction that was terrible but also comprehensible and expressible. More than that, in many stories the outward suffering seems absolutely necessary in order to *make* sin and salvation comprehensible and expressible. The "*Experience of* Frances Curtis" in Dublin makes this necessity very clear. In the beginning, Mrs. Curtis's narrative is virtually indistinguishable from a New England story, trapped as it is within the world of "inward"-ness.

> I cannot but *condemn* my self before *I speak,* I am so *unworthy* of this *mercy.* I have lived *wantonly* in my *youth,* forgetting *God,* doing no good, but all evil, till *Gods hand* was *heavy* upon me for about eleven years; and when in my *outward state* I began to *mend,* still in my *inward* I was much *troubled,* and wished that God had *taken* me *away* by my *former afflictions;* these *inward* were so great, *and a troubled spirit, who can bear?* But afterward I was *much comforted* again.[79]

But Mrs. Curtis hereupon proceeds to a very different kind of *dénouement* from most of those that might be encountered across the Atlantic. If it is the inward trouble that she cannot bear, it is the outward trouble that releases her, that gets her off the seesaw of inner turmoil. Whereas fear of her husband's death is equated with fear of her own guilt for sin, the "*saving* my life, and my *Husbands*" can be explicitly perceived as a sign of redemption. The meanings are clear – neither allegorized nor symbolized but simply found embedded in the outward events of life and therefore (despite the disclaimer about inexpressibleness) conveyed with great conviction.

> In these *wars* I was stripped by the *Rebels* (being *abroad*) and came home so, thorough *sad tempests,* and since have gone thorough *great*

78 Ibid., pp. 12–13.
79 Rogers, *Ohel,* p. 412[10].

> *troubles,* and very many. A while after, *I heard my Husband* was killed by the *Rebels,* which *I* feared was by my *sins,* and so my troubles were *renewed;* and then the *enemies* came upon us, the *Cannon-bullets* flew over my *head;* and in *few days* I was turned out of *doors,* with *my childe in my arms. I* can not express what *God* hath done for me, in *saving* my life, and my *Husbands,* in *hearing* my *prayers* and *tears;* and now in *satisfying* my *soul* with himself. *I* have received such *sweet satisfaction* by Mr. *R.* and have now the *testimony* within me of *Gods* love to me, which makes me so *unfainedly to love him,* and his *ways,* and *desire* to be a *member* with his *people,* in his *Church.*[80]

A similar story, but far more grim in its outcome, still manages with poignant brevity to reach a meaningful conclusion. Mary Turrant confessed at Dublin that in her youth she had "*despaired* of *mercy*" and "thought I *was damned,* and none of *Gods*" until she was "at last *comforted* by *good Ministers,* and the *Word of God.*" Yet, she added, she had to live in a Godless place for seven years, and "*I* do not know, that *I* saw so much as a *Religious man.*" The resolution of her spiritual uncertainty is shocking when it comes, but it is clear: Once again affliction, even in the most horrible form, is the vehicle of insight and peace.

> My *children* were *murthered* by the *Rebels,* and *I* lost my *Husband* by the *sickness,* and yet the *Lord* hath *spared me* in mine *old age;* and now *I* see why? That *I may enjoy* this *great mercy,* which *I* never looked for, to *comfort* me in my *old age.*
>
> I have received great comforts indeed by Master *Rogers* and *I* must needs say, That *I serve my God with a chearful heart, &c.*[81]

For another old woman in New England, however, affliction was neither assimilable nor even fully expressible in this way: Old Goodwife (Elizabeth) Cutter had to relate her experience in negative, abstract terms and had difficulty finding a meaningful resolution.

> And afterward Lord's hand was sad on me husband taken away and friends also to this place. And I desired to come this way in sickness time and Lord brought us through many sad troubles by sea and when I was here the Lord rejoiced my heart. But when come I had lost all and no comfort . . . I saw I was a Christless creature and hence in all ordinances was persuaded nothing did belong to me. Durst not seek nor call God Father nor think Christ shed His blood for me. (p. 145)

Having consulted Shepard and other "servants of the Lord," having contemplated the case of the foolish virgins and that of Abraham, having wavered between "liberty" and "fear," Old Goodwife Cutter eventually learned "to be content with His condemning will to lie at Lord's

80 Ibid., p. 412[11].
81 Ibid., p. 412[11].

feet" and to see "such need of Christ was not knowing whether else to go." Her final words about her experience are that she "desired to submit" (pp. 145–6). These are all perfectly acceptable, even admirable Christian feelings; but the contrast with Mary Turrant's confidence in God's "great mercy," the contrast in the very tone of their narratives, cannot be overlooked. The two narrators – both old, both having endured the grievous losses of women – are not unlike, though Turrant has suffered more. But the crucial difference between their *stories* is that the suffering of Mary Turrant, like that of Frances Curtis or of M.W. in London, is embodied in something external and concrete and is assigned a meaning, whereas Goodwife Cutter's real, external troubles are slowly transformed into something inward, vague, unformed, and unnamed. Mary Turrant's trials are part of a larger, comprehensible structure that she can define and explain; Goodwife Cutter's trials contain and virtually overwhelm her story, rather than being contained by it. To put it in more strictly literary terms, the English saint has found (or has been provided) an objective correlative for her sense of sin and sorrow, whereas the American saint, like T. S. Eliot's Hamlet, has not.[82]

We have been assuming all along that the conversion narrative, although certainly not an example of high literary art, can be treated as an artistic form – essentially, a story people tell about themselves. And we have seen that as a form it presents a certain problem, especially on the American side of its development, having to do with the expression of feeling. To be sure, John Cotton could not have imagined that a problem of art was lurking within his prescription that "in confession of his sinnes (that it may appear to be a penitent confession)" the new church member "declareth also the grace of God to his soule, drawing him out of his sinfull estate into fellowship with Christ"; and yet, the basic demand that produced the conversion story in the first place – the demand that the confession "appear to be a penitent" one – inevitably imposed an artistic standard of performance on every narrator. Along with that standard came the built-in problem, for even though the appearance of penitence had always been a prerequisite for "rightly" taking the Sacrament in

82 To some extent, early America solves this problem with the rise of the Indian captivity narrative in the later seventeenth century. Mary Rowlandson's *The Soveraignty & Goodness of God . . .* (Boston, 1682), for example, seems far closer to the Turrant type of "resolved" story than to Cutter's. Yet even here, the American imaginative mode is distinctive. As I read Rowlandson, she is in a more complicated, "inward" relation to her materials than the English women are to theirs, and she employs Scripture more heavily and more as an integrated structural element than they do. Most important, of course (and most useful), the wilderness metaphor takes on a unique coloring and complexity in the American setting.

gathered churches, there was also a long-standing recognition of the fact that no man could articulate all his sins. "Who can understand *his* errors?" cried the Psalmist, and implied the answer by imploring God, "cleanse thou me from secret *faults*" (Ps. 19:12). According to Erik Routley, Protestant reformers rejected the private confessional for the very reason that "the enumeration of personal sins is not only not necessary, but conducive to a false moral sense: nobody can know the extent of his sins," although "he can know the infinite extent of Christ's power to forgive."[83]

How, then, to make what "may appear to be a penitent confession" in view of the impossibility, not to say false morality, of reviewing all one's sins? The answer had to lie not in mechanical measurement but in the quality of projected feeling: Somehow the penitent, in shaping the public, formal expression of his inward, amorphous experience, had to find a vehicle that could adequately represent to others' eyes his own true sight and sense of sin, which is to say the true seed of his salvation. To complete his conversion narrative, this mute, inglorious artist, perhaps no less than Shakespeare, needed an objective correlative – "the only way of expressing emotion in the form of art."

T. S. Eliot, we recall, defined this phenomenon as

> a set of objects, a situation, a chain of events which shall be the formula of that *particular* emotion; such that when the external facts, which must terminate in sensory experience, are given, the emotion is immediately evoked . . . The artistic "inevitability" lies in [the] complete adequacy of the external to the emotion.[84]

In his reading of *Hamlet,* Eliot found that the hero's real problem could not be worked out in the play because he is "dominated by an emotion which is inexpressible," being "in *excess* of the facts as they appear." That is, he is beset by a feeling of disgust that has been evoked by his "negative and insignificant" mother, but for which she, by reason of her "negative and insignificant" character, is "not an adequate equivalent." Since "his disgust envelops and exceeds her," he is caught in "a feeling which he cannot understand; he cannot objectify it, and it therefore remains to poison life and obstruct action." Moreover, Hamlet's "bafflement" is of a piece with "the bafflement of his creator in the face of his artistic problem"; to this extent, the identity of character and creator is "genuine."[85]

83 "The Confession of Augsburg, 1530," in Routley, *Creeds and Confessions,* p. 25.

84 T. S. Eliot, "Hamlet," in *Elizabethan Essays* (London: Faber & Faber, 1934), p. 61.

85 Ibid., pp. 61–2.

Such is the case in New England conversion stories, wherein the heroes/narrators/personae are dominated by a variety of inexpressible emotions that may be said to be in excess of the facts as they appear (in the stories). In their presentations, the narrators do not know how to account for the fact that the selves whose stories they are telling suffer guilt, depression – which is, after all, inverted anger – and "deadness," and there is no acceptable external object in which to embody these feelings except the whole "situation" in which they find themselves, the whole "chain of events" that brought them to New England in the first place. But they can no more objectify those feelings in New England than Hamlet can objectify his feelings in Gertrude and for a similar reason: New England (unlike England, with its wars, its "parties and factions," its "Enemies") doesn't offer anything bad enough to represent their bad feelings. Indeed, it is partly because New England isn't bad that they are having such feelings. When even such a conscious artist as Anne Bradstreet laments, "I haue not been refined in the furnace of affliction as some haue been, but haue rather been preserved with sugar then brine," is she not offering an unwitting clue as to why "I haue often been perplexed that I haue not found that constant Joy in my Pilgrimage and refreshing which I supposed most of the servants of God haue"?[86] This is the dilemma of Goodman Fessington (John Fessenden), who "being afraid I should not stand in trials" at home, "hence I looked this way" and "so I came" – and who thereupon stumbles into a miasma of guilt, "sadness of heart," and a feeling of "sin and want of God's love" that he never quite overcomes – or articulates (p. 177).[87] It is the dilemma of Goodman Manning, whose excruciating vacillation about whether or not he had "done well" in leaving England is not relieved by "these thoughts," that "though the troubles I had were great, yet I thought some of the saints had far greater, looking back upon the condition of my friends," and yet whose "discontent," on making the voyage, "I found was more burdensome than all crosses and sorrows before" (p. 97).

This "discontent" clogs the narrative like the "stuff" that *Hamlet* is "full of" but "that the writer could not drag to light, contemplate, or manipulate into art." And it, too, is "difficult to localize" because it is "not in any quotations that we might select, so much as in an unmis-

86 *Works,* pp. 23, 7.

87 Thomas Shepard himself expressed similar fears about withstanding the "trials" of Old England but with an ostensibly happier outcome: "The Lord hath set me and my children aside from the flames of the fires in Yorkshire and Northumberland whence if we had not been delivered I had been in great afflictions and temptations, very weak and unfit to be tossed up and down and to bear violent persecution. The Lord therefore hath showed his tenderness to me and mine in carrying me to a land of peace" (*God's Plot,* p. 70).

takable tone."[88] Casting about for an expressive vehicle, New England's perplexed saints cannot transfer the "burdensome" feelings even to the imaginative realm of dreams and devils that is so fertile a source for English conversion narratives, but that remains forbidden territory in early New England. For some people, the only alternative is to retreat behind the claim of a "benumbed condition" (p. 177) – like Goodman Fessington, whose narrative is energized by a taut nervousness that is as far as possible from numbness – and never quite get to the point where "Christ's power to forgive" is made manifest. The resulting conversion stories are probably what Eliot would deem artistic failures, their authors victims of "a problem which proved too much" for them, the problem of an emotion that cannot be expressed in art.[89] Whether they are also religious failures, reflections of an unconverted condition, is not a question we can judge; but we can surmise that for some of the narrators themselves the anguish of inexpressible feelings is compounded by the half-buried suspicion that this is the real problem – that they are not, after all, converted, just *because* they are enmeshed in the tangle of feeling and expression. "He that either cannot, or will not say" something "particularly to show the reality" of his experience, wrote Jonathan Mitchel, "he renders the truth of his faith and repentance suspicious." Invisible grace will out: "*esse, et apparere, non esse, et non apparere,* are all one."[90]

Public performance thus confronted New England's Puritans with literary questions of almost unbearable religious import – and perhaps made feelings just that much harder to objectify. Yet the irony is that the thrust of such intense and unnameable emotion produced the distinctive timbre of these newly American voices. Eliot reminds us that

> the intense feeling, ecstatic or terrible, without an object or exceeding its object, is something which every person of sensibility has known; . . . the ordinary person puts these feelings to sleep, or trims down his feelings to fit the business world; the artist keeps them alive by his ability to intensify the world to his emotions.[91]

In this sense, every convert is a potential artist, and if the "ordinary person" in Massachusetts Bay feared that he was being tempted to "sleep" or to "trim down" the intensity of his feelings, the fact remains that he refused to do so, no matter what he said about it. The earnestness, the poignancy, the unmistakable urgency of these stories are the record of a great struggle to keep feeling alive and to find a new language for it in a new world.

88 Eliot, "Hamlet," pp. 60–1.
89 Ibid., pp. 62–3.
90 "Propositions," in Mather, *Magnalia,* 2:103.
91 Eliot, "Hamlet," p. 63.

5

THE AMERICAN MORPHOLOGY OF CONVERSION

When the eighteenth century looked back upon the Puritans' idiosyncracies, it was struck – sometimes with amusement and sometimes with anxiety – by the saints' apparent propensity for reporting the exact order of events in their conversions. So peculiar did this habit seem that Joseph Addison could vastly entertain the readers of *The Spectator* by recording a fictitious interview between an Oxford student and a Puritan minister who, brushing aside the youth's training in the classical languages, was interested only in "whether he was of the Number of the Elect; what was the Occasion of his Conversion; upon what Day of the Month, and Hour of the Day it happened; how it was carried on, and when compleated?"[1] With infinitely greater sobriety, the young Jonathan Edwards also contemplated the subject, recording in his diary at the age of twenty that "the chief thing, that now makes me in any measure to question my good estate, is my not having experienced conversion in those particular steps, wherein the people of New England, and anciently the Dissenters of Old England, used to experience it."[2] From a distance of only a few decades, friend and foe alike agreed, just as scholars do today, that the Puritans not only had devised a linear scheme that they thought workable but had held to it with relative ease; that "the operation of faith, as recorded in diaries and journals" – and conversion narratives – "did follow the prescription" – so much so that

1 *The Spectator,* 5 vols., ed. Donald F. Bond (Oxford: Clarendon Press, 1965), no. 494 (4:252).

2 *Works,* 2 vols., ed. Edward Hickman (London, 1835), 1:lxxiii. Eventually, of course, Edwards decided that the notion "that comforts and joys seem to follow awakenings and convictions of conscience in a *certain order*" was not a reliable sign of religious affections. See *Religious Affections,* ed. John E. Smith (New Haven: Yale University Press, 1959), pp. 151–63, and Smith's Introduction, pp. 19–21; and Alan Heimert, *Religion and the American Mind from the Great Awakening to the Revolution* (Cambridge, Mass.: Harvard University Press, 1966), pp. 38–42.

"many spiritual narratives of the period were not so much composed as recited."[3]

Yet people in the seventeenth century, no less than the young Jonathan Edwards (if not quite for his reasons), were troubled by the idea of having to schematize their experiences in talking about them. If to hindsight the business of describing one's conversion has looked like a matter of mechanically plodding through a prescribed series of statements, it did not necessarily seem so at the time. Granted that there was supposed to be a morphology of conversion, an established sequence of experiences – which Edmund S. Morgan has summarized as "knowledge, conviction, faith, combat, and true, imperfect assurance"[4] – the question remains: How helpful was such a morphology to the expression of religious experience – to the New England saint's articulation, for himself and for others, of what had happened to him? Could it serve as the basis of a *literary* structure and thereby help to solve "the problem of expression"?

For even so pious a New Englander as Captain Roger Clap, the answer was apparently no. To judge by his vaguely disorganized *Memoirs*, Captain Clap, like people in the Shepard group, from the first had great difficulty both in defining his religious experience and in believing that he had had it – the two sides of the coin that we examined in the last chapter;[5] and this was at least partly for the reason that he, like Jonathan Edwards, could not reconcile the nature of saving grace with the orderly method of its production.[6] Struggling with this problem, he was forced to conclude that

> God doth work divers ways upon the Hearts of Men, even as it pleases Him; upon some more sensibly, and upon others more insensi-

3 Morgan, *Visible Saints*, p. 71; Shea, *Spiritual Autobiography*, p. 106. Thus Jonathan Edwards warned that an undue emphasis on method was distorting people's perceptions to the point that in their relations, experiences were being "insensibly strained to bring all into an exact conformity to the scheme that is established" (*Religious Affections*, p. 162).

4 Morgan, *Visible Saints*, p. 72.

5 Although Clap's memoir is not strictly a conversion narrative, being both a history and an autobiography, I have attempted to discuss here the brief portion of his work that deals directly with his religious experiences in the 1630s, and which might have been offered for public testimony at that time had Clap not already been a church member (see Chapter 1). Alexander Young excluded from his *Chronicles* as irrelevant "Clap's exhortation to his children, and his account of his religious experiences, though excellent in their way" (p. 367, note 3).

6 "We are often in Scripture expressly directed to try ourselves by the *nature* of the fruits of the Spirit; but nowhere by the Spirit's *method* of producing them . . . that indeed is the clearest work (not where the order of doing is clearest, but), where the spiritual and divine nature of the work done, and effect wrought, is most clear" (*Religious Affections*, pp. 162–3).

bly; verifying the Text in the 3d Chapter of *John*, 8th Verse, *The Wind bloweth where it listeth, and thou hearest the sound thereof, but canst not tell whence it cometh, and whither it goeth: So is every one that is born of the Spirit.* Tho' we may hear the Sound of it, that is, be sensible that the Spirit works, or has been at work, yet not know whence it comes, *&c.* If ever there were the Work of Grace wrought savingly in my Heart; the Time when, the Place where, the manner how, was never so apparent unto me, as some in their Relations say it hath been unto them.[7]

Nevertheless, Clap does attempt to "hint a little unto you what I have found" and proceeds to review an autobiographical pattern, if not a full morphology, of conversion with which we are already familiar: a litany of youthful (and unimpressive) Augustinian sins, followed by a strained analogy to Saul's complicity in the death of Stephen, then a desire to hear the Word preached, and, finally, a love to the saints. But the pattern clearly does not serve; the account breaks off; suddenly Clap is speaking of his migration to New England and repeating that

I could not so find as others did, the Time when God wrought the Work of Conversion in my Soul, nor in many respects the Manner thereof; it caused in me much Sadness of Heart, and Doubtings how it was with me; Whether the Work of Grace were ever savingly wrought in my Heart or no?[8]

This time, however, Clap suddenly describes what sounds like a genuine religious experience. It begins (not surprisingly) with a liberating word from "Mr. *Cotton,*" namely, that " '*A little constant Stream of godly Sorrow, is better than great Horrour':* God spake to me by it, it was no little Support unto me."[9] It ends with Clap lying in bed at night telling himself that he would not commit sin even if he could be sure he would not be damned for it – and suddenly sounding remarkably like Mrs. Elizabeth White.

And God's holy Spirit did witness (I do believe) together with my Spirit, that I was a Child of God; and did fill my Heart and Soul with such a full Assurance that Christ was mine, that it did so transport me as to make me cry out upon my Bed with a loud Voice, *He is come, He is come.* And God did melt my Heart at that time so that I could, and did mourn and shed more Tears for Sin, than at other Times: Yea the Love of God, that he should Elect me, and save such a worthless one as I was, did break my very Heart. I say again, When I had most Assurance of God's Love, I could mourn most for my Sins.

Dear Children, Slight not serious Examination: *It is good to commune*

7 *Memoirs,* pp. 21–2.
8 Ibid., p. 24.
9 Ibid., pp. 24–5.

> *with your own Hearts upon your Bed.* That Glimpse of God's eternal Love which I had at that Time, was better to me than all the World; yea far better than Life itself.[10]

In his criticism of Clap's narrative, Daniel B. Shea, Jr., points out that the captain's "principal assurance of grace" comes from this "quasi-mystical experience," whereas "more objective evidence" is too generalized and lacks "the rigor with which the early settlers are said to have examined one another in founding churches."[11] Yet Clap's attempt to express the core of his experience by resorting to a more "English-style" emotional convention is touching just because it *is* "quasi-mystical," which is to say that it is at least a momentary attempt to break out of the bonds of analysis and "steps" and sequence – out of a pattern Jonathan Edwards later described as "first, such awakenings, fears and awful apprehensions followed with such legal humblings, in a sense of total sinfulness and helplessness, and then, such and such light and comfort."[12] Except for the light and comfort, these are not the "steps" Clap is interested in: As Shea observes, Clap's claims that "God has made me sensible that I am a Sinner," and that "Jesus Christ came to save Sinners, and why not me," fall pretty flat.[13] But if Clap is unable either to work up the necessary "great Horrour" demanded by the standard morphology (although not, we recall, by Cotton) or to pinpoint the exact stages of his conversion the way Mrs. White does, his emotional outburst, so like hers, sounds the alarm to remind us that in conversion narratives experience was felt to be more than could be rhetorically contained in a perfunctory arrangement of steps. In fact, the "failures" that Shea finds in Clap's autobiography as a whole[14] may be taken at least partly as a sign of New England's need to depart from established literary structures in order to accommodate a set of experiences that (as we have seen) are unprecedented just by virtue of their taking place in the new land and that must find expression within an imaginative framework only partially defined by the magistrates and ministers.[15]

Nevertheless, it must be admitted that Clap's "quasi-mysticism" and

10 Ibid., pp. 25–6.
11 *Spiritual Autobiography*, pp. 124, 123.
12 *Religious Affections*, p. 151.
13 *Memoirs*, p. 25; *Spiritual Autobiography*, p. 124.
14 Ibid., p. 123.
15 Shea calls attention to this very problem in observing that neither Clap nor Thomas Shepard himself is able to move his autobiography "coherently and comprehendingly from the smaller to the larger cosmos." Clap, he adds, "struggles to articulate a relation between his migration to New England and his new birth in the life of the spirit, but . . . their relationship is never precisely defined" (ibid., p. 119).

his tears do not answer the rhetorical problem: They do not seem suited to the American experience and, mild as they are, would certainly have proved as suspect in New England's churches as dreams, voices, or visions of the Devil. This, at least, is what we are led to believe by Giles Firmin:

> I remember Mr. *Thomas Hooker,* at a Meeting of about forty Ministers, put that question, What *Rules* they would go by in admission of Members into Churches? Will you go by the narration of the work of God upon them in Conversion? Or will you look at the frame wherewith they make their narration? One, saith he, comes and makes his narration with many tears; another he tells you plainly what God hath done, but he cannot shed tears as the other, but yet proves the better Christian, said he. To say no more, Tears are common to Hypocrites, and no infallible sign of soundness of Grace: Many are kept humble and poor in their own eyes for want of tears, when some (I fear) are proud of their tears.[16]

If this sounds repressive, it was an approach apparently understood and accepted by Shepard's saints, whose emotions, unlike Roger Clap's, were almost never directly or simply expressed in conversion stories. Thus Brother Jackson's maid (whose name has not come down to us) repeats outright Hooker's view–and favors it: "And on a fast day hearing signs of godly sorrow consisting not too much in tears as brokenness within nature. This suited my condition" (p. 121). Her flat tone seems to reflect Northrop Frye's definition of the confession as "introverted, but intellectualized in content," and brings to mind the charges of abstractness and impersonality laid at the door of the seventeenth-century conversion narrative. But this is all the more reason to ask: If the emotionalism of "tears" is unwelcome and if "brokenness within" is the desired condition, how is that condition to be externalized and vitalized in the narrative–especially in view of the fact, as Giles Firmin reminds us, that Thomas Shepard, too, was not much enamored of "tears"?

> Mr. *Shepherd* saith, *More are driven to Christ by the sense of the burden of an hard, dead, blind, filthy heart, then by the sense of* sorrows; *because a man rests in* sorrows *most commonly, but trembles and flies out of himself when he feels the other.*[17]

Unfortunately, as we have already seen, that burden of a hard, dead heart is precisely what kept the saints in a deadlock of inexpressible pain, unable to fly out of themselves despite Shepard's dramatic advice.

16 *Real Christian,* p. 86.

17 Ibid. For the original Shepard statement, see *The Sincere Convert, Works,* 1:97.

Burdened as well with strictures against too much emotional subjectivism – strictures that may have been as much self-imposed as imposed by the ministers – where were they to find an expansive, imaginative vocabulary, a lexicon of images, a dramatic vehicle to carry the weight of their experiences? Certainly the felt "lack of symbolic meaning" that marks the struggling soul, the need to build up a pattern associated with something larger than oneself, were not easily satisfied by the ready-made morphology that we have heard so much about – especially in view of the severe distractions of coming to America in the midst of it all. This is why many narratives start out according to the accepted blueprint but suddenly veer off, like Roger Clap's, just at the point of the migration – a "step" in the American morphology of conversion that turns out to be more of a sidestep. Hence almost any New England saint will follow Edmund S. Morgan's description of the "stereotype" to this extent:

> First comes a feeble and false awakening to God's commands and a pride in keeping them pretty well, but also much backsliding. Disappointments and disasters lead to other fitful hearkenings to the word. Sooner or later true legal fear or conviction enables the individual to see his hopeless and helpless condition and to know that his own righteousness cannot save him, that Christ is his only hope.[18]

But few will follow it when describing the central experience, the necessity for which so intimidated Roger Clap: "Thereafter comes the infusion of saving grace, sometimes but not always so precisely felt that the believer can state exactly when and where it came to him."[19] Instead, they sail away to America, where disorientation and guilt paint the whole world gray, and where in their confusion they keep bumping into their own sinful selves.

In this fog there is, however, one rock that the migrants can cling to, and they do cling to it in significant numbers. That rock is the Bible – a source not only of truth and stability but of words, images, symbols, patterns, all the paraphernalia of expression that the saints seem so sorely to need. When Brother Jackson's maid tries to give expressive shape to her "condition," this is the one place to which she can freely turn for help, and, in fact, her testimony is typical both of the women and of the servants in the group in their heavy use of Scripture. Her narrative, though brief, is thickly woven with Bible quotations ranging from Psalms to St. John and calling especially on the Old Testament prophets (not only Isaiah and Jeremiah but also Hosea and Zephaniah) and giving the reader an impression not so much of being marched

18 *Visible Saints,* p. 91.
19 Ibid.

through a morphology as of being led through the Bible. In its small way, the story recapitulates one aspect of Bible structure as well: It anticipates the "happy ending" by beginning with the certainty of eternal life for the "Sons of God" (from St. John's First Epistle, "Beholde, what loue the Father hathe shewed on vs")[20] and by rounding off with John's reassuring gospel message that "the God that is a God to Christ is a God to Christ[ians]" (pp. 119, 121).[21] In between, the saint (like virtually everyone in the Shepard group) tells her story almost entirely through her "hearing" of Scripture, that is, through preaching she has heard but using specific passages almost as if they were concrete objects that she can hold up to show us what she means. At times, the speaker interacts with Scripture in the usual sequential way, by first hearing it, then responding to it in terms of her personal situation:

> And hearing out of 2 Zephaniah – Lord will search Jerusalem with candles.* That place breaking Sabbath he spake against them and so I remembered this sin. (p. 119)
>
> * Zeph. 1:12.

> So feeling many sins and hearing Jeremiah 18 – is there no balm in Gilead† – showed reason why we lie in our wants because there is balm in Gilead. We go not to Christ. So I went on. (p. 120)
>
> † Jer. 18:22.

Such passages are not unlike the Bible references in the English narratives (where Scripture is used fundamentally as a gloss on events), except that here there is more likely to be a hint of emotional urgency that can narrow the distance between speaker and text:

> And after this the Lord sent affliction and frightened me with death. And being in trouble, I knew not what to do though I had prayed and read and frequented ordinances. And so, that affliction was continued and so I prayed to God to add to my days that I might live to make my calling sure.‡ And from Hezekiah's example some report I had that I might live for that end.§ (p. 120)
>
> ‡ Pet. 1:10. § 2 Kings 20:1–6. [Hezekiah, king of Judea, falls ill; he pleads with God, who responds by sparing him for fifteen more years. (Interpolation mine.)]

At still other moments of spiritual intensity, there is a truly integrated feeling, as if the speaker has forgotten that she is in an intellectual

20 This is the Geneva Bible version of 1 John 3:1, clearly echoed in the speaker's words "behold what love Father hath shown us."

21 *Christ[ians]*: my reading. Selement and Woolley give "Christ" here, and do not note the scriptural reference, which is probably John 20:17: "I ascend vnto my Father, & to your Father, and to my God, and your God." The Geneva exegetes explain in a note, "He is our Father & o^{r} God, because Iesus Christ is our brother."

relation with her materials at all, and allows them freely to meld with her imagination, so that we get an outburst like this:

> Hosea 2 – I'll betroth thee to me* – and setting out spiritual marriage of a king, making suit to a poor silly maid do but give thy consent and then care not for other things and Christ would be better than earthly husband. No fear there of widowhood so I took Christ then upon His own terms. (p. 120)
>
> * Hos. 2:19.

Obviously, the picture of a marriage and of a "king, making suit to a poor silly maid" has captured this particular maid's fancy in a way that makes it possible for her to apprehend her relation to God. But so, for that matter, has the New Testament symbol of Christ's kingdom as a pearl – a word she seems to savor, pronouncing it three times (p. 120). These images seem to have a special power for her. They are images of beauty (perhaps a poor silly maid no less than a great poet like Edward Taylor can feel imaginatively starved in Massachusetts), but most important, they are images of love and sacrifice, just as are the more explicit passages about "the sufferings of the Lord Jesus" (p. 120) and the devotion of the disciples, with whom her heart, "melted . . . in private" by the Lord, can identify at the end of her story:

> (1) They forsook all and followed Him.† (2) When Christ was to depart nothing broke their heart so much as then.‡ (p. 121)
>
> † Matt. 19:27; Luke 5:11; Mark 1:18. ‡ John 13:33–8; 16:16–20.

In the introverted but "impersonal" confession form (where even emotionally charged events may be assigned numbers), such Bible images can be the speaker's feelings – and her tears.

Similarly, Mrs. Sparhawk finds passages from the very emotional and vivid Hosea 2 to be "encouragements" – these being among the first direct citations in her heavily scriptural testimony. The first part of Hosea is a brilliantly poetical rendition of God's love for wayward Israel, cast into the metaphor of the long-suffering husband and the faithless wife; and the second chapter, which so captures the interest of both Mrs. Sparhawk and Brother Jackson's maid, is an especially strong blend of dramatic story and rich, sensual poetry, with the explicitly sexual rage of the lover giving way in a sudden, moving *peripeteia* to soaring, merciful affection. Not that Mrs. Sparhawk goes into all this at any length; she merely quotes two passages stressing God's mercy and forgiveness:

> And so had encouragements from other Scripture, Hosea, as He that had brought her to a wilderness would speak comfortably§ and that the Lord would have mercy on them that had no mercy.‖ (p. 67)
>
> § Hos. 2:14. ‖ Hos. 2:23; Exod. 33:19; Rom. 9:15.

But there is a sense that the alluring story has impressed her, like the "sermon of the woman that had the bloody issue" (p. 67); that it resides in her mind's life, that she carries it about with her, and that she may often turn to it (she quotes Hosea again at the end of her testimony). We can speculate about such choices of Scripture that in some way they fulfill a combined psychological and aesthetic need, embodying and vivifying people's feelings and vitalizing the landscape of their minds. That such vitalization is imperative may be indicated not only by the fact that Mrs. Sparhawk cites Scripture no less than nineteen times but by the outburst of these citations only after the central step of her "unwilling" migration (p. 66) to New England. It is as if she steps out of the ship directly into a Bible world; and indeed, a comparison of scriptural use in conversion narratives suggests that this is so, for it shows that in New England there is a dependence on, and an emotional and imaginative involvement with, the Bible that are not matched among most of the English converts.

Certainly there is no question about the fact that New England uses Scripture in conversion narratives with far more frequency and in a greater variety of ways.[22] The Shepard group cites the Bible 544 times – over 100 times more than the Walker group, though actually numbering ten fewer people; hence there is an average of eleven citations per speaker, as opposed to five for the Walker group. The Shepard group is more likely to quote Scripture without exact chapter and verse, that is, as an unselfconscious, integral part of the fabric of discourse. They are more eclectic, calling upon fifty-two of the sixty-six books in both testaments, whereas the Walker group uses only thirty-four books. There is also a slight preference for the Old Testament in the Shepard group, which cites it nearly half of the time, whereas the Walker people cite it a third of the time. In the same vein, of the nineteen biblical characters (apart from Christ and Satan) mentioned by Shepard's group, fourteen are from the Old Testament, but only six of the sixteen mentioned in Walker are from the Old Testament. Moreover, among Shepard's people, the second most frequently cited book is Isaiah, which Walker's group cites only half as many times. (The first choice in both congregations is the Book of Matthew.) We have already had a glimpse of the fact that Shepard's people show high interest in the "minor" prophetic books: They cite eight of The Twelve a total of twenty-two times, whereas Walker's larger group cites four books six

22 The Henry Walker congregation is here used for comparison, being roughly equivalent in size and character to Shepard's group. (The much smaller Rogers congregation uses noticeably fewer scriptural citations than either of the others.) For Shepard, I rely on Selement and Woolley's footnotes and their Appendix (p. 213). For Walker, I have made the equivalent calculations.

times. Hosea alone, the "Prophet of Divine Love," is quoted ten times[23] by seven individuals and is the most frequently cited of these intensely emotional, visionary, symbolical books.

The Shepard group's greater emphasis on the Old Testament is something we might expect, for we are used to the idea that the migrants thought of themselves as reenacting the pilgrimage of the ancient Israelites, with all the imagery that that concept entails. But there is a particular trend here that we ought to note, a particular involvement with the more sorrowful aspects of the Jewish experience that is not at all in line with the exultant "Exodus" theme. We saw earlier that the Shepard people scarcely mention the miraculous crossing of the Red Sea, and we may add that little explicit interest is shown in Abraham's covenant with God.[24] Despite some of the more sanguine uses to which Katherine, Brother Jackson's maid, and Mrs. Sparhawk put the Old Testament, there is in fact more pain than triumph in New England's dependence on the Hebrew Scriptures, a stronger sense of identification with the Jews' suffering than with their having been chosen by God; more, in short, of Babylon than of Canaan. Thus people seem to live imaginatively with the backsliding Jews in Jeremiah, with the wayward Jews in Hosea, with the exiled Jews through their heavy citation of 2nd Isaiah, frequently mentioning the fifty-fifth chapter, wherein God promises a restoration of the covenant when the people return to him. A large number of citations also appear for 1st Isaiah, that part of the prophetic book that concerns God's judgment upon Judah for her sins, and here, too, there is a heavy stress on that peculiarly Hebraic mixture of failure and hope, as in chapter 1:18 ("Though your sins be as scarlet, they shall be as white as snow") and 38:14 ("LORD, I am oppressed; undertake for me").

There is a similarly mournful cast over the picture when Shepard's converts speak of individual figures from the Bible: The majority of these personalities (mostly, again, from the Old Testament) are either exemplars of sin and wickedness, or they are perceived in terms of the trouble, sorrow, or punishment they must endure (whether or not they are eventually delivered from it). This is much less so among the Walker group, whose interest in figures like Job, Caine, and Judas is overmatched by their identification with Joshua, Paul, Nicodemus,

23 Selement and Woolley report nine references to Hosea in their Appendix, but there are ten separate footnote citations.

24 For example, Mrs. Stedman's lukewarm comment, one of only two about Abraham in the Shepard document (the other is by Old Goodwife Cutter), suggests that the idea of the covenant is not very helpful to her. Hearing in a sermon "that great God should enter into a covenant with him [Abram]," she confesses, "I was content the Lord should make what covenant He would . . . Yet I could not believe" (p. 105).

Simeon, Mary, Mary Magdalene, and the Woman of Canaan – all in contexts of favor and blessing. Moreover, no matter what the actual fate of these characters in the original Bible stories, the English saints tend to look for the silver lining: "I likewise took a view of the afflictions of *Joseph, David,* and *Job,* that did much ease my griefe";[25] the American saints as often as not see only the cloud:

> And I wondered the Lord had not cast me to hell and hearing of Jonah – do well to be angry★ – and I was affected. I could do nothing else but sin against God and I thought the Lord would cut me off. (pp. 182–3)
>
> ★ Jon. 4:4, 9.

In Massachusetts, for every happy Katherine who shyly rejoices that she is not like Judas (p. 101) there is more than one tremulous Goodwife Cutter who fears she is not like Abram (p. 145).

But most important is an odd difference in the English and American speakers' ways of relating their own selves to these personalities. The English saint almost always gives a straightforward application of the scriptural example to his own case, either through a formal simile or through a more direct personal conjunction with the figure. But in either case the speaker always keeps his own identity clearly distinct from that of the Bible character.

> Yet it pleased the Lord to bring many promises into my minde, and that example also of *Mary Magdalen,* and also of the Woman of *Canaan* beleeving; that as Jesus Christ had been gracious to them, so he would also be to me.[26]

> And the Lord hath since made me as he did *David,* to be contented as well with *his rod, as with his staffe;* and then, and since, I praise the Lord, I can say with *David It was well for me, that I was afflicted* . . . and I remembred Gods dispensations towards *Job* and *David,* and resolved with *Joshua, that I and my house would serve the Lord.*[27]

The American mode is not quite so cut-and-dried. True, there is some straightforward analogy or application of the English type:

> And so I thought the time of visitation was past and that it was with me as with Esau.† (p. 55)
>
> † Gen. 27:34–41.

> He questioned whether his repentance was right or no or whether no farther than the repentance of Cain and Judas.‡ (p. 36)
>
> ‡ Gen. 4:13–14; Matt. 27:3–5; 1 John 3:12.

25 "*Experiences of* M.K.," in Walker, *Spirituall Experiences,* p. 182.
26 "*Experiences of* E.R.," ibid., p. 367.
27 "*Experiences of* A.J.," ibid., pp. 62–3.

But there is also a tendency to stray across the strict boundaries of analogy, so that we often encounter an emotional urgency (like that of Brother Jackson's maid with the story of the king) that seems to blur the lines. When Goodwife Holmes testifies that

> so going to hear Mr. Wells – thou art Lord our God – and showed a false reliance and true that nothing could content soul that truly relied but the Lord. And that I found, and they had tokens as Tamar's ring* and will not the Lord own those tokens and are these nothing? So I. (p. 80)
>
> * Gen. 38:18, 25.

she is skipping around within a three-part analogy that contains many elements. There is Tamar with her tokens, the ring and bracelets that Judah gave her, and (implied) Judah's response to her reappearance with the pledges after their earlier sexual encounter: These things would be hovering in the background for a Bible-reading audience. Compared to all this, there are the true, reliant souls separated from the false ones and returning to God with their tokens (presumably their desire only for the Lord) and God's response to them. Then there is Goodwife Holmes herself, who thinks she has tokens; but to whom is she comparing herself? In effect she is drawing an analogy between herself and the analogy she has already drawn, but the final "so I" doesn't quite restore order: Is she like Tamar? Like the truly reliant souls? Is she in fact *like* anyone? This is imagination in the garb of linear thinking; compared to it, A.J.'s simile has the clarity of an isosceles triangle: A.J. at one corner, David at the other, the Lord on the apex with his rod and his staff. But to Goodwife Holmes, the logic of it isn't crucial; there is an immediacy of involvement with all the elements of the story highlighted by grammatical shifts in tense, number, and person that virtually blends speaker, regenerate souls, and Tamar all into one.

This tendency to bring real life into the closest possible touch with Scripture affects even very simple associations of the two realms. When Katherine

> looked upon Manasseh† and upon the scarlet sins of Isaiah made as white as snow.‡ (p. 99)
>
> † 2 Kings 21:1–18; 2 Chron. 33:1–20. ‡ Isa. 1:18.[28]

she was, admittedly, "looking into the word" (p. 99), but her language wants to make the book disappear, as if the evil king and the scarlet sins are immediately present before her. William Hamlet, "hearing of Adam's sin that that might make me miserable and this troubled me under my misery" (p. 126), is somehow more directly involved with

28 The phrase *as white as snow,* my reading, conforms to Isaiah. Selement and Woolley give "was white as snow."

our general ancestor than is T.G. in England, who happily "found much comfort in that glorious promise, which God made when *Adam* had sinned, that *The Seed of the woman should breake the Serpents head, Gen.* 3."[29] Moreover, the more emotionally charged the subject matter, the more such blurring of the boundaries occurs: thus with the appearance of Judas Iscariot. Here is Sister (Martha) Collins's line of association with the betrayer:

> And afterward I thought they were too strict in examining of members and at Boston hearing the reasons why they did not receive all that came over which I forget now. And I blessed Lord that followed me and after hearing when Judas was gone out then the Lord spake* and left sin to strike at some eminent ones. And though I did not persecute yet I persecuted God Himself and struck Him and so committed the unpardonable sin and knew not what to do. (pp. 131–2)
>
> * John 13:29–31.

As with Goodwife Holmes, we are faced with questions here that the grammar does not entirely answer. There is obviously a relationship between Sister Collins's doubts about the rules for church membership and Judas's betrayal of Jesus, between the necessity for pure churches and the necessity for Christ to send Judas away before he can speak to the disciples, between the persecuted Boston congregation and the little group gathered in Jerusalem, between the kiss given to Jesus and the blow struck to God. But Sister Collins is not a rationalist (she forgets the "reasons"; she "knew not" what to do); she is involved in soul struggles that require a different kind of mental activity, one that gives the impression, throughout the intermixture of thoughts and feelings and memories, that she is truly identifying with Judas, not merely making an analogy. Her wickedness in questioning Cotton's membership requirements apparently sweeps away all lines of distinction in a flood of self-recrimination and contradiction: She did not persecute, yet she did; she blessed the Lord, but she struck him. If this is merely being *like* Judas, she does not say so; for the moment, his guilt and confusion are her own.

An even more striking treatment of Judas appears in the narrative of Richard Cutter, Old Goodwife Cutter's son, who was about nineteen or twenty years old at the time of his confession. Contemplating his many sins through the filter of John 13, the same chapter that informs Sister Collins's story, Cutter is unable to break through his "obstinacy and hardness" by trying to identify with Peter in his refusal to let Jesus wash his feet (John 13:8). "Nothing stuck till he came to the 30th verse of the same chapter" – the one in which Christ sends Judas out on his terrible errand.

29 "*Experiences of* T.G.," in Walker, *Spirituall Experiences,* p. 314.

> And hearing those that were ready went immediate communion of it. And at the naming of the doctrine I thought I was not ready for Christ. And one reason because all were naturally unready but in use of terrors then – thou that art not prepared shall not enjoy Him – and very sad it was. And my heart did slight it but if I be separated from Christ 'tis that which makes angels stand amazed at it and I stood behind the meeting house. And from Judas went immediately out* and observed that one sin whereby some men pursue their perdition 'tis opposing of His members. And so by this sin many other sins were brought to mind and so could not speak to any. I could apply nothing but what was against the evil. (p. 179)
>
> * John 13:30.

Here again there is a complex intermixture of elements, but all have something to do with the basic theme of the passage, which is separation. Cutter's perspective on the problem of separation is very like Mrs. Collins's: He, too, links the departure of Judas from the circle of the disciples with the distancing of the unregenerate soul from both God and the church members. But in the midst of what might not have been much more than a somewhat muddled scriptural analogy, comes the fascinating information that this terrible sinner, so far from salvation that the angels stand amazed, also felt so much like Judas the betrayer (who "went immediately out" from the holy presence) that he, the speaker, "*stood behind the meeting house*" (emphasis added). What are we to make of this? Was the youth acting out the Judas scene in some access of dramatic frenzy, some wild desire for catharsis? Was he trying to express his own loathsomeness to himself, or to God, by removing himself from the brethren in order not to contaminate them? Was he, in his despair over sin, confusing himself with Adam and Eve hiding behind the trees in the garden? Was he so frightened by his own "lack of symbolic meaning" that he simply felt compelled to perform *some* kind of symbolic act? Or did he not, perhaps, really do it at all – only imagine himself doing it or wish that he had done it?

We can never know for sure the answers to any of these questions, but we can speculate about the last. One of the most significant things about this incident is the very fact that we *can't* tell whether it really happened. There are two possibilities: Either Richard Cutter is symbolizing a real experience, or he is creating a fictional, symbolic experience for his own persona, as if he were the narrator in a Charles Brockden Brown novel whose theme is "the bitterness of sin" (p. 180). But it doesn't matter which is true. Either way, the incident performs the same function for the purposes of the story, serving as a symbolic action that can embody any or all of the feelings described earlier (or others left undefined). To this extent, this swift, tiny stroke of the imagination is a true creative development. But there is another reason why the "real-or-imaginary" question is important. It means that we are no longer dealing just with the straightforward use of Bible content for purposes of analogy nor with the imaginative borrowing of the identity of biblical characters that seems to occur when the speakers have reached a certain emotional pitch. What we have here is a clue to an entire realm of perception from which most of these oddly elusive little narratives seem in fact to be emanating. The clue is not in the specific reference to Judas or in any direct quotation from the Bible but in the faintly mysterious, even other-dimensional quality that seems to imbue this passage. It is in the arresting image "angels stand amazed" and its swift, breathless succession by the stark, unexplained "and I stood behind the meeting house." Not, "I *went* and stood," or "I stood there for *an hour,*" but simply, "I stood"; so that we suddenly see the speaker there, not knowing how he got there; as if it were an incident without duration, without context; as if it were a dream – or a myth. This is why it is not enough to say that the Shepard people use the Bible so intensively because they need a repository of historical types or a lending library of aesthetic and affective images. These considerations cannot quite account for the feeling that we are dealing with a pervasive biblical *sensibility,* a scriptural – which is to say, a figural – way of rendering reality in general. It is more than the direct identification of each discrete event with something analogous in Scripture (this, in fact, is more the English habit), more than a sensual immersion in scriptural stories and imagery. It is the selection and representation of experience as if it were actually being seen through a biblical lens, through an approximation of the biblical angle of vision. Hence Erich Auerbach's noted characterization of Old Testament narrative method might well be applied to the Cambridge testimonies (note its appropriateness to the Cutter passage):

> The externalization of only so much of the phenomena as is necessary for the purpose of the narrative, all else left in obscurity; the decisive points of the narrative alone are emphasized, what lies between is nonexistent; time and place are undefined . . . ; thoughts and feeling remain unexpressed, are only suggested by the silence and the fragmentary speeches; the whole, . . . remains mysterious and "fraught with background."[30]

By contrast, the English narrative, as we have seen, is reasonably well externalized; tends to specify time, place, and detail; expresses

30 "Odysseus' Scar," in *Mimesis: The Representation of Reality in Western Literature,* trans. Willard R. Trask (Princeton: Princeton University Press, 1953), pp. 11–12.

thoughts and feeling with directness, often in conventionalized but useful, shared language; and eschews hiddenness or mystery, though it permits a mild mysticism. In short, it is a kind of narrative well suited to a step-by-step morphology of conversion. But if there is an American morphology, it emerges from an angle of vision and not from an arrangement of steps. It is a literary morphology, a total way of perceiving and talking about experiences rather than a particular, predetermined mold. It comes from the Bible, and yet it is not to be accounted for simply by the Puritans' devotion to Scripture, for the English Puritans were undoubtedly reading their Bibles as avidly as the New English were. It seems rather to have come about with the shift in people's actual situation – a shift that rendered the Bible, at least for a short time, the most comprehensible reality, or guide to reality, that they had. Of course, there are many ways in which devout people may interact imaginatively with Scripture. Joan Webber has pointed out that Bunyan's English Puritan sensibility "encounters" Scripture, or fragments of it, as if it were another person in the real world: At times he struggles and grapples with it directly, at times finds himself serving as "the arena in which the Scripture battle rages." On the other hand, claims Webber, John Donne, with his Anglican sensibility, "assimilates Scripture into himself – makes it speak Donne."[31] But the New England Puritan does neither: Instead, finding his new world confusing, disappointing, or amorphous, he assimilates himself into the Bible world and outlook, dwells there imaginatively, sees through its windows.

As scriptural as the English Puritan mind may be, it does not need to get its bearings in this way when it comes to telling a conversion story. For the English saints, the rock-bottom reality of England itself provides an outlook, and much of the Bible world tends to be relegated to dreams and visions, to phenomena that clearly exist on a different plane from the everyday realm. This allows the English narrative, despite its many imaginative devices, to be much more straightforward and "reality"-oriented in a conventional sense than the American one. Let us take, for example, the fundamental subject matter that we have established for the relation of religious experience – namely, sin and repentance. For T.G. (the same man in the Walker congregation who kept his distance from Adam), the problem is clear and easily expressible:

> I, like an unruly colt have kicked at [God's] fatherly protection, and runne into many grosse and vile sinnes.
>
> The first grosse one was, many kinds of unlawfull gameing, which held mee as a bondslave some thirty years or thereabouts, to the great indangering both of my body and soule; but yet it pleased the Lord to

31 "Donne and Bunyan," in *Seventeenth-Century Prose,* ed. Fish, p. 523.

> look graciously upon mee, and to give me afterwards an hatred against this vice . . .
>
> [The devil then] drew me into a liking of Tobacco, and with it into many other sins, which had almost brought me to as bad an end as the first.
>
> But the Lord . . . gave me an hatred against this vice also, and a resolution, *Never to take any Tobacco more;* . . .
>
> But yet about two or three yeares afterwards (againe) that old enemy of mankind, Satan, that roaring lion seeking whom he may devour, came again with turnings to destroy me, perswading me, that to drinke with my neighbours, was acceptable to God.[32]

And the solution is equally clear:

> First, a sight of my sins: secondly, a griefe and sorrow for them: Thirdly, a resolution to leave them: And fourthly, The Lord set mee, and carryed mee through a way to leave them, which was thus.
>
> I began to call to mind what was the greatest thing I loved in this world, and in the world to come, . . . then I vowed before the Lord, desiring his assistance, *That as I loved the holy Ghost the comforter, . . . I would never drinke above two reasonable glasses, or cups of Wine, or foure cups of Beer in any one place, or at any one time,* without any Equivocation, *And that when I came at any time into the doores of my house, if there were any controversie between my Mother and my Wife, or between the Servants and them, That then I would with gentle perswasions doe my best indeavor to end the controversie.*[33]

Here is a relation in which both matter and manner are orderly, sequential, externalized, commonsensical – everything, as Auerbach would say, in the "foreground." The sins have names and identities and can be recognized, quantified (even by the cupful), and banished. But if we turn to a superficially similar confession from the Shepard group, we find that though it seems to begin with the standard litany of sinfulness, it quickly escapes into a more scriptural-sounding, poetical, intangible space.

> I know I came in the world a child of hell and if ever any a child of devil, I. I had a father that brought me up to eleven years. He gone as I grew in years, I sought a match for my lust; and herein I have been like the devil not only to hell myself but enticing and haling others to sin, rejoicing when I could make others drink and sin. And for ought I know others in hell for them and the Lord might have given me my portion but when I lay in my blood,* love came to me in Cambridge. And hearing that no adulterers, drinkers should enter into the Kingdom of God† and so I knew my condition naught yet my heart was so

32 "*Experiences of* T.G.," in Walker, *Spirituall Experiences,* pp. 308–11.

33 Ibid., pp. 311–12.

naught that I would have my haunts. Yet I have been greatly affected in ordinances and I have had many resolutions then in my base rotten heart. And spirit many a time would have come into my heart and proffering blood and mercy. Yet I would have my lusts and haunts that I would have them dearer than God and Christ and mercy and heaven. And just it had been with God to give me up. (p. 86)

* Ezek. 16:6. ["I said unto thee *when thou wast* in thy blood, Live." The image is of an abandoned newborn infant, Israel, redeemed by God. (Interpolation mine.)] † 1 Cor. 6:9–10.

This confessor, John Stansby, is more inclined to talk about sins of the flesh than most of the Shepard group, but even he provides little concrete detail. He seems not so much to be telling a story of experience as giving an imaginative impression; there is an almost Poe-like imprecision in the incantation of "lusts and haunts," blood and hell, that is viscerally affecting and yet strangely unreal. In fact, there is virtually nothing in Stansby's narrative corresponding to what Erich Auerbach calls the "everyday" world. Auerbach points out that in Scripture "the sublime influence of God . . . reaches so deeply into the everyday" or "domestic" that the two realms are "basically inseparable."[34] This interpenetration of the sublime with the everyday is what all Puritan expression tries to achieve; but Stansby's narrative appears to live almost entirely on a plane of pure language, of mostly scriptural images and metaphors rooted, of course, in "everyday" and "domestic" elements of the ancient holy land but not of seventeenth-century England: The "fount opened," Christ "feeding of his flock," being "under vines and fig trees," God shooting "arrows in my heart" (p. 87). He never brings these figures back to (his own) earth, so to speak; and this is at least one reason why, for all his poetical bent, he cannot achieve in the story as a whole a completeness of expression about his own spiritual experiences, cannot escape from a verbal miasma of sinful-feeling vacillation (even though, like Mr. Sparhawk, he evidently did have a religious experience in Old England [see p. 87]). To the end, he retains some eloquence, describing himself as "a wayfaring man" with "chariot's wheels off" (a reference to Exod. 14:25), yet can only conclude lamely, "When I could not go to Christ yet to gaze for Him" (p. 88). How much firmer is T.G., our straightforward sinner from Walker's church, who simply declares: "I beleeve that God will save mee through Christ for ever."[35]

John Stansby's failure to resolve his narrative is the more poignant just because he is articulate and has experienced gracious feelings. But these things cannot save him – not, at any rate, as a narrator. If he had had or, more properly, if he were allowed to have, a fully mystical

34 "Odysseus' Scar," pp. 22–3.

35 "*Experiences of* T.G.," p. 316.

experience or even a "quasi-mystical" one like Roger Clap's, his temperament and talent might have worked together to produce a powerful expression of religious experience. If he had stayed in London and gone to join Henry Walker's church, perhaps he would have produced a narrative built around, or told through, his experience of the ordinary concrete world. In either case, there would have been some chance to achieve the fusion of experience and expression that a spiritual relation requires. As it is, something is still missing: There is plenty of expression but not much sense of genuine experience.

But if Stansby ends up floating around in a sea of unanchored images, a few others use a figural reading of the world to better advantage. One of these people is Mr. Andrews, the shipmaster. His narrative goes on for a while in the more conventional way: pious parents, religious upbringing, apprenticeship in a godly family, comfort in performing duties, then terror of conscience, hope, and backslidings, all accompanied by scriptural citations from both testaments. In the early part of his story Andrews talks about "going to sea," but all we hear about the experience is that "I had oft temptation to kill myself hence durst not carry a knife about me nor go near water" – a strange spot for a sailor to be in! (and an image that can only make us wonder if we are listening to rote phrases); and that "at sea I got books, searching between a true believer and a temporary," which were studied with alternating degrees of comfort and fear. But then comes a genuine change in the fabric of the story. Having fallen gravely ill in Spain, Andrews was ready to be buried in the sea (to escape the "papists" who "would dig me up or no"), but his health was miraculously restored by God. Lo and behold, he forgot this divine blessing, and the "temptation" came to build a new ship, to try to save himself by his own efforts.

> I built a new ship and my mind much upon it even upon the Sabbath. And I desired to deliver me from this whatever He did with me. But . . . that ship was split and all drowned but a few, four of my men myself naked upon the main topsail in very cold weather and on a morning some on the shore came with a boat. And glad I was that I lost my ship and so lost my sin. (p. 113)

We cannot help but feel, after the more conventional narrative Andrews began with, that we have suddenly plunged into a different imaginative world here, a world that really could be the Bible's. There is the same economy, vividness, and intensity of impression that we get from a Bible story: A simple, universal setting, human foibles and frailties, sparse detail given in high relief, clear strong images that seem to contain much beyond the literal; and yet it is a striking fact that there is no scriptural *content* or even specific language in this passage. Andrews is simply, suddenly looking at things in the biblical way, and this way helps him to trace the moral contours of his experience, to locate a meaning there. This meaning is brought out by treating the facts metaphorically, that is, by seeing the ship as the embodiment of his sin in presuming that he could preserve himself by building it. But the meaning is a hard one, like most Bible truths. Andrews's deliverance comes not only through the loss of the ship and its freight of sin but through the loss of almost everyone's lives; then through an understanding of the losses, and of the necessity for them; not only that, but through (and this is hardest of all) a genuine gladness for them and for the whole scheme that commands them. And all this is behind the one stark line: "And glad I was that I lost my ship and so lost my sin."

This is the first time that we have encountered a real life experience being treated in a metaphorical or tropological way – a way that expands the surface facts into something akin to truth for the speaker and undoubtedly for his audience. And to judge by the rest of Mr. Andrews's narrative, this mode of expression was indeed effective. It is as if, having given utterance to the layers of meaning in that one sentence, Mr. Andrews has fully realized them, for the rest of his narrative is peaceful and joyful. There is no "imperfect assurance" here; the second half of Morgan's morphology ("combat, and true, imperfect assurance") has disappeared. As a whole, the narrative is almost a new breed: part standard morphology, part New England compressed metaphor, part English assurance and peace. Yet it is scarcely like an English conversion narrative. There is, in fact, a seafaring story in the London group, by one T.R., who tells of his adventures in Guinea, Brazil, Ireland, and Virginia. The episodes are brief, colorful, and conventionalized, all filled with terrible trials, all told in minute detail, all ending with deliverance by "the Pilot of Pilots" from "the jawes of death."[36] Compared with the Andrews story, T.R.'s reportorial detail is especially striking:

> Our ship was all eaten with worms, . . . Pump pumping for the space of nine moneths, . . . Victuals was so small, that for one yeare and more we had no bread in our ship, but wee did eate the roots of Trees, . . . and for Beefe, one ounce for a man for a day, which stunke so, that none could have eate it but men in our case.[37]

He goes on to describe the drinking water, the dolphins that God finally provided for food, data about fog and rain and storm. And just as he realistically delineates all that we might want to know about the experiences, so his report on their moral significance explicitly delivers

36 "*Experiences of* T.R.," in Walker, *Spirituall Experiences*, pp. 390, 391.

37 Ibid., pp. 387–8.

all the meaning: Nothing is left unexpressed. This moral meaning is reflected in hair's-breadth escapes from shipwreck and drowning: There is no loss, only "great perill and danger of our lives,"[38] from which, in each case, the protagonists are snatched at the last moment.

> Our poore sick people cryed out, they were drowned, but within one houre after, by the mercy of God, we had faire weather, . . . God set us safe on Land, to our great joy and comfort, that before were almost past all hopes, so that he caused us to say with the Prophet *David, It was good for me that I was afflicted.*[39]

If there is anything of symbolism here, it is of the straight allegorical type: Their salvation from the sea is emblematic, a direct sign of God's favor. Even though it is good to be afflicted, there is no real irony in this situation, no specific moral complexity embedded within the actual circumstances, as with Andrews's story. It is a moral tale and contains a biblical quotation, but it is not biblical in the sense that the American story is, with (again, in Auerbach's terms) its " 'background' quality, . . . and preoccupation with the problematic."[40]

This distinction holds in other cases of suffering and loss; for example, in the war stories of the women we met earlier. Whether there is a narrow escape from disaster, as in Frances Curtis's story, or whether there is true, terrible loss, as in M.W.'s, the moral meaning of the experience follows upon it, is applied to it from the outside, and is fully explicated. The survival of Frances Curtis and her family is like that of T.R. and his ships: Their salvation from the rebels' bullets is emblematic of, paralleled and echoed by, God's "now . . . *satisfying* my *soul* with himself."[41] M.W. cannot make this simple a connection, because she *has* suffered the losses; her method is to go directly to Scripture for the meaning of her afflictions and for the expression of it, either drawing an analogy (she thinks of Paul's willingness to die for Christ in Jerusalem) or directly applying the "severall Promises of the Lord, revealed in his holy Word": John 15:7 ("abide in me") and Matthew 5:6 and 11:28 ("Blessed are they which doe hunger and thirst," "Come unto me all yee that labour").[42] But for Sister Crackbone, in the Shepard group, the impulse is to treat the experience of affliction itself as a symbol, to find, like Mr. Andrews, the moral meaning within it and to express that meaning, like him, in a compressed, metaphorical way and not, as in the English narrative, by laying it out in a full, orderly

38 Ibid., p. 389.
39 Ibid., p. 393.
40 "Odysseus' Scar," p. 23.
41 Rogers, *Ohel*, p. 412[11]
42 "*Experiences of* M.W.," in Walker, *Spirituall Experiences*, pp. 13–14.

explication. Sister Crackbone's experience, however, has an added element: Unlike that of Mr. Andrews, it is symbolically interwoven with the migration itself.

Sister Crackbone testifies that in Old England one of her children died and that she was sure "it was because I had not prayed for them" (p. 140).[43] She thus comes to the new world with an old burden of sin and sorrow, and this contrast is echoed in her house figure: "And when I had a new house yet I thought I had no new heart." The figure can be read a number of ways. First, the house is like herself: She lives inside it as her heart lives inside her. But this is more a conceit than a mere simile: The house is new, like her new location, but the thing inside it, her heart, her inner self, is old, sinful, like the old world and the old Adam. The inside–outside theme is echoed by her use of a common metaphor: "I was under wings of Christ, one of them [the government] yet not under both [she is still outside the church]."[44] Stuck in this halfway position – old self in new place, in the physical plane but out of the spiritual one – Sister Crackbone does next what most good Puritans do: She turns to the means, "prayed to the Lord to make me fit for church fellowship"; but "the more I prayed the more temptation I had. So I gave up." This is the point at which many New England conversion narratives begin to slide downhill, to get lost in confusion and inexpression. Instead, Sister Crackbone gives an extraordinary, spare, but expressive resolution to her story.

> And seeing house burned down, I thought it was just and mercy to save life of the child and that I saw not after again my children there. And as my spirit was fiery so to burn all I had, and hence prayed Lord would send fire of word, baptize me with fire.* And since the Lord hath set my heart at liberty. (p. 140)
>
> * Matt. 3:11; Luke 3:16.

This is not a simple figure. The house-burning does not stand for a straightforward punishment of the kind feared by Frances Curtis: "*I heard my Husband* was killed by the *Rebels,* which *I* feared was by my *sins*";[45] or indeed, by Sister Crackbone herself earlier in her story: "And so being married and having poor means and having afflictions on my child and took from me and so troubled what became of my children. And to hell I thought it was because I had not prayed for them" (p.

43 Evidently there were only two Crackbone children. The one who survived, Benjamin, "was about 5 or 6 years old when His father Joyned here" – and was later disinherited (Stephen P. Sharples, ed., *Records of the Church of Christ at Cambridge in New England 1632–1830* [Boston: Eben Putnam, 1906], p. 12).

44 Interpolations mine.

45 Rogers, *Ohel,* p. 412[11].

140). Nor is it a moral lesson of the kind Anne Bradstreet construed when her own house burned down:

And, when I could no longer look,
I blest his Name that gave and took,
That layd my goods now in the dvst:
Yea so it was, and so 'twas jvst.
It was his own: it was not mine;
ffar be it that I should repine.
. . . .
Ther's wealth enough, I need no more;
Farewell my Pelf, farewell my Store.
The world no longer let me Love,
My hope and Treasure lyes Above.[46]

In Bradstreet's poem the elements–house, flames, furniture, and the poet herself–are presented in linear array, and although the house figure is the controlling metaphor in the poem, pointing to the heavenly house the speaker will one day occupy, it is not identified or merged with the speaker's own inner state. But Sister Crackbone's is a complex metaphor: Like Mr. Andrews's ship sinking under the weight of his sins, the Crackbone house burns by the blaze of her own "fiery spirit," so that, by an act of imaginative expression, the speaker's sin and her misfortune are inextricably intertwined. And like Mr. Andrews's shipwreck, the fire is also a blessing–not only because one learns to bear up under any worldly loss but because it is intrinsically good: It burned up the house that had the sin "in" it. But Sister Crackbone goes even further than Mr. Andrews: Her sin is a remnant of her old life in England, where she "saw not after . . . my children." Now she is freed of the sin by the mercy, both symbolic and actual, of having had her other child spared from the flames, so that the fire symbolically both burns up her old life and self and offers her a new one (symbolized by the child) in the new world. And this new life is itself symbolized by fire: The fire's consumption of Sister Crackbone's fiery spirit–fighting fire with fire, so to speak–has made way for the Holy Spirit to come in, so that her final prayer echoes John the Baptist's promise that "one mightier than I cometh" who "shall baptize you with the Holy Ghost and with fire" (Luke 3:16). In this way, from a literary and expressive standpoint, Sister Crackbone has made an interlocking chain of metaphorical associations and transformations that has activated her understanding, and this understanding, too, "hath set my heart at liberty."

One might even say (or hope) that the earlier "inside–outside" problem is now transcended, that true "liberty" carries the speaker beyond worrying about *where* she is because she has in fact resolved the prob-

46 *Works*, pp. 40, 42.

lems of conversion, of expression, and of the migration itself all at once. This may be too much to claim, but Sister Crackbone's narrative at least demonstrates how these problems can get knotted up together and how a figural way of apprehension can help to relieve the anxiety of being caught among them. In effect, she and Mr. Andrews have taken Shepard's advice: They have "flown out of themselves" by metaphorical means, by imaginatively transforming something real in their experience into a spiritual truth, not something from a dream or from a book – even the greatest, truest book – but from the "text" of their own lives. Given the apparent disappointments and confusions attendant upon *any* kind of experience when viewed through the mists of Massachusetts Bay, this was no mean feat. But it could not have been done without the Bible, without its nurturing of eye and heart in the apprehension and expression of "layers" of metaphorical meaning. Of course, such an approach to religious experience, such an American morphology of conversion, could not be an airtight, lock-step system; but for that very reason, even its failures evince something of the intensity – and the mystery – of the scriptural vision that suited the unknown American experience.

6

EPILOGUE: THE SECOND GENERATION

There is a page at the beginning of Thomas Shepard's notebook on which he jotted down, for purposes unknown, a few words from Scripture. "Looke vpon the glory of woorke," he wrote; "to rayse vp a temple lay foundation of many generations." Shepard was obviously thinking of the prophecy in 3d Isaiah, after the return of Judah from exile, that "thou shalt raise up the foundations of many generations; and thou shalt be called, The repairer of the breach, The restorer of paths to dwell in" (Isa. 58:12), and it may be that he was planning a sermon based on that text. But turning the page, the reader encounters the first of the fifty-one confessions Shepard recorded at Cambridge that we have been discussing here; thus the line from Isaiah seems to express some hope of his that such a collection of religious experiences could itself be a foundation, not only of this particular church but of the future glory of an exiled people restored.

If so, one wonders what Shepard might have thought as he gathered the last few testimonies in his notebook and began to glimpse the spiritual contours of the rising generation of new church members. For there is at the end of even so early a document as his the distinct flavor of a transition between two generational worlds. The break can be detected just after Goodman With's poignant, convoluted testimony of January 7, 1644–5, where Sizar Jones, the forty-eighth speaker in the group and a recent college graduate whose confession followed With's within the year, shows himself to be as garrulous as With is faltering, as unruffled as With is distressed, and apparently as secular-minded as With is scriptural-minded (in four pages of talk, Jones cites the Bible three times, whereas With, in his slightly longer testimony, quotes the Bible ten times). It is as if, in With's confession, something in the first generation of adult saints, some intense and excruciating inwardness, has gone about as far as it can go, leaving the younger generation to veer off in another direction.

This difference shows up not only in the superficial tone and manner of the two men but in their explicit expressions of the meaning of what they are doing in giving a relation at all; and oddly enough, it is the smoother-tongued Harvard graduate who has the greater difficulty with this question. Thus when the elders ask Goodman With "What is your chiefest desire in secret when no other?" he answers concisely, for all his fear and confusion elsewhere in his relation, "That the Lord would manifest himself more to my soul in Christ and power of ordinances" (p. 197). But when the elders ask Sizar Jones "How may it [the soul] know it had true faith?" he cloaks himself in this elaborate reply:

> Though the soul might have many fears, if faith was so built upon Christ as to save it from greatest evil, wrath of God and sin. And this last was when the soul did strive against sin and was at war with sin and Christ delivered soul from wrath when it made it prize favor of God. This did give me some hopes I might have true faith for I saw word was ground of faith and not word but Christ in that word and had delivered my soul from sin and set my soul at enmity from it, not only one but all sin. (p. 202; interpolation mine)

This is, compared with the other, a strangely lukewarm answer: Despite his attention to sin and wrath and "greatest evil" (and his claim to have been delivered from them), Jones conveys, overall, neither the compressed anguish of a Goodman With nor the poetical intensity of a John Stansby. His is a rational, "linear" speech – no conscious "problem of expression" here – but a kind in which the attempt to be logical, expository, and correct is at odds with the crucial and volatile nature of the subject matter. Thus, despite its concentration on the vocabulary of sin, it does not give the impression of being the heartfelt effusion of a truly worried man – much less of one illumined by grace. Goodman With's confession is alive with words like "pity," "joy," and, above all, "love" (even if he does not think he has these things, he yearns for them); not one of these words is uttered by Sizar Jones in all his testimony. In the end, one feels that Goodman With knows why he wants to be saved but that Sizar Jones has lost touch with some vital part of that grave life-and-death question.

The final speakers in the group – Goodman Funnell (John Furnell), one anonymous confessor, and the young William Ames – show similar characteristics even while varying the liveliness of their presentations. All seem to be caught in a web of wordiness and abstraction that spins on too long and from which they cannot extricate themselves. It is as if they simply don't know what to say, even though they are evidently educated, knowledgeable about religious matters, and articulate. There is no complaint here, as there was among the earlier church members, that "I cannot now express myself"; only a feeling that beneath the layers of proper language there is not very much to *be* expressed.

> First sermon here I remember this expression – that many times such was the state of one under misery that he stood between Christ and the devil, Satan pleading it is right that he had been his slave so long and pleading against justice that such a one between Christ and his sin. Yet Christ would manifest His power at last. And though soul could not answer all objections, yet Christ would answer all objections of Satan and his own heart that as he had died to conquer sin and Satan so he would do it and hence exhorted all that had seen their misery to look upon Christ and attend upon the means, which I found to be spoken seasonably to me as being in that condition. (p. 207)

No wonder that at the end of this testimony one of the elders wants to know one simple thing: "When the Lord gave you some hopes of His electing favor?" (p. 208). If this question is an instance of the much-criticized "unreasonable" demand to specify "the time when, the place where, the manner how," it may also be a way of pulling people back to the point, of rescuing them from the smoke screen of their own overworked language.

But in one respect, the expression of the younger saints does retain intensity, sincerity, and directness. As William Ames put it, "When encouragements came in that I was born of good parents in covenant yet I could not but see I might be Esau" (p. 211). This is the emotional heart of the younger generation's testimony, here heightened at the crucial moment by the Bible image of the supplanted son – as well as by our knowledge that this particular speaker is the actual son of the revered " 'Doctor Ames, of Famous memory' " (p. 209). Despite his youth, confesses Ames, "I could not be quiet with fears of eternal death and other death to young as well as old," especially when "I saw young ones wrought up and brought home to God." Similarly, he is able to draw comfort from the thought of "orphans which are helpless, heartless and strengthless and when soul felt itself thus, then Christ would not leave, which encouraged me, for if any ever were so, I was" (pp. 211, 212). Ames, of course, was a semi-orphan (at the age of fourteen, he had migrated to New England with his widowed mother), and it is notable that the one touch of imaginative complexity in his narrative is in this double use of the orphan figure to signify his own two "estates." But even beyond his personal situation, Ames in this respect is typical: The anxiety of being heir to "the foundation of many generations" seems to provide most of the imaginative energy in the few later narratives that have come down to us.

Almost all these later testimonies are from Shepard's own congregation, under the ministry of his student and successor, Jonathan Mitchel

(Shepard died in 1649), and were copied down by Michael Wigglesworth, then a young Harvard tutor, in the early 1650s.[1] Among the handful of people whose declarations of faith Wigglesworth preserved, two were in fact the children of people whose relations appear in the Shepard document: John Collins, the son of Edward and Martha Collins (see pp. 81–4, 130–2), and John Greene, the son of Percival Greene, a Cambridge church member whose relation has not survived, and of Mrs. (Ellen) Greene (pp. 117–18). (A third confessor, Joseph Champney, may have been related to Goodwife Champney [pp. 190–1], although there were two Champney families in Cambridge at the time.) And yet, without this biographical information, we would be hard put to say that the people whose spiritual experiences are set down in Wigglesworth's little diary had anything at all to do with the people whose stories we have been hearing. For as we have begun to see, they seem to live, figuratively and imaginatively speaking, in another world. It is not only that these troubled people seem obsessed with their obligation to live up to the religious expectations of the first generation – something we would expect, which has been amply investigated by scholars of Puritanism.[2] The very existence of such a central obsession

1 This discussion is based on six relations of religious experience, all but one of which were delivered in Cambridge, recorded at the end of Michael Wigglesworth's published *Diary . . . 1653–1657*, as edited by Edmund S. Morgan. Wigglesworth's principles of selection are unclear, although it is entirely possible that only five people joined the Cambridge church during the few years he was there. Fortunately, his notes are very complete and have been scrupulously transcribed by Morgan. However, Morgan's introductory statement (p. xiv) to the effect that all the relations were "apparently" made at Wigglesworth's Malden church is contradicted by the facts that: (1) one anonymous relation is marked "At Cambridge" by Wigglesworth himself; (2) three identifiable confessors (Collins, Greene, and Champney) were Cambridge residents, closely related to people who testified in the earlier Shepard congregation, and all refer by name to the Cambridge ministers and elders; (3) Mrs. Wigglesworth's relation, the last one in the diary, is marked "at Maldon," and would not be thus set apart if all had been given there; (4) Wigglesworth was a resident tutor at Harvard during the years when the first few relations were given. Moreover, though the Malden church records are lost, Collins and Greene are listed in the Cambridge church records as members in full communion as of 1658. (Champney died before the church records began.)

2 References to the "generations" herein are meant as rough designations: on the one hand, to people who migrated as adults and, on the other, to the first people born in New England or those who migrated as children. There are few conversion narratives from this second group, and the ensuing discussion is not intended as a scientific or sociological study of an entire generation. It is speculation about changing modes of literary perception, based on an admittedly small but interesting transitional sample from the very early period. No direct comparison is intended with larger, later groups of "children" treated by Robert G. Pope in his study of *The Half-Way Covenant: Church Membership in*

might even be a link with the first generation: The fathers, after all, grappled with their spiritual expectations of America and of themselves in relation to the new setting; the sons grapple with the fathers' expectations of them in some similar ways. But however similar or different the two sets of problems may be, there is a definite change in the way people are perceiving and talking about their spiritual affairs, the way they are shaping them into an imaginative framework, the way they are telling their "story." And it is this change that makes the later conversion narrative, after only ten years of American experience, a different kind of literature.

At first sight, the extreme concentration on parents and parent-figures seems to operate in the story much as the dislocations of migration had for the fathers: Worries about "their parents going to heaven but themselves shut out,"[3] along with "my sin in not honoring my father and mother" (p. 121) and "great and gross disobedience to my parents," (p. 110) threaten to paralyze both the "expressions and affections" as much as before. But in comparison with their fathers, the speakers seem to have greater surface agility in handling language and, at the same time, a much weaker imaginative life. For example, when Joseph Champney speaks of breaking the fifth commandment, he immediately invokes "first Isaiah The Lord complains of his people that he had brought them up but they rebelled against him I thought the Lord had done so to me but I had rebelled against him and had not known him" (pp. 121–2). This is the familiar analogy between rebellion against parents and rebellion against God, but it is an analogy that leads to no resolution and to no further insight: only to fitful hopes "that he who had been my father's God that he would save me from that wrath due to sin and from sin" (pp. 122–3); only to the recourse of "I told my father of it and he wished me still to seek after the Lord" (p. 123). For all his variations on the theme of the disobedient child, Champney never gets near to "flying out of himself" as Shepard would have wanted. Somehow there is no vital spring, no "inward principle" within his expressive mode.

One immediately apparent problem is the way Champney employs the Bible in a halfhearted associative way that seems to do nothing to enliven or deepen his perceptions. Indeed, one of the striking character-

Puritan New England (Princeton: Princeton University Press, 1969) and by Emory Elliott in *Power and the Pulpit in Puritan New England* (Princeton: Princeton University Press, 1975).

3 "John Green's Relation," Wigglesworth, *Diary*, p. 115. In this chapter, all references are to Morgan's edition of Wigglesworth's diary and will henceforth be cited in the text by page number. Quotations will appear, however, in roman style and not in the italics of the Morgan edition.

istics of the Wigglesworth collection is its heavy, yet relatively unproductive, dependence on the Bible. Thus six people quote the Scriptures about sixty times, and, like the earlier generation of narrators, they select about equally from the Old and the New Testament. Yet these similarities are only superficial, for though the scriptural surfaces have been well mastered, the meanings have not been internalized: chapters, verses, "that place" are scrupulously cited, but the Bible is no longer embedded in the fabric of thought or discourse. This is not to say that Bible truths are not *felt*. Thus John Greene testifies:

> 5 Matthew blessed are the poor in spirit for theirs are the kingdom of God From thence I thought I was one that was poor in spirit that had no grace or good in me no hope or help nothing in me all my prayers and tears were nothing as they came from me nothing but what might cause God loathe me. (p. 116)

Obviously, these words are deeply felt indeed: The passage from Matthew triggers an intense emotional response in the speaker. But, unlike his predecessors, neither does he move ahead within the Scriptures for further insights nor does he continue to employ the scriptural or figurative *mode* of thought (like Mr. Andrews or Sister Crackbone) to reach a resolution of his sorrows. Instead, immediately upon thinking of the scriptural passage, he moves "from thence" *away* from the Bible and the biblical mode and down into his own flatly reported feelings. The speaker is no longer – here or elsewhere in the Wigglesworth notes – "living inside" the Bible or even living intimately with it, as T. S. Eliot said in another connection, lodged inside the cerebral cortex, the nervous system, and the digestive tracts. At times the attitude toward Scripture is even reduced to a kind of polite homage. Thus Sizar Jones "saw word was ground of faith and not word but Christ in that word"; yet for all that, there was literally *not* a word of the Word in the passage we looked at, still less any trace of the expansive, figural method of apprehending reality that comes from being steeped in the Bible. Lip service notwithstanding, the Bible is no longer fully alive in such cases (even though Jones himself, like Ames, is the son of a minister); and this means that if there is to be an intense imaginative and emotional involvement with some pattern, as Northrop Frye says, larger than oneself, it is going to have to sink roots in some other place.

Appropriately enough, we can see such a pattern trying to take shape in the testimony of John Collins – appropriate because Collins was the son of a deacon of Shepard's church, a graduate of Harvard College, and eventually a minister himself: He went to England in 1653 (shortly after delivering his relation) and spent the rest of his life as a pastor, first in Edinburgh and then in a London church.[4] In short, Collins was a figure of transition – between the generations, between the Englands, and, perhaps most important, between old and new ways of apprehending religious experience. Some hints of that transition are apparent in the first sentence of "the relation of Mr. Collins":

> I desire to look at it as a mercy for which I shall ever have cause to bless God that he has pleased to let me live under glorious living gracious dispensers of the Scripture and has out of his grace caused me to be educated under such parents and tutors whose care it was to commend me to be conversant in the holy will. (p. 107)

From here to the very heart of his story, the one thing the reader can never lose sight of is the *people* with whom Mr. Collins is surrounded and through whom he comes to God. Scripture is important, but it is virtually inseparable from its "glorious living gracious dispensers": his parents, Mr. Hooker, Mr. Dunster, Mr. Mitchel, and, above and beyond all these, "that blessed man," Mr. Shepard. Nothing could be more familiar in conversion narratives than the naming of ministers and the recollection of their sermons: In fact, no fewer than forty-five different English and New English preachers are mentioned by the first generation of Shepard converts. But nowhere in all of their fifty-one testimonies is there anything like the emotional involvement with Shepard that appears in Mr. Collins's relation. It is more than emotional involvement – it is virtual apotheosis; for in the course of the narrative, Shepard comes close to assuming the identity of Christ himself, and through that transformation, Collins himself is converted.

The speaker begins in a "Christless condition" (p. 107): careless, neglectful, backsliding, hardened against the day of wrath, formal and hypocritical, and so "corrupted" that "I thought it just with God to bring distraction [*sic*] on the whole country society congregation that belonged to me and I thought that was the cause of all the crosses they met with" (p. 109; interpolation mine). He is, in short, the guilty child of New England, who nevertheless still "thought the Lord might wail over me as a tender father over a . . . son" (p. 109); for this, of course, is the great, the overriding hope throughout: the yearning for the father. But "I had dealt treacherous in his covenant," and "My time was past" (p. 110). Then comes the crisis. Collins suffers a wound or injury of some sort (a punishment for "great and gross disobedience to my parents")[5] and

4 Cotton Mather wrote a brief "Life of the Collins's." See *Magnalia*, 2:139–41.

5 According to Cotton Mather, it was an actual physical injury (ibid., 2:139).

> when I laid so sore wounded it pleased God to show me more of my vileness (when I lay sore wounded) and also to such great pains as God stirred up Mister Shepard to take for me and with me who came and prayed with me and wrestled with God for my life. (p. 110)

This is the turning point, for now that Shepard has prayed, and only now, "the Lord was pleased so far to affect me that I saw something into the nature of sin and what infinite wrong I did to God" and "how foolish I had been to disobey my parents." Now that Shepard has prayed, Collins sees, in a passion of insight, that it is not against parents or ministers but "against thee against thee only have I sinned [Ps. 51:4] . . . It was to him that I had done that wrong" (p. 110; interpolation mine). And now that Shepard has prayed for him, he begins to wonder whether Christ does.

> Though I should be lame all my life yet I thought that exceeding easy that I had my life for a prayer. This the Lord continued by a sermon I pray not for the world [John 17:9] He showed there were a world of men and women that Christ never prayed for much less died for therefore it stood everyone in hand to consider whether Christ Jesus had prayed for him or no I knew no provision why Christ should pray for such a poor vile wretch as I yet I thought it were an infinite mercy if he had . . . but I feared he had not (p. 111; interpolation mine)

But Shepard had. Shepard had prayed for him the way Christ prays for his elect; and infinitely more than that: For now Collins claims that, like Christ, Shepard had died for him – and for *his* sins.

> The Lord stirred my spirit all the time that that blessed man lived from that least visitation of his and when God took him away he struck me with astonishment as [I] knew my sins had deserved it. (p. 111)

At this point, the guilty son's former responsibility for the troubles of "whole country society congregation" has been transferred entirely to the person and death of Shepard – almost as if to Christ suffering on the cross. And indeed, like the disciples squabbling among themselves, feeling lost and broken after the crucifixion, Collins is "sensible of many great outbreakings of my corruptions soon after." A deep depression sets in, almost like the mood of the three days when Christ was in the tomb.

> Mr. Mitchel mentioned those had especial cause to bewail his death whom God had begun to do some good to by him but the work was left in the midst and I feared God &c. Yet God stirred me up to desire he would not leave his own work in me. (p. 111)

And to some degree God does not: At least, from this point on, Collins climbs (slowly and with much backsliding along the way) to a certain tentative "hope that I should see the face of a reconciled father in Christ Jesus" (p. 113). But he never has a joyful experience, never "flies out of himself," only feels a kind of relief, the relief of the incorrigible child who marvels at the fact that his father may finally, actually be willing to forgive him anyway.

There are undoubtedly many explanations for the tentativeness and inadequacy of Collins's conversion (though among the Wigglesworth collection, it is the strongest). Yet the reader cannot help but suspect that the emblemization of Shepard as Christ, as mediator, at the central point of the story has something to do with the diminution, if not of the experience (which ultimately is unknown to us), then certainly of the quality and conviction of its expression. This need to resort to a figural employment of the actual Thomas Shepard – of a living man who was personally known to Collins – suggests that something is happening to the way people think about divine things or to their ability to think about them. The change is subtle but real; we glimpse it even in the words of the minister, for Jonathan Mitchel himself lamented at Shepard's death:

> What a blessed thing it is to have this mediator, the man Christ Jesus to go unto, when I have no friend that I can fully speak to, and open all my complaints and ails into his bosom? I think, were Mr. Shepard now alive, I would go and intreat his counsel, and help, and prayer. Why, now I may go freely into the bosom of the man Christ Jesus, who is able, faithful, tender-hearted above the best of meer men.[6]

Understandably grieved, Mitchel nevertheless conveys the impression, simply by setting up this comparison between Shepard and Christ, that the man, the earthly friend, is somehow preferable to "the man Christ Jesus." Of course mercy has a human heart, pity a human face; but Mitchel's lament reflects a slight shift of emotional weight toward the human part of the equation, toward the tangible, the visible, the worldly – and, most of all, toward the inevitable need to choose between these and the supernatural realm.

For the narrators in the Wigglesworth group, this shift goes even further. It is not enough that Shepard appear as a teacher: "Mister Shepard spoke in his catechize of man's misery by nature" (p. 114); or as a prophet: "mr. shepard spoke to this purpose I tell you young persons that have passed your 20 years and slept out your opportunities tis a wonder of wonders if ever God show you mercy" (p. 119); or even as a living witness: "the Lord spoke oft to my heart by that good man"

6 Cited ibid., 2:91.

(p. 119). In the end, through his own death, he must actually serve in the story as a Christ figure:

> After his death I thought God might just speak to me now no more or if he raised up an other why that he should send him to preach blindness and hardness to me yet after this God did speak to me. (p. 119)

But this miraculous "resurrection" of God's voice is not enough: Neither Collins nor this narrator (whose name is not recorded) is able to express any real change, and for the very reason the anonymous saint gives: "Christ not precious in thought" (p. 119) – at least not as precious as the memory of Thomas Shepard.

This preference for the memory of Shepard over the presentness of Christ is plainly seen in the language and imagery of the later conversion narratives: The delicate balance between matter and spirit, tangible and intangible, sign and meaning, has tipped so far that the "glorious living gracious dispensers of the Scripture" have become more real, more vital than the thing dispensed. They contain, surround, embody the Word; they give it shape as they "dispense" it – and not (not quite) the other way around, as before. Therefore, they and not Christ the Word become the center and the spring of the testimony of religious experience – and they, being "meer men," cannot carry the spiritual load. The attempt to transfer symbolic power from Christ to "meer men," from source to vessel, inevitably leads to a literary dead end, just as does the transfer of symbolic power from the spirit to the letter in the apprehension of the Word: Indeed, in Christian terms, these are the same thing. And this is what Shepard himself would have told them, for when he thought upon his own place in God's scheme, he came to this understanding:

> 'Tis (I saw) an amazing glorious object to see God in a creature, God speak, God act, the deity not being the creature and turned into it but filling of it, shining through it, to be covered with God as with a cloud, or as with a glass lantern to have his beams penetrate through it. Nothing is good but God, and I am no farther good than as I hold forth God.[7]

Shepard's conviction that God shines through the creature, that all phenomena are somehow translucent, extended, of course, to language and most especially to Scripture. In the end, it was the slipping away of that conception of Scripture, symbols, and language in general that diluted the strength of the conversion narrative as a means of expressing spiritual experience. When John Greene "thought of that 130 Psalms. 2. Out of the depth I cried to thee," his impulse once again was to move

7 Shepard, "The Journal," *God's Plot,* p. 111.

directly away from it and to sink into his own confused feelings, from which he could find "no way out."

> [Mr. Mitchel] showed a soul in the depth of his misery should cry to the Lord I thought I was one myself under the power of Satan an enemy to God and so no way out to perish and had no power in myself to look up to God for help altogether miserable and vile as I was in myself when I went to seek the Lord in secret and to hear God's word and nevermore corruption and temptation prevailing. (p. 115)

When Sister Moore, a decade earlier, thought of the same verse of Psalm 130–"Being fearful of being humbled enough–out of depths I have cried to the Lord"–she had at her immediate imaginative disposal the whole psalm, including the seventh verse ("Let Israel hope in the LORD: for with the LORD *there is* mercy, and with him *is* plenteous redemption"). Through it she could hear the answer to the cry "that it was a mercy to be free from depths," and through that promise she was freed to move on to another one: "And from 30 of Exodus when the Lord had laid foundation, nothing between Christ and the soul"; at which point she could make a final imaginative leap, not by simple "application" but by merging herself with the scriptural figure in a metaphorical way:

> And so when the Lord filled the temple* I found Lord had filled my soul with glorious apprehensions of Himself.
>
> * Exod. 40:34–8; 1 Kings 8:10–11.[8]

Sister Moore can "travel" through the translucencies of Scripture to a defined spiritual self; to John Greene, Scripture is opaque: He can apply it or think about it but not enter into it.

The difference in the vitality and fluidity of these two literary modes of perception is a measure of the decline of the conversion narrative. Hence, by the 1650s, what was soon to become "a quaint Speech in the Church"[9] was already losing its usefulness as a way of expressing the meaning of experience. And this meant, in a real sense, that verbal expression was no longer the life of the church in the way John Cotton had envisioned: When the Bible began to lose its translucency, when the Word no longer shimmered with life, then the breath of the Lord would not hold the congregation together.

Perhaps Thomas Shepard feared that this might happen to the "temple" whose foundations of many generations he labored so hard to lay down. For just above those phrases from Isaiah that he had written

8 *Shepard's "Confessions,"* p. 135.

9 Benjamin Coleman, *Gospel Order Revived* ([New York], 1700), p. 8, cited in Morgan, *Visible Saints,* p. 150.

in his notebook, Shepard set down something else, something that must have come from the heart of his experience of the new world. Across the top of the page he wrote: "Cause of New England: want of life." Yet as sad as these words are, they mark not an end but a beginning; for the effort to capture, experience, and express life through vital language – through a language, as Thoreau said, which we must be born again in order to speak – has ever since been the cause not only of New England but of the best of American literature.

SELECTED BIBLIOGRAPHY

PRIMARY WORKS

Allin, John, and Shepard, Thomas. *A Defence of the Answer made unto the Nine* Questions *or* Positions *sent from* New-England, *Against the Reply Thereto By That Reverend servant of Christ, Mr. John Ball*. London, 1648.

Baillie, Robert. *A Dissvasive from the Errours Of the Time*. London, 1646.

—. *The Disswasive From The Errors of the Time, Vindicated from the Exceptions of Mr. Cotton and Mr. Tombes*. London, 1655.

Ball, John. *An Answer to Two Treatises of Mr. Iohn Can, The Leader of the English Brownists in Amsterdam*. London, 1642.

—. *A Letter of Many Ministers in Old England, Requesting The judgement of their Reverend Brethren in* New England *concerning Nine Positions. Written* Anno Dom. *1637. Together with their Answer thereunto returned,* Anno *1639. And the Reply made unto the said Answer, and sent over unto them,* Anno *1640*. London, 1643.

Bastwick, John. *Independency Not God's Ordinance: or A Treatise concerning Church-Government, occasioned by the Distractions of these times*. London, 1645.

Bernard, Richard. "Of the visible Church of Christ under the Gospell." April 1, 1637. Bernard Papers. Massachusetts Historical Society. Boston.

Bradstreet, Anne. *The Works of Anne Bradstreet in Prose and Verse*. Edited by John Harvard Ellis. Charlestown, Mass., 1867; reprint ed., Gloucester, Mass.: Peter Smith, 1962.

Bunyan, John. *Grace Abounding to the Chief of Sinners*. Edited by Roger Sharrock. Oxford: Clarendon Press, 1962.

—. *The Pilgrim's Progress*. London, 1678; facsimile reprint ed., Menston, England: Scolar Press, 1970.

Canne, John. *A Necessity of Separation from the Church of England Proved by the Nonconformists' Principles*. Edited by Charles Stovel. London, 1849.

Clap, Roger. *Memoirs of Roger Clap. 1630*. Boston, 1844.

Cotton, John. *A Brief Exposition Of the whole Book of Canticles, or, Song of* Solomon . . . London, 1642.

—. *Christ the Fountain of Life*. London, 1651.
—. *A Coppy of a Letter of Mr. Cotton* of Boston, *in* New *England, sent in answer of certaine Objections made against their Discipline and Orders there, directed to a Friend*. [London], 1641.
—. *The Grounds and Ends of the Baptisme of the Children of the Faithfull*. London, 1647.
—. *John Cotton on the Churches of New England*. Edited by Larzer Ziff. Cambridge, Mass.: Harvard University Press, Belknap Press, 1968.
—. *Of the Holinesse of Church-Members*. London, 1650.
—. *The True Constitution Of A particular visible Church, proved by Scripture*. London, 1642.
—. *The Way of the Churches of Christ in New-England*. London, 1645.
—. *The Way of Life*. London, 1641.
Crofton, Zachary. *Bethshemesh Clouded, or Some Animadversions on the Rabbinical Talmud of Rabbi* John Rogers of Thomas-Apostles London; Called his Tabernacle for the Sun. London, 1653.
Dorchester, Mass. *Records of the First Church at Dorchester in New England 1636–1734*. Boston, 1891.
Edwards, Jonathan. *Religious Affections*. Edited by John E. Smith. New Haven: Yale University Press, 1959.
Firmin, Giles. *The Real Christian, Or A Treatise of Effectual Calling*. London, 1670.
Fiske, John. *The Notebook of the Reverend John Fiske, 1644–1675*. Edited by Robert G. Pope. *Collections of the Colonial Society of Massachusetts*, vol. 47. Boston: The Society, 1974.
Goodwin, Thomas. *The Works of Thomas Goodwin*. 5 vols. London, 1681–1704. Vol. 4 (1697).
Goodwin, Thomas, Nye, Philip, Burroughs, Jeremiah, Bridge, William, and Simpson, Sidrach. *An Apologeticall Narration, Humbly Submitted to the Honourable Houses of Parliament*. London, 1643.
Hall, David D., ed. *The Antinomian Controversy, 1636–1638: A Documentary History*. Middletown, Conn.: Wesleyan University Press, 1968.
Hill, Don G., ed. *The Record of Baptisms, Marriages and Deaths, and Admissions to the Church and Dismissals Therefrom, Transcribed from the Church Records in the Town of Dedham, Massachusetts, 1638–1845*. Dedham, 1888.
Hooker, Thomas. *The Application of Redemption*. London, 1659.
—. *The Saints Dignitie, and Dutie*. London, 1651.
—. *A Survey of the Summe of Church-Discipline*. London, 1648.
Johnson, Edward. *Johnson's Wonder-working Providence: 1628–1651*. Edited by J. Franklin Jameson. New York: Barnes & Noble, 1910.
Lechford, Thomas. *Plain Dealing; or, News from New England*. Edited by J. Hammond Trumbull. Boston, 1867; reprint ed., New York: Garrett Press, 1970.
Luther, Martin. "The Argument of St. Paul's Epistle to the Galatians." In *The Protestant Reformation*, pp. 88–107. Edited by Hans J. Hillerbrand. New York: Harper, Torchbook, 1968.

Mather, Cotton. *Magnalia Christi Americana.* 2 vols. Hartford, 1855.

Mather, Richard. "An Apologie of the churches of New-England, against the Exceptions of Mr Richard Bernard, minister of Batcombe, in Summersetshire." 1638. Mather Family Papers. American Antiquarian Society. Worcester, Massachusetts.

[Mather, Richard]. *Church-Government and Church-Covenant Discussed.* London, 1643.

—. "A Plea for the Churches of Christ in New England." December 1645. R[ichard] Mather Papers. Massachusetts Historical Society. Boston.

New Haven, Conn. *Records of the Colony and Plantation of New Haven from 1638 to 1649.* Hartford, 1857.

Norton, John. *The Answer To The Whole Set of Questions of the Celebrated Mr. William Apollonius . . .* Edited and translated by Douglas Horton. Cambridge, Mass.: Harvard University Press, Belknap Press, 1958.

Petto, Samuel. *Roses from Sharon.* London, 1654.

Pierce, Richard D., ed. *The Records of the First Church in Boston 1630–1868. Collections of the Colonial Society of Massachusetts,* vols. 39–41. Boston: The Society, 1961. Vol. 39.

—. *The Records of the First Church in Salem Massachusetts 1629–1736.* Salem: Essex Institute, 1974.

R., M. *Memoirs of the Life of Mr. Ambrose Barnes, Late Merchant and Sometime Alderman of Newcastle Upon Tyne.* Edited by W. H. D. Longstaffe. *Publications of the Surtees Society,* vol. 50. London, 1867.

R[athband], W[illiam]. *A Briefe Narration of Some Church Courses Held in Opinion and Practise in the Churches lately erected in New England . . .* London, 1644.

Robinson, John. *The Works of John Robinson, Pastor of the Pilgrim Fathers.* Edited by Robert Ashton. 3 vols. London, 1851. Vol. 2.

Rogers, John. *Ohel or Beth-shemesh: A Tabernacle for the Sun.* London, 1653.

Sharples, Stephen P., ed. *Records of the Church of Christ at Cambridge in New England 1632–1830.* Boston: Eben Putnam, 1906.

Shepard, Thomas. Diary. New England Historic Genealogical Society. Boston.

—. *God's Plot: The Paradoxes of Puritan Piety, Being the Autobiography & Journal of Thomas Shepard.* Edited with an Introduction by Michael McGiffert. Amherst: University of Massachusetts Press, 1972.

—. *Thomas Shepard's "Confessions."* Edited by George Selement and Bruce C. Woolley. *Collections of the Colonial Society of Massachusetts,* vol. 58. Boston: The Society, 1981.

—. *The Works of Thomas Shepard.* Edited by John A. Albro. 3 vols. Boston, 1853; reprint ed., New York: AMS, 1967.

S[later], J[ohn]. *Flagellum Flagelli: or Doctor Bastwicks Quarters beaten up in two or three Pomeridian Exercises . . .* London, 1645.

Taylor, Edward. *The Unpublished Writings of Edward Taylor.* 3 vols. Edited by Thomas M. Davis and Virginia L. Davis. Boston: Twayne, 1981. Vol. 1: *Edward Taylor's "Church Records" and Related Sermons.*

Tibbutt, H. G., ed. *Some Early Nonconformist Church Books. Publications of the*

Bedfordshire Historical Record Society, vol. 51. [Bedford, England]: The Society, 1972.

Walker, Henry. *A Gad of Steele.* London, 1641.

—. *The Sermon of Henry Walker, Ironmonger.* London, 1642.

—. *A* SERMON *Preached in the Chappell at* Sommerset-*House in the* Strand, *on Thursday the* 27 day of June *1650.* London, 1650.

—. *A Sermon, preached In the Kings Chappell at Whitehall, On Sunday last* July *15. 1649.* [London], 1649.

—. *Spirituall Experiences, Of sundry Beleevers.* London, 1653.

Walker, Williston. *The Creeds and Platforms of Congregationalism.* Philadelphia: Pilgrim Press, 1960.

Weld, Thomas. *An Answer to* W[illiam] R[athband] *His Narration of the Opinions and Practises of the Churches lately erected in New-England . . .* London, 1644.

—. *A Brief Narration of the Practices of the Churches in* New-England . . . London, 1645.

White, Elizabeth. *The Experiences of God's gracious Dealing with Mrs. Elizabeth White.* Boston, 1741.

Wigglesworth, Michael. *The Diary of Michael Wigglesworth 1653–1657: The Conscience of a Puritan.* Edited by Edmund S. Morgan. New York: Harper, Torchbook, 1965; reprint ed., Gloucester, Mass.: Peter Smith, 1970.

Winthrop, John. *The History of New England from 1630 to 1649.* Edited by James Savage. 2 vols. Boston, 1825; reprint ed., New York: Arno, 1972.

—. *Winthrop Papers.* [Boston]:Massachusetts Historical Society, 1929–. Vol. 1: 1498–1628 (1929). Vol. 3: 1631–7 (1943).

SECONDARY WORKS

Albro, John A. *The Life of Thomas Shepard.* Boston, 1847.

Auerbach, Erich. *Mimesis: The Representation of Reality in Western Literature.* Translated by Willard R. Trask. Princeton: Princeton University Press, 1953.

Bercovitch, Sacvan. *The Puritan Origins of the American Self.* New Haven: Yale University Press, 1975.

Brook, Benjamin. *The Lives of the Puritans.* 3 vols. London, 1813.

Caldwell, Patricia. "The Antinomian Language Controversy." *Harvard Theological Review* 69:3–4 (July-October 1976): 345–67.

Capp, B[ernard] S. *The Fifth Monarchy Men: A Study in Seventeenth-century English Millenarianism.* London: Faber & Faber, 1972.

Coolidge, John S. *The Pauline Renaissance in England: Puritanism and the Bible.* Oxford: Clarendon Press, 1970.

Delbanco, Andrew. "Thomas Shepard's America: The Biography of an Idea." In *Studies in Biography.* Edited by Daniel Aaron. Harvard English Studies 8, pp. 159–82. Cambridge, Mass.: Harvard University Press, 1978.

Dexter, Henry Martin. *The Congregationalism of the Last Three Hundred Years, as Seen in its Literature.* New York, 1880.

Fawcett, Thomas. *The Symbolic Language of Religion*. Minneapolis: Augsburg, 1971.

Feidelson, Charles, Jr. *Symbolism and American Literature*. Chicago: University of Chicago Press, 1953.

Frye, Northrop. *Anatomy of Criticism: Four Essays*. Princeton: Princeton University Press, 1971.

Grabo, Norman. "The Veiled Vision: The Role of Aesthetics in Early American Intellectual History." In *The American Puritan Imagination: Essays in Revaluation*, pp. 19–33. Edited by Sacvan Bercovitch. Cambridge University Press, 1974.

Hall, David D. *The Faithful Shepherd: A History of the New England Ministry in the Seventeenth Century*. New York: Norton, 1972.

Heimert, Alan. "Puritanism, the Wilderness, and the Frontier." *New England Quarterly* 26 (September 1953): 361–82.

Hill, Christopher. *The Century of Revolution: 1603–1714*. New York: Norton, 1961.

—. *Puritanism and Revolution: Studies in Interpretation of the English Revolution of the 17th Century*. New York: Schocken Books, 1958.

—. *The World Turned Upside Down: Radical Ideas during the English Revolution*. New York: Viking, 1972.

Laymon, Charles M., ed. *The Interpreter's One-Volume Commentary on the Bible*. Nashville: Abingdon, 1971.

Lockridge, Kenneth A. *A New England Town: The First Hundred Years:* Dedham, Massachusetts, 1636–1736. New York: Norton, 1970.

M'Clure, A[lexander] W[ilson]. *The Life of John Cotton*. Boston, 1846.

Miller, Perry. *The New England Mind: The Seventeenth Century*. Boston: Beacon Press, 1954.

Morgan, Edmund S. *Visible Saints: The History of a Puritan Idea*. Ithaca, N.Y.: Cornell University Press, 1963.

Morison, Samuel Eliot. *Builders of the Bay Colony*. Boston: Houghton, 1930.

—. *The Founding of Harvard College*. Cambridge, Mass.: Harvard University Press, 1935.

Nuttall, Geoffrey F. *The Holy Spirit in Puritan Faith and Experience*. Oxford: Basil Blackwell, 1946.

—. *Visible Saints: The Congregational Way 1640–1660*. Oxford: Basil Blackwell, 1957.

Pettit, Norman. *The Heart Prepared: Grace and Conversion in Puritan Spiritual Life*. New Haven: Yale University Press, 1966.

Rogers, Edward. *Some Account of the Life and opinions of a Fifth-Monarchy-Man. Chiefly extracted from the writings of John Rogers, Preacher*. London, 1867.

Routley, Erik. *Creeds and Confessions: The Reformation and its Modern Ecumenical Implications*. London: Gerald Duckworth, 1962.

Rutman, Darrett B. *Winthrop's Boston: Portrait of a Puritan Town 1630–1649*. Chapel Hill: University of North Carolina Press, 1965.

Shea, Daniel B., Jr. *Spiritual Autobiography in Early America*. Princeton: Princeton University Press, 1968.

Stearns, Raymond Phineas, and Brawner, David Holmes. "New England Church 'Relations' and Continuity in Early Congregational History." *Proceedings of the American Antiquarian Society* 75 (April 1965):13–45.

Taylor, John H. "Some seventeenth century testimonies." *Transactions of the Congregational Historical Society* 16 (1949–51):64–77.

Tipson, Baird. "Invisible Saints: The 'Judgment of Charity' in the Early New England Churches." *Church History* 44 (December 1975):460–71.

Watkins, Owen C. *The Puritan Experience: Studies in Spiritual Autobiography*. London: Routledge & Kegan Paul, 1972.

Webber, Joan. "Donne and Bunyan: The Styles of Two Faiths." In *Seventeenth-Century Prose: Modern Essays in Criticism,* pp. 489–532. Edited by Stanley E. Fish. New York: Oxford University Press, 1971.

Woolrych, Austin. "The English Revolution: An Introduction." In *The English Revolution: 1600–1660,* pp. 1–33. Edited by E. W. Ives. New York: Harper, Torchbook, 1971.

Ziff, Larzer. *The Career of John Cotton: Puritanism and the American Experience*. Princeton: Princeton University Press, 1962.

INDEX

(RO) indicates the names of persons whose testimonies are in John Rogers's *Ohel*. (TSC) indicates the names of church members from *Thomas Shepard's "Confessions"*; where the first name is unknown, Shepard's title for that person (Sister, Goodwife) is given. (WD) indicates the names of confessors in Michael Wigglesworth's *Diary*.